HOW TO

HIRE &
DEVELOP
YOUR NEXT
TOP PERFORMER

THE QUALITIES THAT MAKE SALESPEOPLE GREAT

Revised and Updated Second Edition

HERB GREENBERG | PATRICK SWEENEY

New York   Chicago   San Francisco
Lisbon   London   Madrid   Mexico City
Milan   New Delhi   San Juan
Seoul   Singapore   Sydney   Toronto

1 2 3 4 5 6 7 8 9 0   DOC/DOC   1 8 7 6 5 4 3 2

ISBN: 978-0-07-179164-9
MHID: 0-07-179164-7

e-ISBN: 978-0-07-179165-6
e-MHID: 0-07-179165-5

This publication is designed to provide accurate and authoritative information in regard to the subject matter covered. It is sold with the understanding that neither the author nor the publisher is engaged in rendering legal, accounting, or other professional service. If legal advice or other expert assistance is required, the services of a competent professional person should be sought.

—From a Declaration of Principles Jointly Adopted by
a Committee of the American Bar Association and
a Committee of Publishers and Associations

McGraw-Hill books are available at special quantity discounts to use as premiums and sales promotions, or for use in corporate training programs. To contact a representative, please e-mail us at bulksales@mcgraw-hill.com.

This book is printed on acid-free paper.

Library of Congress Cataloging-in-Publication Data

Greenberg, Herb.
  How to hire and develop your next top performer : the qualities that make salespeople great / by Herbert Greenberg and Patrick Sweeney. — 2nd ed.
    p. cm.
  ISBN-13: 978-0-07-179164-9 (alk. paper)
  ISBN-10: 0-07-179164-7 (alk. paper)
  1. Sales personnel—Recruiting. 2. Sales personnel—Training of. I. Sweeney, Patrick, 1952– II. Title.
  HF5439.65.G74 2013
  658.3'11—dc23   2012016251

To our employees,
who inspire us
daily.

Contents

PART | 2

WHAT IT TAKES TO SUCCEED IN SALES

Successful salespeople possess five central personality qualities.

PART | 3

JOB MATCHING

Understanding the requirements of the job and the personal
qualities you are seeking in an ideal applicant will go a long
way toward selecting your next top performer—as we have
demonstrated in two studies published in the *Harvard Business
Review*.

PART | 4

SELECTING AND HIRING TOP TALENT

Have your top performers become your blueprint for your future hiring. From there, recruit more effectively, screen out those who don't measure up, incorporate psychological testing into you hiring process, eliminate interview stars, and make the final, best decision.

PART | 5

BUILDING A WINNING SALES TEAM

Teamwork takes a concerted effort and a consistent approach that includes hiring the right people, playing to the strengths of those on board, recognizing areas where training and development can make a difference, and providing the right incentives so that your values and goals are achieved.

PART | 6

THE SALES MANAGER

Making sure that goals are met, salespeople stay motivated,
talents are developed, the best applicants are hired, and the
future is prepared and planned for constitute quite a juggling
act. The job of sales manager takes a special mix of talents and
personal qualities.

Understanding the difference between managing and leading
is understanding the difference between winning and losing
in cutthroat markets. Pure managers make the system work,
but leaders make things happen. They make the people around
them better.

PART | **7**

THE SUCCESSFUL SALESPERSON IN TODAY'S WORLD

From a business perspective, the boundaries of countries have
disappeared. What does this mean for those who are trying
to succeed in selling? Our studies show that the profile of a
successful salesperson is essentially the same in America as it
is in Japan, Sweden, England, Brazil, Canada, Hong Kong,
or virtually anywhere else in the world. It all comes down to
having the right motivation.

Competing in the global marketplace calls for an ideal blend of
the qualities that distinguish top-performing salespeople and
leaders—at hyper speed.

If you find a job that's consistent with who you are, you'll
never have to work another day in your life. This is at the heart
of our message.

As our gift to you, we are offering you the opportunity to take
our online, in-depth personality profile, which can provide you
with an introductory assessment of your defining qualities.
Consider this to be our contribution to your journey.

Preface

We are very enthused to present our newly revised version of *How to Hire and Develop Your Next Top Performer*, which we originally wrote just over a decade ago.

When our editor, Donya Dickerson, at McGraw-Hill approached us with the notion of updating the book, we shared her belief that now is a particularly important time for this revision. Selling is undergoing seismic changes. The ease of acquiring information on the Internet, coupled with the power of social networking and the evolution of a more borderless global economy, has totally changed how we communicate with one another—and, as a result, how we buy and sell our products and services.

In the past decade, much has changed. And that change continues at lightning speed.

Still, the qualities needed to succeed in sales remain fundamental.

In this new edition we will explore some of the new challenges in hiring top salespeople today, the qualities needed to succeed in sales, the importance of developing a job match, an approach to having your current top performers serve as your model for the future, the value of psychological testing, ways to make your interviews more effective, a method for getting new employees up to speed faster, the connection between sales and sports, the psychology of "A" players, proven ways to improve the performance of marginal producers, ways to develop a competitive yet collaborative team, the challenges of promoting a salesperson to manager, and what this all means for selling in today's global marketplace.

Ultimately, our goal is to provide a clear perspective on what is changing in sales, what remains the same, and how we can bring the past and the present together to stay ahead of our competition.

A QUICK CONVERSATION BETWEEN HERB AND PATRICK ON THIS NEW VERSION OF *HOW TO HIRE AND DEVELOP YOUR NEXT TOP PERFORMER*

Patrick: I believe the genesis of this book, Herb, goes back to the article that you coauthored for the *Harvard Business Review* back in 1964, in which you identified and successfully measured the qualities that distinguish top-performing salespeople.

Herb: In many ways it goes back even farther than that. Prior to founding Caliper, I had a nine-year career as a college professor. During that time, I became intrigued by peoples' attitudes toward their jobs. So, at one point, I had students observe and interview people on their way to work. And we discovered that nearly one-third of the people actually hated their work. They couldn't stand what they were doing. Nearly half of those we interviewed were neutral. They could take it or leave it. Their work was just a paycheck, nothing more. That left about 20 percent of the people who said that they loved the work they were doing. They couldn't wait to get up in the morning and start a new day.

And I thought, *now that's sad*. Why can't the other four out of five people also love what they're doing? How much different would this world be if most of us loved what we were doing? Because that's where *real* success comes from. Unless somebody loves the work they're doing, they'll just get by, just put in their time. And what a waste that is.

To truly succeed, you have to love what you're doing. This is true in any walk in life, and it is absolutely and essentially true in sales.

Patrick: Herb, it's so interesting to hear you talk about that because I truly believe that you were, in fact, a pioneer in the area of redefining work. Particularly back in the early 1960s, most people just thought of work as a job. You know a j-o-b. Just something you did to get by that you hoped wasn't too painful. But you introduced the notion that work could be an expression of who we are, that it could actually be fulfilling. You asked the question that hadn't been asked before: Why can't the rest of us be like those 20 percent who really love what they're doing? And that notion has now helped to transform the way we think about what we are doing.

Herb: That was always my desire. The starting place is to think about who you are—not just what you have done. Don't limit yourself by what you have done. Consider your potential. Understand your strengths, and play to them. And become more of who you are.

Patrick: So that was what motivated you to start Caliper?

Herb: Not completely. I was always had in the back of my mind that question about why most people were not working in jobs that fulfilled them. And I was always trying to figure out if there was something I could possibly do to change that.

Then, one day, I was minding my own business and just enjoying myself as a professor at Rutgers University when a colleague asked if I could help him conduct a consulting project for a major insurance firm. They were trying to determine if there were any personality tests on the market that could predict whether someone could sell. So I readily agreed to work with my colleague on the project.

After a thorough review of what was in the marketplace, we turned in our analysis, which essentially said that there were not any assessments that could accurately predict sales success.

Then, recognizing the clear need, my first business partner, David Mayer, and I decided to try to develop an in-depth psychological assessment that could accurately tell whether someone had the personality qualities needed to succeed in sales. We first determined that an individual needed to have three essential qualities—he or she needed to be able to understand where someone else was coming from, he or she needed to be driven to persuade others, and he or she needed to be able to bounce back from rejection. With that premise, it took us four years of intensive research, assessing salespeople across multiple industries, to develop an assessment that could, indeed, predict sales success.

Patrick: So you had a concept that was proven with academic rigor. And you knew that you could apply your assessment to the real world—and have a significant impact on identifying people who had the potential to succeed in sales. You knew you had an approach that could change the way businesses hired salespeople. And, as a result, help those businesses become much more successful. That was an enormous discovery. So how did you introduce your approach to the business community? How did you move from being an academician to an entrepreneur?

Herb: The first thing we needed was someone to believe in us. We needed some backing. And after many doors were slammed in our faces, some more forcefully than others, we were able to persuade a small real estate broker to lend us $15,000 in return for majority ownership of our stock. That was over a half century ago. And even back then, $15,000 didn't go very far. It went far enough, however, to give us the opportunity to present to Gail Smith, who was vice president of merchandising for General Motors, and he had the courage to give us our first shot. With him, we had our assessments and predictions validated, testing sales applicants for Buick and tallying the results on the IBM 1620 computers that General Motors Institute was using at the time.

Patrick: And that has opened so many doors.

Herb: It has. Since then, we have assessed the potential, strengths, and motivations of over 3 million applicants and existing employees for over 25,000 companies—from startups to Fortune 500 companies. And we now have a dozen offices around the world.

Patrick: And the focus still remains on identifying and developing an individual's potential. And on helping companies surround themselves with top performers. It is that unique place where who we are aligns with what we are doing—where the personal and the professional connect.

Herb: It truly is.

Patrick: And that brings us back, full circle, to the first article you coauthored in the *Harvard Business Review.* It was in 1964, and for the first time, you presented, tested, and proved the concept that in order to succeed in sales, an individual needs to possess certain innate qualities.

Herb: This book, in many ways, is an extension of that concept—updated to reflect what has changed and what remains essential.

Patrick: Much certainly has changed in the way we buy and sell, particularly in the past decade since we originally wrote this book.

Herb: That's absolutely true. Still, while you always have to keep your eye on what is changing, I believe that the fundamentals apply now more than ever.

Acknowledgments

This is where we run into one of the biggest risks of writing this book, which is leaving out so many of the people who helped us to make this dream a reality.

Given Caliper's history of over a half century, it is virtually impossible to acknowledge all the people who are responsible for the experience and knowledge we have acquired and are presenting in this book.

This having been said, however, there are a few people and a few institutions that must be singled out, given the fact that without their contribution, Caliper would never be the company it is today.

First and foremost, we want to acknowledge our over 200 employees around the world who have made Caliper what it is and who teach us so much every day. Their voices ring loudly in this book.

We also must mention the late David Mayer. It was David who spent four years with Herb Greenberg conducting the research that led to the development of the Caliper Profile. It was David who, together with Herb, borrowed $15,000 to found Caliper, and it was David who traveled to countless places with Herb, attempting to sell the idea that there was, in fact, an in-depth personality assessment that could predict sales success. (It also was David in the early years of Caliper who would pick up on the other telephone extension with Herb so that both of them would have something to do on the rare occasion that a client called.) And it was David who with Herb coauthored the landmark article in the July–August 1964 issue of the Harvard Business Review, *"What Makes a Good Salesman?" which contributed so enormously to Caliper's success. It is certainly safe to say that without David, Caliper would not be here.*

Caliper also would not exist were it not for the confidence of the late Gail Smith. Gail, an executive at General Motors, had enough confidence to say, "Let me see which division is hurting badly enough to try this." And it was he who called one day in late December, when there was literally no money left to continue the business, to ask David and Herb to come to Detroit to start a program with the Buick Motor Division. All of us feel the enormous debt of gratitude to this executive with the vision and courage to try something new.

Early in 1962, when Caliper was located in New York City, on the corner of West 13th Street and 7th Avenue in a small one-bedroom apartment, we received a call from a leading research firm. The caller said that the Buick Motor Division of General Motors assigned their research firm to vet Caliper because of the substantial contract GM had given us. A young man came to the apartment and spent a couple of hours with us. Evidently we vetted successfully because we retained the contract with no further questions. Now let's fast-forward to early 2000 when Herb and one of his colleagues were having a meeting at the office of J.D. Power and Associates. We were speaking with the founder's son, Jamie, when Dave Power, the founder himself, walked in. Herb stood up and extended his hand saying, "It's an honor to meet you." Dave laughed and said, "What do you mean 'meet me'? I've known you for 41 years!" It turns out that the young man who vetted us in 1962 came home from his job with the consumer research firm one night and told his wife that he needed to quit. He was earning a great salary and had a wonderful future ahead of him, but he wanted his research to be even more meaningful. So he and his wife mobilized their scant savings and founded the startup company, J.D. Power and Associates. And the rest is history.

We also will never forget the contribution of Leon Levy and Jack Nash, who in 1962 were senior partners with Oppenheimer and Company. They believed in Caliper when we were virtually unknown, and we are proud to say that Oppenheimer remains a valued client to this day.

We are also extremely grateful to Jack Pohanka, chairman of Pohanka Automotive Group, and the late Henry Faulkner, Jr., former chairman of The Faulkner Organization, who, in 1962 had the confidence to believe in our work. Their companies remain valuable clients and a treasured part of Caliper's history and future.

For over a quarter of a century, Bill Weston also has been a loyal and dear colleague, representing Lynn Insurance—now Lumbermen's Insurance. We met Gene Lynn in the early 1960s, and his company has been a valued client, and Bill has added a wonderful depth of friendship to this relationship.

Joan Brown, who in 1964 was an executive at the Office of Economic Opportunity in Washington, and Gerry Sentari, an executive at Sales and Marketing Executives International, also should be acknowledged. Together they provided Caliper with the opportunity to embark on our ongoing efforts to help people rise from poverty and join the mainstream of productive society. They, along with the U.S. Department of Welfare and the National Alliance of Business, were responsible for Caliper working for two years in Puerto Rico in what was called the New Opportunities Program, which led to the extensive New York City program that resulted in the placement of over 3,500 "hard-core" unemployed individuals in 55 job categories with 52 companies. This program provided us with the experience to continue our efforts today in a number of welfare-to-work programs.

It was Gordon Gund who gave us the opportunity to demonstrate that our job-matching concepts, so successful in business, could translate to the sports arena. He had enough confidence in us to ask for our help with his Minnesota North Stars hockey team and his Cleveland Cavaliers basketball team. It was our success with these two teams that made it possible for us to expand our work into the sports arena and which led to the assessment of over 50,000 athletes on the college and professional levels.

Harry Weltman, who collaborated with us when he was the general manager of both the Cleveland Cavaliers and then the New Jersey Nets, incorporated our assessment approach into the selection and development of his players.

Joe McIlvaine, former general manager of the New York Mets, one day asked Herb to advise him on five minor league players who were causing him some problems. Herb pinpointed where the problems stemmed from in four of the five players. For the fifth player, however, he couldn't find anything wrong. In fact, his assessment gave every indication that he would be a very strong individual contributor and an exemplary team player. When he heard this, Joe laughed and said, "You got them all right. There is no problem with that last player. I just threw him in to test you!" That player, it turned out, was Tim Bogar, who went on to have a long, successful major league career and is currently on the coaching staff of the Boston Red Sox. So we passed Joe's test, and the Mets became a client.

We had the pleasure of honoring many of these individuals in person at our Fiftieth Anniversary Gala event. The tone of the evening was profoundly expressed by Governor Gaston Caperton, former governor of West Virginia, former owner of McDonough-Caperton Insurance Group, and current president of the College Board. The night of our gala, he also had plans to celebrate his wife's birthday. Still, he said that he could not miss at least touching base with our fiftieth anniversary party. So he came and gave a wonderful speech to kick off our celebration, sharing stories and insights from his initial contact with Caliper until the present day. Then he was whisked away to his next event. We are exceedingly grateful to Governor Caperton for his belief in us, the opportunities to work closely with him throughout the years, and his endearing friendship.

One of the cornerstones of Caliper's growth also has been our abiding relationships with dozens of professional and trade associations. While there are so many that could be mentioned, we feel that we must acknowledge two in particular, which we also honored at our Fiftieth Anniversary Gala event—namely, the Independent Insurance Agents & Brokers of America (IIABA) and the Material Handling Equipment Distributors Association (MHEDA). IIABA has worked with us since 1973, and Herb was honored by receiving a Chairman's Award as a major contributor to the insurance industry. Liz Richards, executive vice president of MHEDA, has been a trusted advisor, a valued colleague, and a dear friend, as was her predecessor Dan Reilly.

We also would like to thank immensely the deep and meaningful contributions of Philip Ruppel, president of McGraw-Hill Professional, and our editors Mary Glenn and Donya Dickerson. Again, people and projects can only move forward when other people show confidence, and Philip, Mary, and Donya have continually expressed their belief in us, offered sound advice, and helped enormously to complete this project on time, which we freely recognize was an enormous undertaking, particularly given the easily distracted nature of these authors.

We have necessarily left out so many people who have taught us so much and people who have provided us with so many opportunities to learn and share with you what is in this book. You can only imagine the numbers of people that could be mentioned if we simply say "thank you" to all the executives of the more than 25,000 companies who look to us for advice on hiring and developing their top performers, "thank you" to the general managers at the dozens of major league sports teams who we help with their draft choices, and "thank you" to the executives of scores of professional and trade associations who endorse our work. For their belief, faith and confidence in us, we are eternally grateful.

A New Introduction

HOW SALES IS CHANGING *BEFORE OUR EYES*

The accelerated speed of communication and our ability to access information with just a few keystrokes is changing everything—including the way we buy and sell. In the meantime, our economy has become borderless as the reach of global companies has altered the competitive landscape. As consumers, we have access to more information, faster—and feel, as a result, that we can make many of our buying decisions without ever talking with a salesperson.

And when we do need to deal with a salesperson, statistics from Eric Berridge, cofounder of Bluewolf, reveal that 70 percent of a customer's buying decision is made before the customer even starts a conversation with a salesperson.

Not surprisingly, Jim Dickie, managing partner of CSO Insights, shares that the percentage of sales representatives making quota has dropped from 61 percent in 2007 to less than 51 percent last year. Going out on a limb, but probably not too far, Gerhard Gschwandtner, CEO of Selling Power, predicts that of the 18 million sales jobs that currently exist in the United States, only 3 million will be necessary within 10 years.

What does this mean for the sales profession?

The game is changing.

To remain competitive, sales leaders and sales representatives need to be fluent operating virtually, in the online world, have a clear understanding of how the buying habits of customers are changing, and realize that how they succeeded in the past may have very little to do with how they will succeed tomorrow. Gerhard shared with us: "The Internet has created tools that help customers educate themselves. This is part of the self-service movement that started in the 70s when gas stations offered you a choice: Do you want somebody to fill your tank, or would you like to save a few pennies per gallon and do it yourself? And the self-service movement is being perfected by businesses selling to consumers, such as Amazon.com, where you can buy virtually anything at your convenience, whenever you want, without talking to a salesperson. So the customer is more in charge of the buying process."

"Added to this," Gerhard said, "is that there is intelligence at work providing customers with information from other customers. So customers are less influenced by salespeople and more influenced by the persuasive comments from other people who have purchased the same product or service."

And businesses selling to other businesses are starting to exploit these technologies in new ways.

As a result, when salespeople are needed, those who succeed today need to be bright, empathic, versatile, curious, flexible, and able to connect with clients, in person and virtually, in all parts of the world.

And that's just for starters.

The most effective salespeople today are using new technologies to engage in online conversations with prospects, keep up on what their competitors are doing, arrange appointments, and create client demos on the fly,—all in real time.

The future belongs to salespeople who can thoroughly understand, embrace, and take advantage of this new technology to enhance their relationships with their customers. Selling, as always, is about understanding the way your customers want to buy. What is most important now is that those ways are changing.

The relationships in sales will become, by necessity, deeper faster. And for the best salespeople, technology will enhance these relationships. More sales calls will become virtual, with a dozen prospects sitting in different places, viewing a document or a demonstration online, and altering what they are seeing to meet their needs.

Successful salespeople today certainly need to be more technology savvy while also being able to absorb more information faster and make connections quicker.

Somewhere between Google, Bing, Yahoo, LinkedIn, Twitter, Facebook, and corporate websites, salespeople can find all they need to start meaningful conversations with their prospects, including what other companies they have worked for, what schools they attended, what connections they might share, where they live, how they communicate, how they treat their customers, how they position themselves and their company, what others say about them, what their philosophy is, how their company is growing, and what the latest news items are on their firm. And these threads can all be tied together with the ease of a few clicks.

You doubt how much or how quickly you can find out something about someone on the Internet? Or how quickly they can find something you weren't even aware of about you?

Just ask Colleen Aylward. She is interested in dragging talent management from the dark ages into the light of the twenty-first century. An author and the founder of the recruiting firm Devon James Associates, she tells of a sales executive who was in one of her seminars and doubted her ability to find anything on him on the Internet. He insisted that since he did not use social media, she would come to a dead end when trying to find out about him and others like him. So, in front of the class, she looked him up. And there he was, with a photo that was decades old, kissing a girl in college. "I didn't plan it that way. It was just so funny. And he was mortified and said, 'That's not me. Turn it off,' as he turned red."

Laughing, she added, "I still use that in my slide shows, and people still crack up every time."

The instant access to information has arrived not a moment too soon to help address the immediate needs of most prospects and clients. Colleen says, "One of the things about this economy is that executives are only thinking right in front of their faces. 'How do we solve this problem? How do we make our next sale? How do we stay in business?' They're not doing a lot of long-range planning. So their short-term needs are 'How do I get this issue solved now?' It is a much more immediate frame of mind than it has been for a long, long time. So it is important to understand that. To get the immediacy of that. The urgency."

It is easy to see why, amid all these technological advances, many sales executives are also questioning whether there are, in fact, fundamental differences in the generations. On top of everything else, do executives now have to worry about managing younger people differently than they did their peers to get the same results? There is, some feel, a sense that young adults entering the job market have grown up having their needs instantly gratified, and they've been able to access anything online at the snap of a finger. As a result, they do not have much patience with waiting their turn as they climb the corporate ladder.

Adam Unger, a talent consultant and twenty-something himself who was drafted by the Yankees in 2003 and has studied opera with one of Pavarotti's teachers, told us, "My generation, we're used to being in the spotlight, being on Facebook, instant messaging, constantly reaching out, seeking perpetual connection and gratification. My friend Brandon Yankowitz actually made a movie called *Trophy Kids* about this, because when we played soccer, we all got a trophy. Not just the winner, but there was a sixth place and a seventh place ribbon, and everybody was fantastic. And our parent's refrigerators were full of our artwork. And now, not surprisingly, we're not just interested in taking a job, any job, and seeing where it leads us. We want to find work that is personally meaningful, something that we're passionate about, something that we love doing."

HOW SALES IS STAYING THE SAME *BEFORE OUR EYES*

For a salesperson to succeed, he or she does not have to be incredible. But he or she absolutely has to be credible.

Do I trust you? Do I think that you know what you're talking about? Do you convey expertise? Do I believe you? Do I feel that you will come through? And follow through?

We know, through our more than a half century of assessing potential and talent, that top-performing salespeople all possess three qualities. They need to be able to connect with people, to read them, to understand where they are coming from. They need to be driven to persuade others, to bring them around to their point of view. And they need to view rejection as just something that happens, another learning experience, another bump in the road, something to overcome. Then they need to be able to carry on, even more determined than ever—to connect and persuade another prospect or client.

Our cross-industry studies demonstrate that fewer than half the people currently making a living in sales possess those three essential qualities.

As if to mirror our findings, nearly half the companies today say that they need to improve their ability to consistently hire salespeople who succeed, according to Jim Dickie of CSO Insights, a research firm that has surveyed over 1,400 companies worldwide to reveal best practices in sales and marketing.

And even on the part of companies that are hiring the right people, there is a frustration with getting them up to speed. According to Jim, just shy of half the firms surveyed reported that it takes in excess of 10 months to get a new salesperson to full productivity (defined as new reps generating the same amount of revenue as experienced reps).

"We did an analysis for a software company that was facing this 10-month ramp-up time. And the chief sales officer shook his head and said, 'In order to plan for growth next year, I would have had to have hired new reps back in February of last year.'

So, now, sales executives are consumed with not just will this new person I've hired be one of the two who will succeed? But, if they do succeed, can I help them succeed faster?"

Adam Unger, a talent consultant, says that uppermost in the minds of sales executives who are hiring right now is one thing: efficiency. "Everyone is interested in hiring the right people *faster*. And bringing them up to speed *faster*. And not making mistakes along the way."

Still, what remains the same is the essential talent needed to succeed in sales—and the search for people who have what it takes.

"A winning attitude is the number one trait that I look for," Jean-Yves Ghazi, director of the Empire State Building Observatory, told us. "What is the mix I'm looking for in an ideal sales candidate? Give me 75 percent attitude and 25 percent skill, and I'll make it work. A positive, upbeat, can-do attitude is definitely the starting place. After that, everything follows."

That right attitude, though, is not something you can give somebody. We asked Jean-Yves if he could give us an example of someone with the right attitude.

"I have one salesperson who is a very active listener, which makes him excellent at developing relationships. So he hears what others are saying, can read between the lines, and is able to translate their needs into experiences we can deliver."

How did this translate into success for this salesperson?

"He just designed a program to respond to the Student & Youth Travel Association's needs, which generated over 20,000 students visiting the Empire State Building this year alone."

That's being able to listen and deliver on what is heard. What did he hear that lead to such a huge sale?

"He heard exactly what they needed from the time they arrived until they had to leave for their next destination. He understood their time constraints, and the importance of their getting the most out of their trip to New York City. And he created an experience that stood out from their memories of visiting New York."

If you don't mind our asking, what is the competition for a salesperson for the Empire State Building?

"We're competing for tourists. Over 60 percent of the people who visited us last year were international, and 40 percent were domestic. Europe is driving our growth this year. But Brazil, Argentina, and China are growing substantially. So when people come to visit New York City, it is a matter of which sites are they going to see. And we have to make sure that we deliver an exceptional experience. And our sales team needs to help create packages that bring those expectations alive."

When people take that 57-second elevator ride from the second floor to the eightieth floor of the Empire State Building, then get in a queue to go up to the eighty-sixth floor to experience the view of the city and beyond, what are they looking for? The views are iconic. Are they imagining King Kong, hanging onto the building, battling airplanes to protect the actress who befriended him? Or wondering what would have happened if Cary Grant and Deborah Kerr had met there?

There definitely is romance in some sales positions.

And that brings us back, with a renewed sense of urgency, to the premise for the article that Herb wrote in the *Harvard Business Review* nearly a half-century ago. Why are some salespeople so incredible, whereas others are obviously in the wrong job? What do the best salespeople have that others do not? What does it really take to succeed in sales? What remains the same? And what has changed?

PART 1

THE SALES ENIGMA

Why is it that some people succeed in sales, whereas others, who work just as hard, seem to get nowhere? What do the best have that others do not? What does it really take to succeed in sales?

"I think the best salespeople are those who are motivated by a higher purpose. It is a given that top-performing salespeople are motivated by accomplishment and by achieving results. But, at their very core, I believe the very best salespeople are driven to create an impact. They believe in their products or services and their intrinsic value for the customer," says Alyson Brandt, executive vice president, general manager Americas at Forum Corporation, a pioneer in linking learning to strategic business objectives.

Sales is a career with enormous opportunity. For those who are ambitious and too impatient to inch their way up the career ladder, sales is an extremely attractive profession—if they have what it takes. With a sales career's high income, personal freedom, and limitless opportunities for recognition and advancement, why is there any problem recruiting and retaining highly productive professional-level salespeople?

CHAPTER 1

The Opportunity and the Challenge

In striking contrast to most corporate positions, sales provides an opportunity for those who want to operate with a good degree of autonomy and independence. It remains the only profession where individuals are judged according to a dollar-and-cents standard. And for those willing to sacrifice the security of a consistent paycheck, sales can be extremely lucrative.

Listen to what David Oreck, inventor of the famous lightweight vacuum cleaner, told us he thought the three most wonderful words in the English language were: "I'll buy it."

His approach to selling starts with listening to his customers. One of his customers asked him, "How can I get my teenager to clean his room?" At first David just laughed. Then he thought about it and designed an upright vacuum cleaner with a radio and headphones in the handle.

The key, for him, was convincing people that they needed his product but just didn't know it yet.

"Whether you are offering a product or a service," he told us, "success is all about persuading. You have to be able to sell your ideas—usually to people who haven't the faintest idea that they need them. Never underestimate the power of ideas. Ideas have started religions and nations." Then he said, "We've all heard that if you build a better mousetrap, the world will beat a path to your door. But that isn't true. The world has to first get the message."

Does that message resonate with you? Then perhaps you are built for sales.

For fast trackers who are looking to make more money than their peers, are seeking increased responsibility, and are too impatient to slowly climb their way up the corporate ladder, there is only one option—sales. As inviting as all this sounds, though, sales is not for everyone.

It takes a special kind of person to succeed in sales.

Let us tell you about a few such individuals.

What was it about sales that appealed to Tom Gartland, president, North America, of Avis Budget Group?

"I started in sales over 30 years ago because it is the one job where you have complete control over your own destiny. It's just a matter of understanding the skills you have available, honing them, and putting in the effort necessary to be the best. If you're willing to put in the time and the effort, develop yourself, reach out to others, take advantage of the training, tools, and other resources your company offers, and give it your all, you can create your own destiny. That, to me, is why I love the sales side of any business. But you have to be willing to put in half-days."

Half-days? That sounds like a part-time job.

"No, no. Half-days mean a 12-hour day. It has to do with your work ethic. It's working harder than your competition. It's demonstrating a real commitment. That's how you stand out."

Did he always know he wanted to pursue a career in sales?

"Absolutely, when I was 14 years old, I went to work for a place called Robert's Rent-A-Tux, and in no time I was making incremental commission by selling cufflinks, shoes, and bow ties. I was on commission. It was awesome. It's just part of my DNA. It's always been."

Another 14-year-old who discovered that selling was in his DNA is Jussier Ramalho. He had to quit school in fourth grade because his mother could not afford to pay for his transportation. His father had abandoned the family, leaving them in one of Brazil's poorer neighborhoods in Natal. At the time, he had the nickname Windcutter because he was so emaciated. So, to help make sure that he, his mother, and his two sisters had enough food, he started selling cookies on the street for a bakery.

You sold cookies on the street?

"The baker would give me several boxes of cookies. Then I would go out on the street and try to sell them. At the end of the day, I would give the baker a certain amount of money for each box that was sold, and I could keep whatever money I made on top of that."

Was he the only one doing this?

"No, there were lots of people on the streets trying to sell cookies. It was very common. So, to stand out, I started giving away samples. I figured that if I gave people a free taste, they would like them and want more. And it worked. Soon, I was selling 100 boxes of cookies a day, using about three of those boxes as samples. I learned that if you gave someone a taste before buying, then they would trust you and buy more."

He went on not only to learn how to read but also to buy a newsstand, become a noted motivational speaker, and write a book called, *You Are Your Best Mark*, in which he helps people understand that they are their own best product.

"Whenever you are selling," he says, "you are not selling a product or a service. You are selling yourself. It's all about trust. You have to trust in yourself in order to have people trust you. At its very best, he describes selling as similar to mouth-to-mouth resuscitation, where you are breathing life into someone else, giving them something that can change their lives."

Still, it is worth noting that not everyone who succeeds in sales was born with a sales gene planted in their DNA. Some of us develop our ability to sell our products, services, solutions, or ideas via a more circuitous route.

Alisa Barry, chef and creator of Bella Cucina, admits to having mixed feelings about sales. After studying culinary arts in Spain and then with Alice Waters at Taunte Marie in San Francisco and then working in the Bay Area for a few years, she returned to Atlanta to reconnect with her family before deciding what to do next. While there, she needed to make some money, so she started selling salads and sandwiches out of a basket.

"I rented a kitchen and worked with an organic farmer, who would drive up in his pickup truck, and I'd buy whatever he had. Then, throughout the week, I'd wake up every morning at 5:00 and decide what I wanted to cook that day. Then I'd prepare my sandwiches and salads and walk with my two baskets through Virginia Heights, a neighborhood where I could sell lunch to the retailers and their customers."

She has gone on to write several cook books and have some of her creations featured on Oprah's television show. One could certainly say that her food is so splendid that it sells itself. Still, she told us, "The truth is, I hate to sell. But I love to talk about my products and what I do. And I think because I'm so passionate about the ingredients and the products and what we do that it is translated into sales. And I believe that passion is the foundation for creating and selling. Because if you're not truly passionate, you really can't sustain the level of energy and intensity and authenticity you need to stand out from the crowd. I think you really have to believe in what you're selling and love it in order for it to translate to other people. And then they will understand. I always say, 'I will educate as much as possible, and I truly enjoy that. But then it's really up to the person to make a decision. It's my job to share as much as I can, to share my knowledge and my passion. To show them why I love it.'"

Still, you say that you hate selling? Maybe it depends on how you define selling.

"That could be. In order for our business to thrive, somebody has to buy from us. And it is interesting, as I think about it, because the one piece for me that is part of the creative process is actually putting our products out in the world, whether it is Williams Sonoma or Crate & Barrel or our own shop, and having them be discovered."

If the creation is not sold, then no one discovers it.

"I do like to sell things. I definitely like that. But I don't like to feel like I'm selling, if that makes sense."

That paradox is probably at the heart of why Alisa is so good at selling. She is not trying to. The truth is that there are as many ways to sell as there are successful salespeople. What is most important is that how someone sells has to be natural. It has to come from within. Just trying to follow a playbook will come across as being hollow and fake. And we can all sense a fake a mile away.

As you can see, salespeople have a different way of looking at the world. They sense opportunities where others fear rejection. Frowns are not signs of discouragement; they are something to be changed. Where others see obstacles, salespeople see challenges.

This is why, more than anything else, salespeople must believe in themselves. And the best salespeople we have encountered know themselves very well—they know how to play to their strengths.

And because of who they are, as salespeople grow in their positions, they are constantly seeking new opportunities. In a recent study, we found that most top executives have come up through the sales and marketing ranks. This is so because the best salespeople and the most effective corporate executives share many of the same qualities, including initiative, drive, imagination, and a willingness to work hard.

But what attracts successful people to sales? What do they have that others do not? What, ultimately, does it take to succeed in sales?

We intend to give you a clearer picture of exactly who the best salespeople are. We will explore what drives successful salespeople, what differentiates them from people in other professions, and perhaps most important, what distinguishes the best salespeople from the rest of the salespeople. In addition, we'll explore why some people excel in sales, while others, who seem to work just as hard and enthusiastically, fall short of meeting goals.

We have counseled over 25,000 firms on these questions throughout the past half century. And in this book we will share our findings.

As our economy shifts and adjusts, what it takes to succeed in sales has become a little more complex than it once was. One certainty is that there is a growing need for the human touch. As the Internet opens new doors, the nature of sales is changing. Customers find themselves looking for someone to guide them through the labyrinth of possibilities they face. Many products and services today are difficult to distinguish from the competition. So, above all, this sales process depends on trust. This trend underscores the growing importance of truly professional salespeople.

This is so because what is being sold in today's economy is not really products or even services. What the best salespeople truly sell are solutions—solutions that uniquely meet the particular needs of each client.

Throughout this book we will be taking out our psychological pens and sketching portraits for you of the kinds of individuals who have what it takes to make it in this game—a game where there are few clear-cut rules and where the odds are inextricably stacked against success, but where the opportunities and challenges are virtually limitless.

What we are about to describe for you are rare individuals, but they are not impossible to find. In our work, we have found that approximately one out of every four individuals today has what it takes to succeed in some form of sales, either consultative, or relationship building, or display sales, or the hard and fast-driving closers. However, only a few of those select individuals with sales ability end up using their innate talent. And, as we are all well aware, far too many people who are completely lacking in sales ability wind up selling. The result is that sales has received a professional black eye. But more about that later.

For now, we would like to concentrate on those who do best in sales. For starters, they do very well—make that exceedingly well—financially. The truth of the matter is that it is not uncommon for top salespeople to earn more money than their sales managers. Sales superstars sometimes earn even more than the owners of their companies. The possibility of making so much money prompts the question: What special skills or motivations explain why many salespeople earn more than we pay the president of the country?

Sales, perhaps more than any other profession, is a psychological testing ground. Two decades years ago, a survey rated product knowledge as a salesperson's most important attribute. But product knowledge has been surpassed by honesty, integrity, and professionalism. The best salespeople tell us that they would leave their jobs if they did not wholeheartedly believe in their product or service.

Prospects, meanwhile, go through a precise psychological order when making a buying decision. First, they judge the salesperson's integrity. People today simply will not do business with someone unless they are sure that they can depend on the person. Then prospects will determine whether the salesperson's company can back up its product or claims. Next, they determine whether what is being offered, regardless of price, will take care of their needs. Price becomes the final determinant of whether they will place an order.

The salesperson who succeeds is the one who works as a partner with his or her clients, helping them do their jobs better. To accomplish this, salespeople bring several qualities to the table, including empathy, persuasiveness, persistence, and resilience.

And the very best salespeople make it look so easy, so . . . natural. While thoroughly understanding the advantages of the products or services they represent, they are also well versed in the weakness of their competitors—and they seem to anticipate their customers' evolving needs. To top it off, they make it look as though they could do it all while walking in their sleep.

Still, top-performing salespeople always need to be on their feet, ready to respond to the requirements, and adapt their selling style to their customers' requirements. In other words, if they are in a consultative mode but their customer just wants to take care of a transaction, then they need to drop the consultative mode and adapt to a more transactional approach. On the other hand, if they are thinking that a situation calls for a transactional approach but by the quality of their prospect's questions it becomes clear that a consultative approach is needed, then they need to switch gears.

Salespeople need to be much more adaptive now than in the past.

The best are extremely attentive to each client's needs and totally intent on seeking an ideal solution to each client's unique problems. In the end, such individuals are problem solvers. They are the ones who uncover solutions for their clients better and more quickly than their competitors.

For such work, salespeople enjoy an unusual degree of independence, a chance to make money commensurate with their abilities, and limitless opportunities. They are, in many ways, their own bosses. When it comes down to it, few individuals in other professions can say the same.

The picture that develops is of highly paid, independent professionals who are trusted confidants to their clients. Such individuals are out there proving themselves every day. They are on the cutting edge, in a black and white world, where either they make it or they do not. There are really few jobs that hold this level of continual suspense. But that is what the best salespeople thrive on.

So, for all its advantages, why has sales, historically, received such a bad rap? Why are there so many jokes about the traveling salesman? Why are there so many negative phrases about the profession, such as "selling you a bill of goods," "selling you down the river," and "selling out"?

Our studies show that the real reason that the sales profession has suffered in terms of prestige is because four out of every five people now selling should be doing something else—for themselves, for their company, for the profession, and certainly for the sake of the prospects they encounter. Because these salespeople do not have a natural talent, they try to fake it and, in the fast-talking process, sell themselves, and all the rest of us, short.

Unfortunately, these are the kinds of salespeople whom we all seem to come across more frequently than we encounter the true professionals. They are the type that make you want to ask, "Why don't you do all of us a favor and get another job?"

Jeanne Frawley, director of the Sales Education Foundation, told us that the first job for half the students graduating from universities today is in sales. However, nearly two-thirds of them fail. "They don't fail because they're not bright enough," Jeanne says, "And they don't fail because they don't work hard enough. They fail because it was a fall-back position for them." Entering sales was not a deliberate decision for most of these graduates. They didn't intend to get a job in sales. They just tripped into a sales position. Their other options were closed. So they try sales, by accident, and not surprisingly, most of them don't even come close to succeeding.

More than 50 universities have come to recognize this as a missed opportunity. They have recognized that there is an enormous gap between the jobs available to new graduates and the preparation they have received.

With the goal of recognizing sales as a profession, these universities have begun offering sales programs, with courses such as Introduction to Professional Selling, Key Account Management, and Negotiation. They are also providing internships. The students are not just studying but practicing sales. And when they graduate, they are ready to pursue their calling. Added to this, according to Jeanne, 90 percent of the graduates from these sales programs are being offered jobs.

There are very encouraging signs for the profession of sales, which is clearly undergoing seismic changes.

We hope that this book will add a clear understanding of what it takes to succeed in sales. If nothing else, we hope to help eliminate the hackers and pave the way for true sales professionals. We hope to provide insights that will enable managers to uncover people with natural sales ability and that will help individuals to determine whether they have what it takes to succeed. If we can contribute in the slightest way toward this goal, we feel that we will be providing an enormous service to the business world and to the unfortunate customers who unwittingly come across the lion's share of mismatched and ill-equipped salespeople.

But why is it so hard to hire and develop top performers?

For starters, you can get a master's degree in business administration without ever learning two of the most important things in business, which are how to hire the right people and how to avoid hiring the wrong ones.

Over the past half century of working with companies around the world, we have found that most recruiting practices start out by looking in the wrong places for the wrong things.

In the hiring process, we have found that there is, almost universally, entirely too much concern with external superficialities (what salespeople are supposed to look like) and not enough concern with what is inside (whether they are motivated to succeed in sales). This seems to have been the case throughout time. For instance, an article in the premiere issue of *Sales and Marketing Management* 90 years ago noted, "Large men command attention, providing that they are physically well organized and their muscle tone and health is [*sic*] all that it should be. Large salesmen are most likely to depend upon their size and bluff to succeed than they are to make use of every ounce of their gray matter. Smaller salesmen must make up for this deficiency in height and brawn by using their minds more effectively. They must either have more courage and self-reliance, more tactfulness and friendliness, or more intellectual resourcefulness."

An editor at another magazine told us just a few years ago, "I got a letter from a plastic surgeon who avows 'more salespeople than ever before are utilizing plastic surgery to improve their sales.' Then he proceeds to outline just what he can do for a salesperson who needs a lift (face, that is) to shore up sagging neck skin, a sure sign of . . . aging. Particularly striking, in the words of the good doctor, are thin lips ('not trustworthy') and weak chin ('not reliable')." The editor went on to ask, "Is the suggestion of plastic surgery just another version of the old wheeze that looks and patter are more important than substance?"

Sometimes the more things change, the more they seem to remain the same. We can only assume that the continued emphasis on external factors, such as size and appearance, is due to a lack of understanding that sales is fundamentally a game of motivation.

If we can convey one thing in this book, it is that succeeding in sales has to do with what is inside you. When push comes to shove, no one can give a salesperson the desire to succeed, the need to persuade, the ability to bounce back from rejection, the ability to understand the needs of others, or any other of the qualities that are needed to succeed in sales. These are all inherent gifts that some of us have in larger quantities than others. But they are not gifts that we can neatly package and give to someone else.

In addition, we have found that the best salespeople, regardless of their field, share one other characteristic. Ben Feldman, one of the most successful insurance salespeople in the world, summed it up best when he was asked, "What is the best shortcut you've discovered for getting to the top?'"

"Shortcut?" Feldman repeated. "I've never been able to discover any shortcut around hard work."

It is important to keep in mind that both a piece of coal and a diamond consist mostly of carbon. But it would be fruitless to give a jeweler a piece of coal and ask her to polish it until it becomes a precious gem. That, however, is what many sales executives are asked to do every day—to create salespeople out of individuals who are not fundamentally suited to the task.

Having assessed the potential of over 3 million applicants and employees, we are convinced that most people have the potential to be winners in this world. What it takes is understanding our inherent strengths and then getting ourselves into positions where our limitations are not of consequence and our strengths are allowed to shine.

The goal is to understand what drives us—to determine our strengths and potential. And the strengths and potential of those with whom we surround ourselves.

Our goal is to provide insights that will enable managers to uncover people with natural sales ability. And to help individuals determine whether they have what it takes to succeed in sales.

Ultimately, for people who have what it takes, sales can be a very lucrative profession, offering a world of opportunities.

CHAPTER 2

So Why the Revolving Door?

I f the sales profession is indeed so attractive, offering the high income, personal freedom, and limitless opportunities discussed in Chapter 1, why is there any problem in recruiting and retaining highly productive, professional-level salespeople?

Whenever sales and marketing executives get together, poor productivity and high turnover are invariably key topics for discussion. These executives are constantly seeking ways to reduce the incredibly high cost, in both time and money, of recruiting, selecting, and training salespeople, only to have the majority leave, be terminated, or at best, turn out to be mediocre producers. While striving to solve these problems, they nevertheless seem to accept, as a fact of business life, that the overwhelming majority of a company's sales are made by the top 20 percent of the sales force. The staggering, wasteful costs stemming from this situation are endured because they are thought to be inevitable. The resulting high turnover among those 80 percent who are fumbling along is, in turn, accepted as a necessary cost of managing a sales force. The fact is that neither the universally accepted poor productivity among sales forces nor the high turnover need be inevitable.

Our studies show that 55 percent of the people earning their living in sales should be doing something else. Quite simply, they do not have the personality attributes that are needed to succeed in sales. Another 25 percent have what it takes to sell, but they should be selling something else. These individuals could be successful in some selling situations, but they are only marginal performers in their current sales position. This leaves only 20 percent of salespeople selling the products or services best suited to their personality.

Jim Dickie, managing partner of CSO Insights, told us that, unfailingly, the top 20 percent of the salespeople generate 60 percent of a company's revenue. He reflects, "The message is clear. Too often we are relying on what we refer to as the 'rainmakers' to pick up for the lack of performance from the rest of the team."

Consistently, a small percentage of each sales force is overwhelmingly successful, whereas the vast majority barely hangs on, leaves, or is terminated. But it need not be this way.

A realistic goal can be that a majority of a company's sales force can consist of people as effective as the highly productive 20 percent. The benefits of having such a sales force are exciting to think about. Just imagine two-thirds of a company's sales force selling at the level of the current top 20 percent. We leave it to you to do the math. The final figure would not even include the reduced costs that would result from fewer turnovers and less recruiting, training, and managing of novices.

A more objective approach to recruiting and selecting sales personnel can result in a significant increase in the percentage of productive people. It is a matter of looking at the sales profession in a new way.

Before looking at the way to dig out of this hole in which the sales profession finds itself, though, let us try to understand how we got there. Why is it so difficult to identify people who have what it takes to succeed in sales?

We have found that most salespeople are hired for the wrong reasons. Most hiring approaches do not predict whether someone has what it takes to succeed in sales.

RELYING ON EXPERIENCE

Regardless of how selective companies might be, they cannot hope to make correct hiring decisions if their selective criteria are incorrect from the start. These companies often use extensive application forms, have multiple interviews, check references carefully, and in short, take many of the steps that are required in making logical, thoughtful hiring decisions. This process is often costly, but it is considered worth it, again because of the importance of the decision. As most human resource executives and sales managers will confess, despite all the time, money, and effort, wrong decisions are the norm, so the poor productivity and high turnover endure.

One of the most common hiring mistakes is to rely too heavily on experience. There is a mistaken belief that an experienced individual will hit the ground running. Our advice is to do yourself a favor and do not steal from your competitors unless you want them to thank you.

Think about it for just a minute. When you're putting together a "help wanted" ad, what is the first thing you write? "Needed: A salesperson with at least one year of experience." No, wait a minute. This is a much more important job than that. Let's say "need five years' experience." Experience is what we look for in job candidates. If two candidates seem equally qualified for a position and one has slightly more experience, the decision seems easy. Experience wins. Some executives even look in their competitors' back yards for individuals who are ready to make a move. Conventional wisdom is that an experienced individual will hit the ground running.

But the price can be high for taking this easy road. After all, how often have you come across people who have 12 years of experience, which adds up to just one year's bad experience repeated a dozen times?

We have a tendency to think of experience in a way that is really too limiting. What we should be looking for is not direct experience but transferrable skills. In sales, for instance, it is not whether someone has sold the same product or service before, but what have they carried with them. Are they able to initiate relationships easily? Can they get a client to open up? Do they know how to identify and solve problems? These are some of the transferrable skills that can take an individual successfully from one position to another and even from one career to another.

As Laurie Dalton, vice president of human resources for Gate Gourmet, the world's largest independent provider of catering for the transportation industry, told us, "It has become increasingly important to hire for attitude. Aptitude we can train for. But you can't give someone the essential qualities needed to succeed in sales, along with the right attitude. Without those qualities, and the right attitude, success will be hampered by many roadblocks."

In the end, effective hiring has less to do with experience and more to do with potential. Ultimately, hiring is one of the most important business decisions we make. Yet all too often those decisions are forced under deadline pressures with a pressing need to fill an empty chair. We know that such an empty chair can be scary. But filling it with the wrong person can be a lot scarier and a lot more costly. We recommend crossing off your hiring to-do list "hire only someone with the right experience" and replacing it with "hire someone who has the potential for growth and has the same qualities as your top performers."

Consider the cautionary words of John Beattie, former vice president of human resources at GMAC Insurance. He said, "I use to hire from my competitors. And what I was getting was the dregs of the sales industry. They were stuck in their old ways, unable or unwilling to change. And they did not bring the contacts, business savvy, or anything else we hoped they would have developed through their years of experience. Instead, all I was doing was a huge favor to my competitors—by relieving them of an underperforming salesperson and wasting time trying to have them produce for us."

To hire top performers, don't focus on experience. Think instead in terms of an applicant's growth potential—what the applicant is capable of doing, not what he or she has done. Does the applicant have what it takes to grow into your position?

You have to delve below the surface to discover if an applicant has the character strengths, flexibility, empathy, persuasiveness, persistence, problem-solving ability, resilience, and optimism to grow with your company.

Just imagine what it would be like if you didn't accept the way things are and rely on the top 20 percent of your salespeople to sell 60 percent of what you sell. Just imagine what it would be like if 50 percent of what you sell were sold by 50 percent of your salespeople. Just imagine what it would be like if most of your salespeople were producing at the level of productivity currently represented by your top 20 percent. Just imagine.

WHAT IT
TAKES TO
SUCCEED IN
SALES

Successful salespeople possess special personality attributes that enable them to succeed. Unlike many jobs where mediocre performance can be disguised and an individual is able to get by despite intensely disliking the job, a salesperson's success or failure is revealed immediately by bottom-line numbers. The very nature of the sales job precludes success for those who do not possess the fundamental motivation to sell.

In this part, we will first talk about motivation in general and then discuss the three central qualities that are key to success in sales. As we discuss these qualities—these key motivational forces—it should be kept in mind that possession of these qualities is essential to sales success. Without them, someone succeeding in sales would be like someone trying to defy gravity. Keep in mind, though, that possessing these qualities alone does not ensure success in sales. It takes additional qualities to succeed in specific sales jobs.

CHAPTER 3

The Motivation
to Succeed

The key element that separates the top 20 percent of all salespeople—the 20 percent who consistently sell most of what is sold—from the rest is their motivation to excel in a very special way. Only by understanding what motivates an individual from within can we know what it really takes to succeed in sales or any other occupation.

Companies are continually looking for ways to motivate their people. Motivational speakers are featured at company meetings and industry conventions. Incentive plans are developed, and contests are held. In most companies, there is an endless sequence of carrot and/or stick programs designed to motivate. Unfortunately, virtually all this attention to motivation deals with external factors rather than internal motivation. Our work over the past half century has proven beyond question that the real key to productivity is not external motivation but, rather, that which is generated from within the individual—what we term *internal motivation. Motivation* is commonly defined as an incentive that persuades someone to do something. We pay salespeople commissions to motivate them to sell—a positive motivation. On the other hand, there is the threat of being fired if people do not come to work on time or if they fail to work diligently. The annual review serves as another motivator, theoretically driving people to do their best for the purpose of earning salary increases or promotions. These are the classic carrots and sticks.

But it is our view that entirely too much emphasis is placed on these externals and not nearly enough on what is the critical key to effective job performance—internal motivation. In the long run, the external motivations have little bearing on how well or how poorly an individual will perform. Of course, people want promotions. Of course, they want higher commissions. And of course, they do not want to be fired. However, these carrots and sticks do not lead to effective, productive work.

The true motivation that causes individuals to excel comes from within. It is this inner motivation that distinguishes the 20 percent of those who succeed in the sales profession. Internal motivation is what drives us from within to act.

However, because inner motivation seems so difficult to understand, many managers focus on the more obvious but less effective external motivations. For instance, many sales organizations set aside a particular month as "supersales month." All the salespeople are listed on a board, and each person's sales are noted on a daily basis. This public display is, of course, designed to motivate everyone to compete. At the end of the month, the top producer will receive an all-expense-paid trip for two to Hawaii with all the frills.

As expected, everyone works hard during that month, sales increase, and someone wins the glamorous trip. Aside from the wonderful time the top producer has in Hawaii, however, the story does not have such a happy ending. Two results somehow tarnish the luster of the exercise in external motivation. First, to no one's surprise, the winner of the contest has been the top producer consistently for two years. Second, and much more important to the success of the company, although sales increased during the contest month, they dropped substantially over the next couple of months, and the year's final results were the same as they would have been without the contest.

What the external incentive did was generate some additional activity for a short period of time and caused people to either delay sales in order to close them in that month or hurry to push them into that month. But the overall totals were not affected. Simply put, sales, and individuals, found their level.

It is much easier to hire motivational speakers or to set up contests of this kind in the hope that such external processes will increase productivity. External incentives are tangible, so we reach toward them as solutions. Everyone walks out of the room feeling wonderful after being exposed to a dramatic motivational speaker. Still, we cannot help but wonder whether the productivity increase is any better than it would have been if the participants had gone to a Broadway play or a special concert, after which there is also a wonderful feeling.

The truth is, though it is much more difficult to uncover, that the inner motivation determines how well an individual will do in a specific job. Inner motivation is much harder to deal with because you have to delve below the surface to uncover and understand that motivation. Interviewing, conducting psychological testing, and checking résumés and references are all focused on uncovering some of a person's inner motivations. How effective we are in this quest determines how successful we will be in our hiring. The plain truth is that if we hire people whose motivations and abilities suit them to the position, then and only then can some of those external motivational approaches have a long-lasting, positive effect on productivity. Without the proper internal motivations, external motivations can create motion but not consistent achievements.

To help better understand internal motivations, think for a moment of the laziest person you know. Most likely, that individual is working for your company. When you look at this "lazy person," ask yourself if he or she is too lazy to get up at 4:00 in the morning to go fishing, or to stand in the hot sun swinging a golf club, or to work in the garden, or to play bridge, or to do one of a hundred other enjoyable things. The answer is, "Of course not." What you are really saying when you think about that lazy person is that he or she is too lazy to do what you want him or her to do. The reality is that this so-called laziness, with few exceptions, is really a lack of inner motivation. Provide people with an activity that connects with their inner motivations, and they will work as hard as anyone else.

This is our basic thesis. If an individual possesses the inner motivation to do a job and is given the proper training and supervision, he or she will succeed. On the other hand, if an individual does not possess the proper inner motivation required to perform successfully in a specific job, all the training and incentives in the world will not make that individual highly productive. That lazy person's willingness to work hard at fishing or golf is really typical of all human beings. We will work at what is fun for us—at what we enjoy. If we enjoy our work because that work satisfies our inner motivations, we need no one to tell us to work harder—we will do it because we want to, because it is rewarding. If, on the other hand, we hate what we are doing because it runs counter to our basic motivational forces, we might go through the motions, we might do our best because it is our responsibility, but we will never really be happy and will never really achieve at a top level regardless of the external motivations.

We want to underscore the point that money motivates virtually everyone to some degree. But truly effective individuals in any field are motivated by more than money. For them, money is a symbol of achievement, not a motivational factor in and of itself. This is our basic thesis. If an individual possesses the inner motivation to do a job and is given proper training and supervision, he or she will succeed. On the other hand, if an individual does not possess the inner motivation required to perform successfully, all the training and incentives in the world will not make that individual highly productive.

We should add here that as strongly as we deny the power of external motivations to create productivity, we have seen situations where external motivations can place serious limits on that productivity. It is certainly possible, for example, to set up a compensation system that runs counter to the motivations of the people receiving that compensation. If highly driven salespeople, with tremendous persuasive motivation and entrepreneurial orientation, are placed on a salary, even a high salary, with little upward mobility, this will demotivate them. The incentives—the commissions—will not in and of themselves act as a motivation, but their absence, for certain individuals who need enormous up-end potential, can act as a disincentive.

A number of years ago we ran into a classic case of this disincentive with one of our clients. We were asked to do a study on the company's sales operation to solve a problem that had plagued the company for more than a decade. The company felt that it was hiring effective salespeople. Most of the new hires started quickly and were highly productive over the first couple of years. However, counter to the experience of most companies that lose salespeople early in their careers, this company found that there was a high level of turnover between the third and fifth years of its salespeople's careers and a parallel flattening out of sales productivity.

When we tested the sales force, we found that the company did have an unusually high number of strongly driven, highly motivated people. Instead of the usual 20 percent of effective salespeople, the staff consisted of more than 50 percent whom we would have recommended for hire on the basis of their sales dynamics. When we investigated further, we found another unusual fact: The high turnover rate in the third to fifth years was largely among the salespeople with strong dynamics. The marginal people, those who were just getting by, were hanging on and were making a career of their mediocrity. This was puzzling. Normally, people leave because they are not succeeding. Here, it was the productive people who were leaving.

As we studied the situation further, the reasons became clear. All signs pointed to the company's sales compensation plan. What occurred simply was that when a salesperson's level of sales became "too high," the person's sales territory would be split. The reasoning, as we found out from interviewing management, was that a salesperson could not possibly handle too large a territory because continuous follow-up was involved in most sales. Thus, once a salesperson had too many clients, the reasoning went, that person could not possibly service all those additional clients.

As rational as this sounds, the net result of splitting the territories was to totally remove the most productive salespeople's incentive to do well. People with drive are normally willing to work for little or no money at the beginning, but they cannot tolerate limits on their top potential. This splitting of territories created an absolute upward limit and therefore destroyed the motivation of those people the company counted on to be most productive. On the other hand, the mediocre salespeople probably never reached a high enough production level to require a split of their territory, so they hung on with their mediocrity.

We suggested that rather than split the territory of the highly productive people, the company provide these top producers—these inner-motivated people—with a service assistant whose job would be to help in the ongoing servicing and follow-up of accounts. Rather than destroying up-end incentives, we felt that it was important to give the top salespeople the ability to deal competently with their ever-expanding book of business. The result was that, within a year, the turnover among the productive salespeople was reduced by two-thirds. As might be expected, productivity increased substantially in proportion to the increased tenure of the effective salespeople. Within one more year, the company was able to gain important savings through reducing the number of senior account representatives and supporting its talented sales staff with lower-paid service assistants.

PERSUADING ONE STEP AT A TIME

Mario Moussa, one of the directors of Wharton School's Strategic Persuasion Workshop, shared a compelling story with us about how understanding the motivation of someone you are trying to persuade can change history.

We're taking you back to December 1776. With very few victories under his belt, General Washington could hardly feed and clothe his army. The winter was brutal. At the end of the month, most of the men would have fulfilled their tour of duty. There was little hope in sight, little reason to continue this struggle. The straits couldn't have been more dire.

"I believe there's a lot of wisdom in this story. It is at a pivotal point in the war when Washington was asking himself, 'How am I going to keep this army together?' He considered all his options, which were few. Then he and his officers hit upon was the idea of offering an incentive to sign up for six months more of duty. So they offered the soldiers $10, which at the time was not a completely insignificant sum. Then he mustered his men together, and one of the officers announced their plan to the soldiers. Then, with a roll of drums, he asked them to take a step forward to indicate their agreement. So they announced this incentive scheme, and they roll the drums, and they stop, and they're waiting for soldiers to take a step, and nobody is moving. And Washington is observing this scene, asking himself how am I going to keep this army together? And he takes a moment to gather his thoughts, and he then delivers one of the most powerful speeches in military history and, even more generally, in rhetorical history, and he says, essentially, 'Men, I understand you've made great sacrifices, you're starving, you're freezing, you've been apart from your families, and you've lost friends, but I can't pursue the cause of liberty without you. The cause of liberty needs you, and I won't be successful unless you stay with me. I asked you for six months of duty. And I understand that is a lot to ask.' Then he paused and said, 'Just stay with me for one more month. Take, with me, a small step for liberty.' And then one man stepped forward. Then another. Then virtually the entire army stayed with him for that month."

He changed the deal. He knew how to connect. He persuaded by understanding the motivations of his men. And as a result, he changed history.

"That month lead to the next and beyond. Most of them stayed for longer than the six months. Most stayed for the rest of the war. There's been a lot of discussion in the psychological literature about the aftermath of that scene. But the point is that the six months at that time, under those conditions, was too big an ask. One month, however, was something the soldiers could commit to. Then, once they made that commitment, those commitments grew legs, as psychologists put it."

Persuading, whether in sales, leadership, or on a personal level, starts with understanding your strengths, your potential, and your motivations. Then it is equally important to thoroughly understand the strengths, potential, and motivations of those who you are trying to persuade.

"Exactly. Another lesson learned in this story is that it's hard to change people's minds. And, for the most part, people change their minds in small ways. Some of us, on a very rare occasion, have a dramatic changes of heart or faith or belief. For the most part, though, we're pretty much who we are, and we don't make dramatic changes. We change in small ways, and that's very important to keep in mind from the point of view of persuasion. It is realizing that most people need time to make small changes. Then, ultimately, what drives those small changes in the way we think is small changes in actions. This is the one-small-step idea. So, if I'm trying to persuade you, it's really important for me to find ways to get you to take a small action step that will lead you to begin to think differently. Then you will align what you think and believe with what you are doing. So, focusing on those small ways I can get you to change is much more effective than asking you to make large, dramatic changes."

Mario tells another compelling story about how understanding the motivation of someone you are trying to persuade recently changed history. This story is about Bono, the lead singer of U2, who is known for his philanthropic work. Whenever Bono comes into a situation he is trying to change, Mario told us, Bono's first question is: "Who's the Elvis?"

What exactly does that mean?

"That's an important question that Bono always begins with. He wants to know who the key player is who has to be convinced. A few years ago, Bono identified Jesse Helms as the key person to get on board with a United Nations initiative to save people who were dying from malaria in Africa."

So how did Bono connect with Jesse Helms?

"First, he did a lot of preparation. And, interestingly, before he went to meet the senator, Bono asked his driver to make a couple of turns around the block, as he re-checked his facts, making absolutely sure he was prepared. Then they sat down together, and you can picture them, knee-to-knee, this very conservative, elder senator and the rock star with his wraparound sunglasses, greased back hair and earrings. And Bono is extremely deferential, you know, saying Senator this and Senator that. Then he starts with his 'pitch,' if you like, which was very fact-oriented. He was reeling off figures about how 5,000 people were dying from malaria each day. And he was delivering in a kind of rapid-fire machine gun style. But it wasn't connecting with Helms. In fact, the senator literally started nodding off. So Bono switched from fact-orientation to value-orientation. And he started telling stories from the Bible, and he shared what he knew about orphans traveling from village to village, searching for food and shelter. That's how he began to connect with Jesse Helms. And, as he continued telling some of their personal stories, tears began to run down the senator's cheeks. Then the elder statesman stood up and threw his arms around Bono and said, 'Whatever you want, I'll give it to you.'"

True persuasion starts with a real connection. You need a strong sense of who you are, where you're coming from; and, at the same time, you also need an equally strong sense of where the other person is coming from. And you need to meet in between those strengths.

We'd like to close by sharing a story about someone who has figured out how to sell the first stage of persuading.

Claudia Timbo, an entrepreneur and call-center expert, has created and sold several businesses that were designed for the expressed purpose of arranging meetings for salespeople to meet likely prospects. It all began nearly three decades ago when she answered a phone that was ringing in her husband's home office. He was a traveling salesperson, working for a firm that helped customers reduce their real estate taxes. "The caller was from Buffalo, and he needed advice because his taxes were going to be raised. My husband was away on a business trip. So I made the appointment for him. Then I got to thinking: If this person was going to have his taxes raised, there were probably other businesses in Buffalo in the same situation. So I started making calls. And by the time my husband returned from his business trip, I had four more appointments in Buffalo for him. Then I started arranging similar trips. And after a few months, his manager saw my husband's numbers climbing and asked what he was doing differently."

Since then, Claudia went on to open call centers that succeeded because they had a very personal touch. While most people cringe at the notion of cold-calling, she has reinvented the model. She focuses on hiring superior talent, which most businesses would envy, including retired executives with significant business credentials and people with disabilities.

What Claudia and her team are selling is a meeting. They are selling the opportunity for a salesperson to meet with the right person in a company. "Salespeople need to have a lot of appointments. And most salespeople are very good in front of their clients, but they don't like to do the cold-calling. So we are selling the appointment for them, making it easier for them to succeed by freeing them up to do what they are most effective at—which is presenting to the prospect, following up, and making a sale," she told us.

So Claudia has broken the sales process down into its component parts. And she has made a sale out of the first part of the selling process—creating a meeting.

Her sale is setting up the sale. And she's made a business of it. Several businesses, actually. It all starts with being clear about what you are selling.

Persuading is about making something happen. So it starts with changing someone's mind. That leads to the change we are seeking, changing actions, and ultimately, changing the way things are.

Persuading starts with understanding where people are coming from and how they would like to change. And, sometimes, persuasion can change history.

Now let's dive into the traits that are the foundation for this internal motivation to succeed in sales.

CHAPTER 4

Empathy:
The Guidance System

The first key quality we found to be of critical importance to sales success is empathy. *Empathy* is the ability to read others. It's knowing what drives them. It's being able to intuit their strengths, limitations, potential, and motivations. Empathy is the ability to pick up the subtle clues and cues provided by others in order to accurately assess what they are thinking and feeling.

People with real empathy would not walk into an antique shop and ask, "What's new?" *(OK. We couldn't help ourselves.)*

It is important to keep in mind that empathy does not necessarily involve agreeing with the feelings of others, but it does involve knowing what their feelings or ideas are. Empathy is not sympathy. Objectivity is lost in sympathy. Sympathy involves a feeling of loyalty to another person and thus the loss of objectivity. If you identify with and feel the emotions of others, you cannot view them in a dispassionate, objective, and helpful manner.

Thus, in order to sell effectively, you must understand how a prospect or client is feeling while still maintaining your own sense of identity, your own purpose, and your own objectives. A salesperson simply cannot sell without this invaluable and irreplaceable ability.

Because sales involves concerns, questions, and objections, salespeople need to be empathic and flexible enough to adjust their presentation and approach. Understanding the needs of individual customers and selling them an appropriate solution is part of a building-block process that starts with someone who is empathic enough to really hear what is being said and really feel the needs of prospects, including clear recognition of unspoken agendas and objections. It is those unexpressed agendas and objections that often can defeat a sale. Only with sufficient empathy to recognize the real needs of a prospect can those needs be met.

We would like to underscore something very important that we have learned about the way salespeople integrate empathy into their approach to connecting with prospects and clients.

There are three distinct ways salespeople can come across as being empathic.

Individuals who are genuinely empathic have very high levels of flexibility, openness, and sensitivity. They have natural warmth, which others immediately sense and respond to. When someone who is empathic asks how others are, they often receive a real, sometimes surprising answer. We sense that they care, and as a result, our relationships can become more open and meaningful.

We also have come across successful salespeople who have what we would measure to be a moderate level of empathy, but when the situation calls for it, they turn up the volume on their empathy. And their situational empathy allows them to tune in, when needed, to pick up the subtle clues and cues that others might miss.

In addition, we have worked with salespeople who succeed because they have a natural intellectual curiosity and are very accommodating. Such individuals can come across as intrigued by how things work and fascinated to know why things are the way they are. And they also can get people to open up.

The results of understanding where a client is coming from can be very similar for all three of these individuals as long as they are being true to themselves, playing to their natural strengths. All three—those with genuine empathy, those who know how to turn up the volume on the empathy they have, and those who are intellectually curious and accommodating—are able to connect with their prospects and clients, often creating a desired level of trust and confidence. What is important is that they are being genuine, not trying to be something they are not. Nothing can turn us off more than someone who isn't really interested but is trying to be. We can all sense a fake a mile away.

That being said, we want to emphasize that we are naturally drawn to people who possess genuine empathy. Empathy is the starting place for connecting. Salespeople who are empathic will make more real and lasting connections with their clients.

Amalia Sina, president of Sina Cosmetics in Brazil, describes selling as "the universal concept of connecting with someone else. It is all about making a true connection. Wherever you are in the world, selling is ultimately that one-to-one connection. And there is nothing that can replace it. It starts with understanding the interests of someone else. Then it is connecting, through your natural enthusiasm, with their dreams, their ideas, their hopes."

During the course of our early research, we identified empathy as the single basic ingredient common to all effective salespeople. Empathy alone, however, does not create sales. The successful salesperson, while he or she may genuinely like the prospect and sincerely may want to serve the prospect well through the product or service, nevertheless sees that prospect as a means of achieving the end of making the sale and, therefore, as a means of gratifying the salesperson's ego needs. A salesperson who loses sight of this goal, though he or she may be well liked, will be less effective in overcoming objections and closing sales.

Let us share a story from one of our clients that illustrates this point. A sales manager was coaching one of her salespeople who failed to close a sale with an important prospect. The sales process evidently had been going on for more than three months. In response to the manager's coaching, the salesman explained that the president of the prospect company was extremely busy. He went on to describe the absolutely staggering schedule the president followed and how difficult he found it to add to the president's pressure. He then explained, "When I do get to see him, I feel that I only have part of his attention and that he actually has one foot out the door." What was happening here was that the salesman so identified with the customer's pressures that he failed to keep his objective in mind, which was to provide a service that would, in the long run, actually help to alleviate some of those pressures. The overidentification with the customer's busy schedule prevented the salesman from meeting his own objective, which was to make the sale.

At the other end of the spectrum are people who choose to perform on the surface of life. They deal with what is tangibly in front of them and tend to accept what is said and what is done at face value. They are not interested in exploring what might lie behind a statement or action and spend little of their energy thinking about the motivations or needs of others. These individuals might be perfectly nice, friendly, and even outgoing individuals. They might even be right there when someone needed help, especially physical help. The key, however, is that they do not probe beneath the readily recognizable aspects of life. If someone falls and is injured, they will respond to this, but they are not likely to recognize or want to become involved in the psychic pain that another might be experiencing.

On the other side of the coin, there are individuals who are motivated to read and understand others. They probe beneath the surface and are constantly asking questions and listening because they are genuinely interested in others.

"Unless it is a very simple transactional type of sale, people still want to do business with people. It's that simple. And they want to work with people they trust. That does not come about without a deep personal connection. And empathy is a huge component of that. Am I understanding you? Are you getting me? Are we connecting? Without that real connection, which starts with empathy, a lid will be put on how successful a salesperson can be," Bill Ecstrom, president of the EcSELL Institute, told us.

Andrew Skipp, president and CEO of Hubbard-Hall, Inc., a leading chemical manufacturer, distributor, and service provider, told us how empathy has been at the heart of his company culture since its founding in 1849, and therefore, empathy infuses how the company comes through for its customers.

"Everything we do is really about making our clients more successful. How can I help make the person I'm working with be more successful in his or her job? How can I provide a solution that will make his or her life better? It is really about developing those individual relationships in a way where you help them succeed. And that comes from trust. It comes from having real expertise. And it comes from being able to listen and gain a true perception of what your client is trying to accomplish. I remind our salespeople to seek first to understand, then to be understood. By that, I mean that trust requires someone believing that they are truly heard. You have to take the time to understand the person, their concerns, what they want to accomplish, and the challenges they are confronting. Then you have to be able to look beyond just a straight line. By being a little more abstract in your thinking and being able to tie in other aspects and solutions from other companies in which you've dealt with, and recognizing a parallel situation. It is about being able to look clearly at the challenge at hand while also being able to see beyond the dimensions that your customer might be presenting to you."

Empathy is the starting place for connecting with a client, as well as for being able to understand his or her unique problem and being able to see beyond the obvious. Inside of empathy is a genuine interest and a real curiosity.

"We are trying to understand what the ultimate goal of our customer is, what they are truly trying to accomplish. And many times that means understanding the needs of our customer's customers. What are the requirements of *their* customers? Because they may see their customer's requirements as one thing, but we may be able to lend a new perspective that could help them come through for their customer in ways that they hadn't even considered before. So we are able to make them more successful by coming through in a bigger and more unexpected way for their customer."

To provide an unexpected solution, you need a real understanding of the problem. And only through real empathy can you get at the problem. Or the problem behind the problem.

"By way of example, one of our top salespeople had a client who was purchasing massive amounts of several different raw materials from us. Now some salespeople might just say, 'That's wonderful.' Then do everything they could to make sure that we were delivering our material on time. But this particular salesperson wanted to delve below the surface and deepen her relationship with our customer. So she asked why they were purchasing these particular materials. And she discovered that they were mixing them to create another product. But that process was complicated for them, involving exact amounts of specific quantities, and there was a lot of waste in the procedure, let alone time lost. After consulting with our chemists, our salesperson was able to come back to our customer with an idea of how we could blend these raw materials for them, creating their base mixture and delivering it as they needed it, eliminating any need for storage and waste. So we've been able to come through for our customer in a way that is a great win-win. We're selling them tanker loads of the mixture they need, and they've increased their manufacturing capabilities while decreasing their production cycle."

It all starts with empathy, with really listening and connecting on a deeper level.

Ed Kaplan, group vice president of human resources at K. Hovnanian Homes, a nationally recognized homebuilder for over a half century, told us about a critical selling path he teaches that has 22 steps. And each of the steps starts with empathy.

"We are heavy into relationship selling. You know, you can go to a department store, pick up a purchase, go to the cash register, and check out. You don't do that with homes. For our buyers, who are having a home built for them, the process can take up to nine months. The buyers need to get comfortable, looking at all the ins and outs and considering that home against a wide variety of similarly priced homes."

So it all has to start with the relationship that the salesperson develops with the potential buyer.

"It's all about creating that relationship, keeping the home buyers coming back on a regular basis, being keenly aware of their wants and needs, keeping them excited, and ultimately, introducing them to the right home for them. If they believe in you, you have an opportunity to make a sale. If they don't, you won't."

Buying a home is the largest purchase most people will make. So the salesperson has to be able to connect with the potential buyers in a way that is real and genuine, getting to know who they are, what they're about, their hopes and dreams. "If you are buying a home to be built for you, our salesperson will have an active relationship with you anywhere from six to nine months while your home is going up. There are various touch points. Most people come to visit their home as it's being built on a regular basis. So the salesperson accompanies them, keeping them informed, addressing each and every concern, and maintaining their enthusiasm. That takes a real connection. Genuine empathy. And that has to continue through the end of the sale and beyond. That's for two reasons. One is that our homes are under warranty. So the salesperson is still responsible for the sale for 5 or 10 years down the road. And second, every successful salesperson knows that even though there will be basically one payday per customer, the depth of the relationship will be reflected in the amount of referrals that come afterward."

The empathy is never designed to end. In relationship selling, empathy is at the heart of the relationship.

"I tell all our sales consultants that the ultimate goal is to be invited to the open house. When the people move in and celebrate their new home by having friends and family over, if you are invited to that open house, that means you did your job right."

It is all about asking questions that come from a genuine curiosity, from a place of real empathy, adds Edilson Lopes, founder and director of KLA Business Education, one of the largest training companies in Brazil.

"Some people can ask a question and get a one-word response. Others can ask the same question and get someone to really open up. As a result of that opening up, everything changes. It has to do with having empathy, with being genuinely curious, and with allowing those qualities to come through and shine."

It is a matter of being truly interested. That's something that can't be faked.

"Even if it is as simple as buying an automobile. One salesperson might be asking you questions about what color you would like, while another could be getting you to open up about the car you always wanted to own when you first started driving. It all starts with being curious about people, truly interested, and knowing how to make a real connection. The difference is whether you are tapping into the latest fashion or someone's true passion."

Empathy is the first ingredient of the sales equation.

There are many people who possess real empathy, however, who struggle at sales. This is so because empathy alone won't make the cash register ring. For every successful salesperson, there are several who, on the surface, seem to have the same qualities but can't quite cut it. They are outgoing, friendly, and curious and have a way of making their prospects and customers feel very special. However, they rarely close a sale. They know how to educate their buyers and work with enormous energy, but when the customers sign on the proverbial dotted line, it is often with another salesperson.

Why is that?

While empathy is absolutely essential to sales success, empathy by itself is not enough. The best and most effective salespeople use their empathy as the guidance system for their sales process. But empathy is just one ingredient necessary for sales success.

CHAPTER 5

Ego-Drive:
The Motivational Force

What is it about salespeople that set them apart from other professionals? Why don't they look for jobs in which they can drop an anchor in calmer waters and face a judgment of their abilities only when it comes time for an annual salary review? Why do they endure rejections even though they could be avoided? The answers to these questions are one and the same—ego-drive.

Ego-drive is a unique quality that makes a salesperson want and need to make a sale in a very personal way. Individuals with ego-drive feel that the sale has to be made. So the prospect is there to help fulfill a personal need. To the top salesperson, getting a prospect to say "Yes" provides a powerful means for ego enhancement. His or her self-image improves dramatically by virtue of achieving that yes and diminishes slightly with each sales failure. Whether the yes involves commission is far less relevant than the yes itself. To the ego-driven individual, "Yes, I will go out with you" or "Yes, I will join your club" or "Yes, I will vote for your candidate" or "Yes, I agree with you" is just as satisfying as "Yes, I will buy your product or service." If an individual really has ego-drive, he or she needs that yes—regardless of what the yes is—as a key means of satisfying his or her ego-drive.

How people view themselves underlies most of their ambition and motivation. We seek approval, we want acceptance, and we enjoy our associates' acclamation for a job well done. For the fortunate among us, the path we choose in search of self-enhancement becomes our career.

Engineers are gratified by designing complex bridges or buildings. Artists achieve gratification by expressing themselves creatively. Teachers achieve gratification through the accomplishments of their students. Carpenters and tailors achieve gratification by exercising their craftsmanship. In the same way, top salespeople enhance their egos through persuading others, frequently in face-to-face, one-on-one situations.

What salespeople seek is an opportunity to turn others around to their point of view. This is why top salespeople never really retire. Characteristically, after reaching the mandatory retirement age, they may head a local fund drive, put their energy to work fighting for one civic cause or another, or perhaps even enter into politics for the first time. Even when he or she no longer needs the money earned in a life-long process of persuasion, the salesperson is still strongly driven to persuade. Persuading is like breathing for the ego-driven individual.

When we asked Peter Byloos, M.D., CEO of Handicare, "What is it about convincing someone else that gives you a kick?" he didn't miss a beat. "It's the achievement," he said, definitively. "It's all about winning." He paused for a moment and then added, "It's not about the money or the title or the rewards or any of that. For me, it's just about winning. I guess everybody has their own motivators, but winning a deal is just great fun. To win when you know your competition was in there trying to get the deal and knowing that you won. That's as good as it gets."

Mike Ferguson, CEO of VXI Corporation, a company known for delivering best-in-class headset solutions, told us that he learned a lot about the way he persuades when he was in his first sales job and having a difficult time making ends meet. "I was really struggling. Then, all of a sudden, one day, it all clicked in, the light went on, and I suddenly understood what I was doing right and what I was doing wrong. What I discovered about myself was that in the normal part of my life, the part where I wasn't trying to convince people, I was actually very persuasive. I was able to convince people to do things or give them advice, and they were appreciative and would take it. I was persuading naturally. And what I was doing was helping them to see solutions to problems. I was painting a picture in words and sharing what I saw and what I knew. But I was able to do it with a kind of take-it-or-leave-it approach. And it worked beautifully. When I needed to sell for a living, though, I was forcing it. I found that I was actually trying to sell somebody something. And my approach was not working. I was getting in my own way because I was not being natural. I wasn't being who I was and using my innate persuasive abilities. So I said to myself, 'Tomorrow, when I wake up, I'm going to change the way I approach my customers in the marketplace. I'm going to be who I am.' And I would say to them, 'Here are your options. This is the option that makes the most sense to me because of the following reasons.' Then I'd ask them what they thought. And maybe they'd agree with me or maybe they would come up with another option. But we worked on it together. And all of a sudden I was convincing customers in business like I'd been doing all my life in normal everyday situations. And that's when I became a successful salesperson."

This need to persuade, ego-drive, however, should not be confused with the usual perceptions of drive, willingness to work, and aggressiveness. For example, a bank president may be extremely ambitious, driven, hardworking, and aggressive but still not have an inner need to persuade. Ego-drive is a particular means of gaining self-enhancement through persuasion of another person; it is not to be confused with a general desire to get ahead or to achieve.

It should be kept in mind, however, that strong ego-drive alone does not ensure success in selling. Ironically, unless it is properly balanced with empathy and other key personality characteristics, too much ego-drive can spell disaster in selling. The reason is simple: Salespeople whose ego-drive is in overdrive are "too hungry" for the close. They are so driven to conquer in a one-on-one situation that they tend to bowl customers over, rushing toward a close without listening to possible objections or not even relating the product or service to the prospect's needs. Such a salesperson, by the sheer force of his or her personality, may produce some sales, but he or she will miss many sales that a more sensitive, more balanced salesperson would have achieved in similar circumstances. Such salespeople often offend or alienate potential customers and, in the process, burn territory for their companies.

Clearly, a balance must exist between ego-drive and other basic personality characteristics if a salesperson is to be genuinely successful. We can illustrate our point here by considering the case of Jack, a salesman for a major computer firm. On first appearance, Jack would impress any potential employer with his prototypical sales abilities. Yet he was among the least productive members of the sales force. When we examined his personality dynamics in detail and then checked his personality profile against his job, the reason for his low productivity was clear: Jack's job was to sell large computer installations to the government. Success was defined as selling two major installations per year. The financial rewards for these two sales were enormous, but Jack's ego-drive was so intense that he simply could not tolerate the infrequency of closings. In his desperation to achieve a quick sale, his need for the close impelled him to push too hard, so he met with failure.

This does not mean that Jack had no value as a salesperson. It simply means that his personality dynamics were wrong for the particular sales job in which he was slotted. He was transferred to another division of the company that provides time-shared computer services—payroll, accounting, and the like—primarily to small and medium-sized businesses. His success was almost immediate. The reason was that he had several closing opportunities per day and, given his level of ego-drive, was able to convert more than his share. The reality for Jack was that his up-end financial opportunity was somewhat less in the new situation, but the opportunity for satisfying his ego-drive was greater.

We have learned from dealing with thousands of Jacks and their employers that the salesperson with an overabundance of ego-drive can, if his or her drive is tempered by other qualities, be exceptionally successful with essentially hard-sell and small-ticket products.

The evidence is clear that no single salesperson would be equally effective in all sales jobs. (This is one of the most critical and often overlooked factors in attempting to build a sales force.) Some people's personality dynamics suit them to a particular kind of selling, but no person is ideally suited to all kinds of selling.

With this fact in mind, we will in later chapters discuss the various personality characteristics that are needed to succeed in different types of selling. Nevertheless, empathy and ego-drive are the two most important characteristics for identifying the basic sales personality.

ARE THESE QUALITIES IN OUR DNA?

The question that invariably arises in discussions about the dynamics of a successful salesperson is this: Are these abilities inborn, or are they developed? Is ego-drive something—a genetic quality, perhaps—that exists in the individual from birth, or is it something that can be developed in anyone through training and motivation?

There is no way to know the exact role that genetics or socialization plays in any behavioral trait. The answer probably lies somewhere between nature and nurture. Undoubtedly, there are some inherited qualities that provide the kind of climate in which ego-drive is more likely to develop. Yet there is not sufficient evidence to prove that genetics alone is responsible for ego-drive. What appears to be the predominant factor in the existence of ego-drive—as in the development of other personality characteristics—is childhood and early adolescent experiences.

We know one young man who has grown up to be a professional musician. While in college, he would turn his ego-drive on at least once a month to get a gig playing in a local club and make enough money to pay his rent.

That ability, indeed desire, to persuade served him well. While he did not pursue sales as a profession, his ability to persuade was something he could pull out of his back pocket whenever he needed it.

His mother recalled when he was selling cookies for an elementary school fund-raising project. She was amused at how he could turn on his ability to persuade at just the right moments. She laughed recalling a telephone call she got from one of her neighbors who said, "Your son will never starve. He just left my house, and I bought more cookies than I'll ever know what to do with. In fact, I don't even like cookies. I never have. But he somehow convinced me that I couldn't do without them."

Was he born with that ability, or did he learn it at a very young age?

All we can tell you for certain is that he had it as soon as he needed it.

Putting aside "born" or "made" theories, we know that ego-drive exists in young adults to the precise degree that it will continue to exist for the rest of their lives. A person who is not basically motivated to persuade others cannot be trained to derive primary satisfaction from selling. You cannot train people to use what they do not have. Only a person with ego-drive can be trained to use what he or she has in a maximally effective way.

Ego-drive is to the salesperson what fuel is to an automobile engine. Without fuel, the automobile engine cannot move forward. With fuel, but without steering, the automobile constitutes a hazard and is valueless. In selling, ego-drive is that fuel, whereas empathy provides the steering.

CHAPTER 6

Ego-Strength:
The Key to Resilience

When all is said and done, selling is a game of trying to beat the odds of rejection. Rare indeed is the salesperson who can close a sale in two contacts. Any person who is attempting to persuade another individual is more likely to be rejected than to be accepted. What happens, then, to the persuader (the individual who likes himself or herself better as a result of getting someone else to say "Yes") when the inevitable rejection occurs? The individual feels diminished. But the key here is that the salesperson must never feel totally diminished. When one fails, one obviously does not feel too good, but the essential question is: Does that person have the resiliency—or what we call *ego-strength*—to bounce back from rejection?

People with resilience—and it is extremely difficult to succeed at anything in life without it—view rejection as something to get over, to get through, to get on the other side of. At the end of the day, this quality has a lot to do with defining who we are. Top performers—in sales, management, leadership, whatever your pursuit—learn from negative experiences and turn them into defining moments.

Succeeding has much to do with how we handle adversity. Do we shut down? Or open up? Do we put our head down and just keep doing what we were doing before? A little faster? A little harder? Or do we look around and discover a new path? The difference has to do with how we succeed—and who we become.

To succeed, we have to be able to handle situations we wish we didn't have to. It's knowing that rejection, and even failure, is just part of the game. Nothing personal.

Resilience, or *ego-strength*, is the degree to which an individual basically likes himself or herself. If an individual possesses a high level of ego-strength, then failure can motivate that person toward the next try.

Persons with ego-strength feel as bad as anyone else would when they encounter failure, but they react to that failure much as the hungry person does to missing a meal: They are that much hungrier for the next opportunity.

The failure, though disappointing, does not destroy their positive view of themselves. The failure is not personalized but rather creates a disappointment—a lack of fulfillment—that the next opportunity will correct. On the other hand, when people do not have sufficient ego-strength to react with resiliency—if they don't have enough positive feelings about themselves—they take the rejection personally. They feel that the *no* is a no *to them* personally, so they take it to heart. They are therefore very hesitant to seek another situation that could incur yet another rejection because even if they have a desire to persuade, the pain of the potential rejection is simply too great to run the risk.

It is important to note that many people confuse resilience with toughness. Toughness is an aspect of resilience, certainly. Being tough can be an advantage in certain circumstances. But only to a certain point. This is so because toughness also can create an armor that deflects emotion. And it can cut us off from many of the resources we need to bounce back. Most important, it can cut us off from the people around us.

Resilience, by contrast, is very different. Resilience is not about deflecting challenges. Resilience is about absorbing those challenges and rebounding even stronger than before.

In our first article in the *Harvard Business Review* in the early 1960s, we identified ego-drive and empathy as the two key traits needed to succeed in sales. Then we ran into a situation that taught us in a most dramatic fashion the importance of ego-strength.

We evaluated a sales applicant for a client and strongly recommended that the client hire the individual. He had outstanding empathy and possessed more than enough ego-drive to close sales effectively in that company's situation. He also had a strong sense of responsibility and clearly possessed the desire to succeed.

Sure enough, the young man started out like a whirlwind. Within a month after the training period, he was in the top 10 percent of the sales force, and to say the least, we had a very happy client.

Three months later we received a bewildered call from the sales manager. To paraphrase, the manager said to us: "Jim simply stopped producing about a month ago. As you know, we thought he would be one of the best salespeople we ever hired. But all of a sudden it all seemed to come apart. He has not made a sale in the last month, and what is making it worse is that he is beginning to come in late and take very long lunches. He obviously has the ability. But what do you think could have happened?"

We reevaluated his personality assessment and determined, again, that Jim had all the ego-drive and empathy that we originally thought he did. But what we began to see as we examined the results of his behavioral test was that he really did not have positive feelings about himself. His ego-strength was clearly lacking. As we discussed the situation in more detail with the manager and interviewed Jim, the picture became clear. Given his ability, Jim successfully closed a number of sales in succession. Someone with less ability would never have made those sales, but anyone, regardless of ability, could not continue at that sales pace. Inevitably, rejection pushed Jim out of the super-sales level. Statistics being what they are, those rejections came in three out of every four sales attempts, and simply put, Jim's lack of ego-strength made it impossible for him to deal with such rejection. He was not able to simply look at the rejections as statistics inevitably catching up with him but rather saw them as a truth finally being told. The early successes he viewed as simply a fluke, and the real Jim was represented by the failures.

As a means of desperately trying to turn his situation around, Jim pressed too hard and literally drove away prospects that he would have sold earlier. The more he pressed, the more he failed, and the more he failed, the more he came down on himself. Finally, despite his obvious sales talent, Jim was terminated.

The case of Cathy illustrates the role of ego-strength in quite a different way. When we evaluated her personality attributes, we saw an individual who had excellent empathy, was highly intelligent, and possessed both a strong sense of responsibility and fine personal organizational skills. Our only doubt related to her ego-drive. She definitely had some persuasive motivation, but she lacked the intense need to persuade that characterizes most highly productive salespeople. She got pleasure from the close—from getting the "Yes"—but not the typical kind of intense satisfaction that strongly ego-driven people receive. Thus we felt that she might miss some closes because of this lack of intense drive.

Given her other strong qualities, especially her strong sense of self (her good ego-strength), we suggested to our client that Cathy be hired. We also suggested that if at all possible, she be provided with training in the area of closing skills to try to bolster her moderate ego-drive.

Cathy was hired, and for the first month or two, we and our client were concerned because she started extremely slowly. Finally, she made her first sale—although, as our client described it, she did have a number of prospects on the line.

Slowly, however, the situation began changing. A few of the prospects became customers, and her number of prospects increased steadily. Within six months, Cathy was functioning in the middle of the sales force, and by the end of the first year, she was high in the second quartile. At this writing, four years later, Cathy is still functioning well in the second quartile of the sales force, and although not a top producer, she is well above average and an important, strong contributor to the company's bottom line.

Unlike Jim, Cathy's rejections came early. Because of her lack of intense ego-drive, she did not close sales early and often. Rather, she experienced the rejections and failures that are so typical of novices. But again, unlike Jim, because of her strong sense of self (her good ego-strength), she did not view the rejections in a personal way. She saw her failures as the inevitable result of inexperience and of the price she had to pay to gain that experience. Because of many other strong personality attributes, she would not accept no as a final answer but continued to consider her prospects as potential customers in need of follow-up. And of equal importance, she was able to continue looking for more prospects without fearing their rejection. In the long run, she had enough ego-drive to convert some of those initial rejections to closings and, with increasing know-how, to slowly but steadily improve her initial conversion ratio.

The difference between Jim and Cathy can be summed up this way: Jim obviously had more drive and possessed the potential to function near the very top of the sales force. His lack of ego-strength, however, made it impossible for him to actualize that talent because he could not deal with the inevitable rejection that even a superstar must experience. On the other hand, Cathy, with less inherent persuasive talent, could function near the top of her potential because she felt good enough about herself and strong enough within herself to do so.

Chris Pierson, director of sales for Stratix Systems, a technology company that focuses on document and information management, told us, "We look for salespeople who have demonstrated earlier in their lives that they know how to compete. That they're in it to win. But they know how to take defeat. They are driven to win. So the setbacks don't define them. They're just something to get over. People who are resilient bring their sense of self-worth and pride and drive to any situation. And they know how to make it better. That's who we look for. People who are built that way."

He added, "This quality is particularly important in these tough economic times. They have to view it as an opportunity to win new business from your competitors, who may not be as strong as you. It's a chance to go to the clients of your competitors and make sure that they feel that they're being treated fairly, that they're getting the best products and service. It is actually the best time for someone who is resilient to get in front of prospects and to tell their story."

Salespeople, in particular, salespeople with a strong sense of resilience, view rejection differently from most people on this planet. Most people, when they are rejected, say to themselves, "Well, that wasn't a whole lot of fun. I don't think I'm going to try that again."

But successful salespeople view rejection as a learning experience. Nothing personal. When they are turned down or lose a sale, they are walking out saying, "I know what just happened. I didn't know enough about my prospect, or my competition, or the marketplace." And if they could, they'd go through a revolving door and replay the situation all over again—with a different ending this time.

It's like their mind is a tape recorder, and if they could, they'd like to tape over the experience of being rejected with a new experience of being accepted.

Ego-strength is, quite simply, an individual's ability to feel good enough about himself or herself to accept rejection not as a personal affront but as part of life. The individual with ego-strength has the ability to leave the rejection behind and go on from there. Those who accept themselves, who possess ego-strength, operate freely and fully, allowing themselves to function at or near the top of their capacity.

CHAPTER 7

Integrating the Dynamics for Success

No one person, regardless of his or her personality dynamics, can be equally successful in all types of sales situations. Let us look at why this is so. The personality characteristics that we have been discussing do not exist independently. They affect one another—sometimes positively, sometimes negatively. These qualities exist in a dynamic relationship.

Let's look at a number of possible combinations of just two of these qualities—empathy and ego-drive.

First of all, there are, of course, top-performing salespeople who have a great deal of both empathy and ego-drive. As long as they also have sufficient levels of ego-strength and other key qualities needed for a specific position, they will invariably do well in sales.

Then there are salespeople with fine empathy but too little ego-drive. They may, of course, be splendid human people, but in many cases they will be unable to close effectively. They are usually well liked and, from all appearances, should be among the best salespeople on the staff. But they never quite make it. While they develop very good relationships with prospects, they rarely convert those prospects to clients. Salespeople with fine empathy but very little ego-drive get along with and understand their prospects, but they lack enough inner hunger to move those final few inches to a completed sale.

This is not to say that such individuals will never sell anything. In fact, there are some sales situations in which these individuals may perform reasonably well. They may succeed in detailing doctors for a pharmaceutical house, for example. This is an instance where service and relationship building are more vital than the close. But where fast and frequent closes are the requirement, such individuals will not succeed despite their congeniality, personableness, and sensitivity.

Then there are salespeople with enormous ego-drive but too little empathy. They will be sheer forces of personality, bulldozing their way through to some sales but also missing a great many more. And the real concern for such salespeople is that in the process of making an occasional sale, they may cause enormous damage to their employers' professional reputation.

Again, there are some specific sales situations in which these bulldozers can be reasonably effective. For instance, they may do well selling used cars in a busy auto dealership. In other words, they may succeed in situations where the immediate close is the name of the game, the potential market is unlimited, and the likelihood of repeat business is minute. But their strength begins to wane as soon as the sales situation requires follow-up, service, and relationship building—in short, where repeat business and the development of a stable market are important. Then, even if their number of sales seems acceptable, they can be like termites, causing unseen harm to the firm's professional reputation.

Finally, there is the example of a salesperson without much empathy or ego-drive. In all honesty, such individuals simply should not be in sales. A potential employer would save much time and money by determining this in advance, before hiring, training, and then losing such an individual. This, of course, does not mean that such individuals are failures as human beings. They might be excellent at hundreds of other pursuits: engineering, accounting, computer programming, technical work, operations, or any number of nonselling activities. But they are destined to fail at selling. It is tragic that many such individuals, with little or no chance to succeed in selling, nonetheless carry on a perennial and futile quest for success. This makes for a double waste. First, they fail their employers at the sales job they have chosen, and second, they fail themselves by not choosing a profession at which they could succeed.

Our studies have shown that these individuals without sufficient empathy and ego-drive account for 55 percent of the individuals now attempting to earn a living in sales. Ironically, within the same companies in which they work, there might be any number of openings for jobs they could fill with distinction and profit.

The bottom line is that an individual cannot sell successfully without possessing empathy and ego-drive. However, it is also important to keep in mind that we are not talking about a case of all or nothing. It is not as though someone has, for example, empathy or is completely devoid of it. We all function on a continuum. As we look at someone's ability to sell, we have to look at how much or how little of each quality that person possesses—and how those qualities integrate with the strengths of the person's other qualities.

For certain sales jobs, an individual might have too much ego-drive, with other sales jobs calling for as much ego-drive as possible. Certain sales jobs require only moderately strong persuasive motivation, but a high degree of service must go along with it. Some sales jobs can tolerate somewhat reduced levels of empathy, but others demand very high degrees of that quality.

In short, few people possess optimal amounts of all these essential qualities. As we look at an individual and determine whether that person is suited to a particular sales job, we need to look at how much of each of these central qualities he or she possesses and how these attributes may interact with one another to produce a motivational pattern within that individual. Next, we need to look at the real requirements of the sales job to see how that pattern fits those requirements. Then we still must go to the next step and look at additional qualities beyond these central dynamics that might be required for success in the specific sales role. Then and only then can we predict with some degree of certainty whether an individual is indeed suited to the specific sales job and would most likely succeed.

CHAPTER 8

Other Personality Qualities and the Job Match

As we underscored when discussing the central qualities required for sales success, the possession of empathy, ego-drive, and ego-strength does not ensure success in a particular sales position. When people possess these qualities, they certainly should do well in a position in which persuasion is central to success. What that specific position is, however, depends on the possession of a number of other attributes.

Let us look at some of these qualities that can be as crucial to success in specific sales jobs as the central dynamics themselves. These attributes include the ability to grow on the job, to be an effective decision maker, to be adept at working with details, to organize work and time, to communicate effectively, to work as a team member, to be willing to risk and try new things, to be assertive and aggressive where necessary, to be shrewd in sizing up situations, to possess a sense of urgency or a drive to get things done with all due haste, and more.

GROWTH

Whether an individual has the ability to grow in a job should be a major concern. In fact, it is one of the key qualities we would advise looking for in a promising job candidate. You certainly want to focus on whether an applicant has the qualities needed to succeed in a specific job. Then the next thing you want to know is, Can the person grow with your company?

The ability to grow—to see new possibilities and to want to improve continually—is a necessity in most sales jobs and in virtually all management jobs. While growth is related to one's ability to acquire new information and view situations from a fresh perspective, however, it is not merely a reflection of IQ. Some individuals, while possessing an outstanding IQ, are so opinionated, rigid, and dogmatic that they use their intelligence to reinforce and defend their preconceptions. In other words, they use their intelligence to build a wall around themselves, selecting evidence supportive of what they already believe to be correct and ignoring all conflicting ideas and facts. Such individuals use their intelligence to keep themselves from growing. We have come across individuals whose IQ was in the genius range but who were incapable of growing beyond their current job. Growth involves intellectual capacity, of course, but it truly manifests in empathy, sensitivity, and the flexibility of mind that ponders and seeks new ideas and methods.

Tom Gartland, president, North America of Avis Budget Group, shared with us, "You have to keep in mind that you're hiring someone for a certain position, but you're also hiring that individual for the future. Knowing everyone's growth potential is vital to the growth of our organization. Right now, I have five assistant vice presidents who run Canada and the United States, and each of those people is managing about $1 billion worth of car rental volume. So, if anything were to happen to any of them, I need to know what we would do. Our company's success is based on my having a clear vision and understanding of who the next leadership team is. Who could be next in line? We need to be absolutely sure that we are putting our people in the right roles along the way, developing their skills so that they're ready to step up when we go through the promotion process. Right now I'm thinking about one of our very best account managers. She is in her late 20s and has been with us for five years. The next promotional decision we make for her can have the potential of impacting her career for 20 years. And it could also have an impact on our company for the next 20 years. So we've got to get that right. We have to be committed to her. It is our job to identify our most talented individuals and grow the hell out of them."

TRUST

"Our company has been around for over 160 years," says Andrew Skipp, president and CEO of Hubbard-Hall and chairman of the National Association of Chemical Distributors. "That's a legacy that is built on trust. And our salespeople all represent that legacy. In order to connect with our clients in a way that is real, meaningful, and creative, our salespeople start by engendering trust. And that trust occurs on several levels. It has to do with our ability, it has to do with knowing that we have our clients' best interest at heart, and it has to do with coming through for them—time and time again." It is this trust that establishes the relationship and that strengthens the connection. Andrew adds, "It is the trust we establish with our clients that allows them to open up, then allows us to consider opportunities which our customers might not have even considered for themselves."

Trust is at the heart of any meaningful relationship. In sales, it is a make or break factor. It is the start or stop of any relationship. Do you really believe that what I'm telling you is true? Do you trust me? Do you believe that I have the ability, skills, and talent that you need? Do you believe that I have your best interest at heart? Do you believe that I will be true to my word? That I will come through for you? Do you trust me?

To the extent that trust is there, our relationship will deepen.

To the extent that it is missing, all bets are off.

DECISION MAKING

Another element that helps to define a salesperson's approach is his or her decision-making ability. In many situations, the ability to make quick, correct decisions can save a sale from being lost. Should the price be cut? Should a special guarantee be offered? Should the close be pushed for? Should another meeting be scheduled at which technical assistance can be brought in? Is this customer a genuine prospect that should be pursued or one that is just picking the salesperson's brains for technical information without any real interest in buying? What should the salesperson do when the purchasing agent wants to refer him or her to the vice president? How does the salesperson react when a customer accuses his or her company of providing poor service? Even with generous shares of empathy and ego-drive, a poor decision maker can fail as a salesperson by acting too impulsively and be even more destructive by not acting at all, out of fear of making a mistake. An overly impulsive salesperson may immediately cut price, wildly promise extravagant benefits, accuse competitors of outlandish practices, and behave in a way that is irredeemably embarrassing and totally unprofessional. This hasty, impulsive, impatient decision maker tends to be poor on follow-up. Yet, given empathy and the ability to grow, such individuals may learn from their mistakes.

With experience and a course in time planning, such impulsive salespeople may partially or even fully overcome this tendency. But the non–decision maker has less opportunity to learn from mistakes because those mistakes are due to inaction rather than judgmental error. Consequently, the results are difficult either to trace or to measure. Because such overly cautious individuals cannot decide to make a fractional price cut, they may fail to secure a million-dollar order, but still no one can accuse them of having made a "mistake."

It is hard for anyone to learn from mistakes that are camouflaged or rationalized out of existence. It is this failure to learn that poses the largest problem for the overly cautious decision maker. Overly cautious people fear the possible results of their actions and therefore never act decisively. So they lose critical opportunities and rarely sell effectively. Shrewdness and judgment are also critical attributes that play a part in the decision-making process. Since we want to balance willingness to act with a strong sense of responsibility in order to temper hastiness, we also want to include the shrewdness, insight, and good-judgment components of good decision making. We look for an individual who will take a risk, learn from whatever mistakes are made, and by and large make astute decisions.

DETAIL

Now let's focus on detail. The ability to handle a certain degree of detail work is also important in many sales jobs despite the stereotypical view that salespeople despise and, indeed, cannot cope with even the smallest amount of detail. And many salespeople do, indeed, exemplify this stereotype. To the hard-driving, impulsive salesperson, detail is an abomination; it is a form of torture to fill out an expense report. Yet there are thousands of very fine salespeople who are capable of coping with detail adequately, and some of them are even quite good at it. In thousands of sales jobs, detail is an inescapable part of the operation. For example, how could a real estate salesperson sell a house or a commercial property without involving himself or herself in detail? How could a person begin to sell complex equipment and machinery and stay clear of detail? Without the ability to handle details, is there any way, even with an abundance of drive and empathy, that a registered representative could sell securities, a wholesaler sell mutual funds, or an agent sell estate planning programs?

Of course, some sales jobs require less ability to handle detail than others.

Car salespeople, if they have a sales manager to back them up, need only moderate detail ability. Telemarketers, retail salespeople, and soft-drink route people all have the required details directly in their canned presentations, and they need relatively little inherent detail ability. All this clearly indicates why knowledge of an individual's ability to handle detail is critical in assessing potential in any given sales job.

ORGANIZATION OF WORK AND TIME

Now let's turn to organization of work and time. The ability to organize one's own work, in combination with initiative, also needs to be considered in determining a person's sales potential. Most retail sales jobs, by their very nature, bring customer and salesperson together and so permit the salesperson with significant ego-drive a reasonable number of customers regardless of whether he or she has done preparatory work.

In many other sales jobs, however, even outstanding salespeople could starve while they waited for the customer to come to them. The nature of those sales jobs requires that salespeople find customers and then use their ego-drive to close sales. In these sales situations, individuals without the ability to organize their work are likely to sit all day waiting in vain for a prospect to persuade.

The case of Sandra exemplifies this point. An insurance agency asked us to assess its entire sales and management staff. Sandra, we found, possessed outstanding empathy and ego-drive, exceptional intelligence, and all the prerequisites of an outstanding salesperson. Yet she was not succeeding.

Why, in view of Sandra's strong central dynamics, was she failing? She was an impulsive, driven salesperson who intensely disliked detail, had little or no capacity for self-starting, and had a low level of organizing talent. She was simply incapable of going through customer cards or prospect lists with painstaking care or engaging in routine follow-up activities.

Although the job was called sales, the primary means of retaining and expanding business was through what is known in the industry as *x-dating*. What this means is that the salespeople had to keep close tabs on their account files so as to be aware of when their policies were coming up for renewal (the *x-date*). It was at that point that the salespeople were supposed to contact the customers, discuss their current insurance, and look to opportunities for increasing amounts or broadening coverage. Sandra's lack of detail ability and personal organization made such careful recordkeeping and follow-up virtually impossible. She much preferred the rejections involved in looking for new customers to the painstaking detail work involved in working through customer record cards.

We advised the CEO that Sandra would never be appropriate if her job continued to involve detailed follow-up. Yet we did not want our client to lose an individual possessing Sandra's high degree of sales dynamics. Sandra was installed in a purely outside sales role, going after new business. And we were able to uncover Sandra's replacement inside the agency. There was a customer-service representative who had been working there for a year, so he knew the business but was starting to feel restless and held back in his career goals. When we assessed him, we discovered that he had enough ego-drive to step into the inside sales role. Besides knowing the customers and the business, he also possessed the detail ability and personal organization skills needed to follow up on x-dates. So it became a win–win all around.

Without these job shifts, the agency would have lost a valuable salesperson in Sandra because she was attempting to fill a sales role with a job description not suited to her personality. The agency also would have lost a customer-service representative who had too much drive to function in a purely service capacity. With these shifts, both people were retained and given the opportunity to succeed by fulfilling their potential. Sandra filled a role not requiring so much detail ability, whereas the customer-service representative was placed in a role using his detail ability and personal organization skills while also allowing him to satisfy his persuasive motivation.

COMMUNICATION

The ability to communicate, of course, is critical to succeeding in sales. In virtually all sales situations, the ability to connect with a prospect and communicate the benefits of the product or service will determine success. The ability to receive accurate feedback from a customer, coupled with effective presentation skills that address the customer's reaction, is two-way communication at its best, at least in selling.

When the salesperson lacks empathy, the conversation that is thought to be a meaningful sales dialogue is in reality several alternating monologues: The salesperson is talking at the customer, the customer is talking back at the salesperson, and no real communication is taking place. On the other hand, if the salesperson has empathy and so genuinely understands what the customer is thinking and feeling but is unable to translate that understanding into good presentation skills, the empathy could be wasted, and the sales failure would be just as complete as if the empathy did not exist in the first place. Thus real communication involves both the ability to gather vital feedback from the customer and the ability to use that feedback to communicate the product or service effectively in terms of how it will meet that customer's needs.

TEAM PLAYER

When we asked Roger Staubach, legendary quarterback of the Dallas Cowboys and founder of the enormously successful real estate enterprise The Staubach Group, which sports analogy makes the most sense to him, he responded, "Competition is certainly important. Being clear about your goals is crucial. But for me, the key to developing a successful organization is all about team building. It's all about the people you surround yourself with. Succeeding in business, in sports, is a matter of pulling together people you can trust, who are honest, who have their priorities in line, and who have the talent, ambition, and desire to reach beyond themselves and make something really big happen."

We have found that one of the most overlooked attributes of a successful salesperson is the ability to function as a member of a team. The ability to collaborate with others can make the difference between success and failure. The ego-driven salesperson, by definition, wants the thrill of conquest and is more often than not the ultimate individualist. Yet questions often arise to which the salesperson does not know the answer. Perhaps the most intelligent, most credible (and most honest) answer that any salesperson can give is, "I don't know, but I will find out." Unfortunately, some salespeople appear to be constitutionally incapable of this kind of reply. Instead, they are more inclined to blunder along, faking answers they don't have, frequently misleading the customer, and quite likely, losing him or her forever. It follows that one of the key requisites of a successful salesperson is the ability to bring in technical help when necessary and to make use of the manager's skill and experience. In short, the salesperson often must be able to play as part of a team, not just as a wheeling-and-dealing individualist.

The sports world offers a close analogy. Many a ball team laden with superstars has stumbled and failed because each star played for himself instead of submerging his strength into the body of the team. So it is with a salesperson.

ASSERTIVENESS

Many people may possess ego-drive (the motivation to persuade) and yet may not be assertive enough to ask for an order despite their intense desire to get that order. A time comes in every sales situation when, after the presentation, the gathering of customer information, and all the other elements that go into a sale, the prospect has to be told, "Please sign here." It is at this moment of truth that the customer gives the final yes-or-no answer, when the salesperson's assertiveness or lack thereof can be the difference between success and failure.

The term *assertiveness* is frequently confused with *aggressiveness*. Assertiveness is not pushiness and, in fact, never should be perceived as pushiness or aggression. Rather, assertiveness is the ability that enables an individual to get other people to do willingly what they might not do spontaneously on their own. Assertiveness allows an individual to have a special effect on others that commands their respect and admiration and causes them to respond in a positive way to what that individual is asking or suggesting. Assertiveness involves the ability to get a positive response from others and use that response to bring about a desired attitude or course of action. Putting it in simplest terms, the assertive salesperson is willing to ask for the order and is capable of asking for it in a sufficiently effective way to ensure that the prospect will willingly give that order.

AGGRESSIVENESS

Aggressiveness, on the other hand, is often confused with *assertiveness*. The two, however, are distinctly different. Where assertiveness involves getting people to do what you want them to do without pushing, aggressiveness is precisely that pushing. Aggressiveness is the willingness to actively oppose someone else's position, interests, or point of view, even if it could adversely affect that other person. Unfortunately, too many salespeople, particularly those with somewhat deficient empathy, are purely aggressive, as opposed to genuinely assertive. People do not want to be pushed into making a decision, so the psychological difference between real assertiveness and pure aggression is far more than an academic distinction. Yet there are sales situations in which aggression of a certain kind is essential. For example, there are many telephone sales situations in which the salesperson is simply blocked from talking to the potential prospect. Pounding away at the locked gates often requires simple, though polite, aggressiveness. After all, you cannot use empathy, ego-drive, and assertiveness on a prospect with whom you have no contact. This can mean multiple conversations with a secretary before finally wearing him or her down and getting through to the boss, the prospect. Interestingly, once the door is opened, the prospect often will say, "How could I say no after such persistence?" and "You really must believe in what you're doing if you were willing to work that hard to arrange a meeting." One can look at these multiple calls as simple persistence, but the reality is that while persistence certainly was involved, each conversation had to include a pushing (polite, but still a pushing) toward the goal of eventually talking to that secretary's boss. Simple persistence (the willingness to make 18 phone calls without the aggressive push) probably would not have achieved the goal.

Here again is a perfect example of why, though we talk about individual qualities, they cannot really be viewed separately. The aggressiveness we just described would have done no good without persistence and without empathy. There had to be ego-drive to persuade the secretary to let the call through, empathy so that the secretary did not become angry, and persistence to keep trying. All these qualities, not just one, had to come into play to achieve the goal. In fact, we should mention another quality used in this situation—ego-strength—because there was a great deal of rejection on the road to achieving the goal.

INSIGHTFUL

Being *insightful* is the ability to read between the lines and to further process information rather than accept it all at face value. There is certainly a relationship between this attribute and empathy, and yet they are very different in the sense that empathy deals with understanding of the person, while being insightful deals more with the understanding and perception one brings to a situation. Here again, the combination of empathy and insight really makes for an ideal salesperson, particularly when you are dealing with more complex conceptual sales as opposed to the sale of a simple, tangible product.

Often a prospect will tell the salesperson what is needed on one level, but insight will allow the salesperson to read between the lines and get to the next level of real need. In fact, many salespeople will relate instances in which their insight allowed them to ascertain needs of which the customer was not even aware. Insight and empathy allow the salesperson to act as a consultant, helping customers to discern their real needs and meeting those needs through the product or service being sold.

Again, there are many sales situations in which insight is less important because the situation is simple and what is on the surface is all that is really there. In other situations, however, the insights a salesperson brings to the situation can prove to be as important as some of the central sales dynamics themselves.

SENSE OF INNER URGENCY

Now let's turn to a sense of inner urgency. The individual with a great deal of *inner urgency* needs to get something, make that everything, done "right now." This individual has a need to move quickly and finds delay extremely frustrating. Typically, he or she cannot stand long deliberation over a subject but rather is motivated to act and keep acting until a successful outcome is achieved. To individuals with inner urgency, there is no waiting for a call; instead, there is a move to action—to pick up the phone and make the call themselves.

Okay. That's the extreme.

Let's go to the other extreme. Individuals with very little inner urgency will be much too laid back, complacent, and even passive. Even if they, somehow, possess ego-drive, they are likely to feel that closing opportunities will present themselves, and they feel little need to actively seek out those opportunities.

When such individuals are presented with a prospect, their ego-drive will allow them to close effectively. If they seriously lack inner urgency, though, they will not be proactive but rather will only be waiting for an opportunity to present itself.

On the other hand, individuals with too much inner urgency could be so bent on immediate response that they could make bad judgments because of the immediate need to respond. In trying to get an immediate decision, they could end up with a negative outcome.

To completely understand inner urgency, we should look at this quality in relationship to ego-drive and to impatience, with which it can easily be confused.

Ego-drive is the need for victory, but this does not necessarily imply that that victory has to be immediate. Ego-driven individuals with the right amount of inner urgency will not let grass grow under their feet—they will move with all deliberate speed.

On the other hand, they will not act recklessly and perhaps wrongly just for the satisfaction of this need for immediacy. However, we have seen many potentially successful salespeople, even with a great deal of ego-drive, who simply do not possess enough inner urgency to impel them to actively seek ways of satisfying that drive. For example, we can recall one young man whom we tested and found to have ample amounts of empathy, ego-drive, and ego-strength. He turned out to be, in fact, a reasonably successful salesperson, although, as our client told us about a year later, he never achieved the top performance level that would be indicated by his level of ego-drive. After some investigation, we found that his conversion ratio (number of closes to number of contacts) was quite high. What we also found, however, was that his number of contacts was among the lowest on the sales force. After interviewing him, it became apparent that he made no effort to maximize the number of calls he would make in a given day. If one call was completed at 11:30, rather than try to make an additional call before lunch, he would use that time to take a somewhat longer lunch. If a call was completed at 4:30, he would not rush to get to a prospect's office by 4:55 but instead would take the opportunity to beat the traffic and go home.

Individuals with inner urgency probably would have made those additional two calls because they would have the need for immediacy that would drive them to use the time to get work done. The result, given this young man's conversion ratio, likely would have been at least one additional sale per day.

What we see here is an individual who is making full use of his ego-drive; once he was in front of a customer, he closed that customer effectively. His lack of inner urgency, however, substantially reduced the number of these closing opportunities. The result was adequate, though not outstanding, sales performance.

As we said earlier, inner urgency is also confused with impatience. The difference is that the individual with inner urgency will act to obtain immediacy, whereas the individual who is simply impatient may be bothered by delay but not necessarily do anything about it. An individual, for example, may be terribly impatient while experiencing the inordinate waits typical in doctors' offices, but the individual with inner urgency is likely to walk over to the nurse, tell her it's impossible to continue waiting, and either get taken earlier or reschedule the appointment. Mere impatience does not denote action.

Inner urgency, for good or ill, most often leads to action.

Laurie Dalton, vice president of human resources at Gate Gourmet, the world's largest independent provider of catering services for the transportation industry, told us, "One of the most important distinctions for people who succeed in sales is a bias toward action. And in my view, that is not something you can learn."

By the time somebody is old enough to apply for a job, they either have it or they don't.

"A real sense of urgency, a strong bias for action, will help a salesperson succeed here." Laurie paused and then added, "If you think about it, we are servicing the airlines, and their entire focus is to be there on time. So we need that quality to come through for them."

SELF-DISCIPLINE

Self-discipline involves the inner motivation to do what needs to be done whether or not the task involves something that the individual really wants to do.

Self-discipline can be expressed in many different ways. It has to do with an inner sense of what has to do be done, what is important at the time.

As we said earlier, each and every one of these qualities does not function independently. They are all connected to each other. What we want to focus on here is the connection between urgency and self-discipline.

If a salesperson has enough self-discipline, he or she might try to make that final 5 o'clock meeting, even though the inner urgency to do so is absent. This salesperson would do so because he or she *should*, not because there is the inner desire to do it.

On the other hand, the individual with inner urgency will make that meeting because he or she wants to—because such a person has the need to get that little extra done during that day.

As you read this, you might ask, "What is the difference?"

If the salesperson in fact makes that meeting, aside from academic interest, why do we care if it is because of inner urgency or self-discipline?

We do, in fact, care, because—as is the case with so many things we are discussing in this book—we do things we like and want to do much more effectively than things we have to do or are forced to do by external pressure. Thus, if the individual makes that meeting at 5 o'clock because he or she is compelled to by an inner sense of urgency, he or she is likely to pursue that meeting full tilt, making every effort to make that meeting effective and successful to satisfy his or her need for immediate results. On the other hand, if the individual makes it to the meeting because it was the proper thing to do, the process may be carried out in a pro forma way, lacking the genuine enthusiasm required to close the sale.

The difference has to do with understanding where the result comes from. Is it self-discipline or urgency? As a manager, you want to know what is driving your top performer. Obviously, if someone possesses both the right level of inner urgency and the self-discipline to plan and organize work and time efficiently, you have the best of all worlds.

COMPETITIVENESS

One last quality we'd like to touch upon us *competitiveness*.

Curt Nelson, founder of the Entrepreneurial Development Center, has a wonderful way of describing how this quality comes out in top performers. "Top performers are always competing with what they believe they should be capable of."

By their very nature, top salespeople are very competitive. They want—make that *need*—to win.

It's part of who they are.

The best are always competing. But we want to provide just one cautionary note about people who are always competing.

The question that needs to be asked is: Who are you competing with? Yourself? Or someone else?

The answer matters. People who are competing with themselves will continually try to improve. It's in their makeup. It's part of who they are. That's how they show up. And that competition never ends.

Those are the individuals you want to surround yourself with.

One of the most important goals for a sales manager is to harness that competitive spirit and make it a vital part of their team.

A competitive spirit creates an energy that is contagious.

There is just one cautionary note: You want to make sure who your salespeople are competing with. If they are always competing with others rather than themselves, that can be a concern. Because some competitive people don't know how to turn the competition off. To keep it where it belongs—focused on the competition. As a result, they can stir up real conflicts—inside their organization. We have been brought in to consult with teams where some of the top performers were competing with others on their own team—rather than with the competition. This can be extremely destructive.

It is important to keep that competitive spirit focused on your competitors—where it belongs. This is when everything can move ahead, exceeding expectations. When salespeople express their strong competitive drive in a positive, can-do way, possibilities abound.

Paul Knee, managing director for Verathon, a company known for designing, manufacturing, and distributing state-of-the-art medical devices and services, told us, "My top-performing salespeople all have that competitive drive. They're enthusiastic. And always driving to improve, to do better. They accept challenges for the sake of the challenge rather than what they're going to get out of it. So, whenever I am looking for salespeople, I am always looking for that competitive spirit. It's something that either they have or they don't. And when they have it, it comes through in whatever they do—and it makes all the difference in the world."

There are several other qualities we could touch on as we discuss the qualities that distinguish top performers. But we hope that the foregoing discussion has essentially made the point that as important as any of these qualities are (including empathy, ego-drive, and ego-strength), they are all interrelated. None of them alone can predict success in sales or any other pursuit. And it takes a unique blend of these qualities to determine whether an individual will be successful in a specific sales job.

So let us turn now to the process of predicting success on a job—by determining whether an individual's unique personality attributes are matched to the specific requirements of that unique job.

PART **3**

JOB MATCHING

As we discussed earlier, one of the key reasons for poor productivity and high turnover in so many sales organizations is the inappropriate approach management takes to hiring salespeople. In this part we present job matching as the remedy to these endemic problems. We will explore how to understand the distinct requirements of your particular sales positions. Then we will return to an understanding of the personality attributes required to succeed in a particular job. Then we will focus on the essential equation—matching the strengths of an individual with the functional requirements of the job and determining if any dominant flaws might prevent success. We will conclude this part by demonstrating the bottom-line results of replacing the traditional approaches to hiring with job matching.

CHAPTER 9

Understanding the Sales Job

Although all sales jobs involve, at their core, the ability to persuade, the breadth of these jobs is virtually limitless. Sales jobs range from quick-closing, hard-selling, short-term, commission-only positions to the opposite extreme, where the persuasive element is much more subtle and takes place only a few times a year at the end of a long process. Similarly, many sales positions require little technical background, while others require the salesperson to be a technical expert in a particular product or service. Some sales jobs presume that the individual customer will buy once and likely never again, while in most other sales situations, a one-time-only buyer would be disastrous. Numerous additional examples of these extremes could be cited, but we hope that these serve to make the point that saying a position involves sales is far from adequate for understanding the nature of that position.

As we begin to look at the job-matching process, it is important to understand the key elements that are necessary and some of the key questions that must be asked to develop an understanding of the specific sales role and the personality attributes required for an individual to fill that role successfully. These are the elements that will go into creating a realistic job description, which then becomes your blueprint for finding the ideal candidate.

While this may seem very fundamental, we have been continually amazed at how many companies come to us with job descriptions that are very *unspecific* and, as a result, set the stage for disappointment.

One quick way we have uncovered this is by asking a manager what the three most important responsibilities are for someone reporting to him or her. Then we ask the person reporting to manager the same question. Very rarely do we get the same three answers from both the manager and the person reporting to that manager. Then, on those rare occasions when we do get the same three responses from the manager and the person reporting to him or her, it is *extremely* seldom that we get them in the same order.

This is amazing when you stop to think about it.

If you are looking to hire someone and you will be managing that person's expectations, don't you think that it's crucial that both of you are clear on the three major job responsibilities? And that you know what the most important one is?

But it is the exceptional case where all three of those responsibilities are aligned.

Another reality of most job descriptions is that they are terribly dated.

Just think about it. When you have to place a help-wanted advertisement to replace someone who has left your company, what's the first thing you do? Brush off the old job description so that you can create the ad with some specific details about the responsibilities and the kind of person you are looking for? On one level, this makes sense. If you stop to think about it for a minute, though, how long was the previous person in that position? For five years? And has the job changed in those five years? Your company certainly has changed over the past five years. So how has that position changed? And how would you like to see it change in the next year?

Don't just hire based on the past. Push the pause button. Use those hiring opportunities to help you reflect on the past and envision a new future.

With this in mind, here are some important aspects to consider as you focus on defining the new sales position.

PRODUCT OR SERVICE

The first question to be asked, as you consider defining the job is, What is the nature of the product or service to be sold? It is not enough to say, for example, computers, or automobiles, or real estate, or pharmaceuticals. Within these broad categories of products and services are numerous subdivisions, each of which requires many differing individual qualities and work processes to sell successfully.

For example, it is a far different job to sell personal computers over the counter in a retail store than it is to sell large mainframes directly to business and government. Both can be technically categorized as computer sales, but there the similarity ends. Thus, as simplistic as it may sound on the surface, it is important to understand the full nature of the product or service being sold—as well as the nature of the potential customers.

This critical difference was brought home to us in one of Caliper's first consulting engagements over 50 years ago. Before engaging us in a consulting project, a pharmaceutical firm asked that we assess a statistically significant cross section of its "pharmaceutical sales" force. Since this was in part a test of our accuracy, we were not provided with performance data for each of the salespeople we were assessing. The company was looking to see if our assessment of potential lined up with the performance of its salespeople.

Given this lack of information, all we could do was evaluate people on the basis of their empathy, ego-drive, and ego-strength and assume that people who were strong in these dynamics would, in fact, be the best salespeople. It turned out, however, that our predictions landed far from the mark, and in fact, in many instances, people with strong ego-drive were at the bottom, whereas people with moderate to extremely mild ego-drive were performing exceptionally well. Empathy seemed to hold up as a predictor, but ego-drive and ego-strength failed, so our overall judgments did not prove out.

However, after we were provided with job descriptions, we realized the underlining reason for our lack of predictive accuracy in this particular case. What quickly became obvious was that the sales force we evaluated really should have been broken down into two sales forces: proprietary sales and medical detailers. The job for proprietary salespeople was to visit pharmacies, present the company's proprietary products, and persuade the pharmacist to purchase more of those products. The salesperson literally was charged with walking out with an order from each visit. The sale was tangible, and success or failure was determined by the dollar value of the contract with each pharmacy. Several closes a day was the name of the game.

On the other hand, the medical detailers literally never closed a sale. They would visit doctors, leave samples of various prescription drugs, and talk with the doctors about the value of the drugs. Their goal was to convey the improvement of the new product, leave samples, and hope that the doctor would think of their particular antibiotic or blood pressure pill when next prescribing to patients. Since they never closed sales, these salespeople only got feedback about whether or not they had succeeded in general by quarterly, semiannual, or annual reviews of how their area was doing.

So when we could see these two radically different job descriptions, both called "pharmaceutical sales," we were able to quickly determine why our earlier analyses had to be incorrect.

For the detailer position, if an individual had too much ego-drive, he or she simply could not tolerate the lack of closing. What is needed to succeed in this position, besides product knowledge, of course, is the empathy to connect with the doctor and his or her staff.

This is just one example. The list of similar titles with drastically different job functions goes on and on. Suffice it to say here that to make a rational judgment on who can fill a particular sales job, you need to understand the product being sold, the nature of the prospects being solicited, and the very process through which success can be attained.

FREQUENCY OF CLOSE

Related closely to the foregoing is the issue of how many opportunities are present for closing the sale. As we said earlier, many sales jobs require multiple closings per day to be successful, whereas many others offer relatively few but all extremely important closing opportunities. If, for example, an individual has extraordinarily intense ego-drive and perhaps possesses the impatience that frequently goes along with that kind of drive, that individual hungers for closes as a key means of satisfying that drive. Thus, regardless of the compensation, a sales situation that provides two or three closing opportunities per year simply would not satisfy that individual's ego-drive. He or she would not have sufficient fun; there would just not be enough closings to keep that person happy. On the other hand, for the individual who has moderate ego-drive but possesses great consultative skills, service motivation, and persistence, the job requiring frequent closes might prove too taxing. That is, fundamentally, why it is critical to determine the frequency of closing opportunities so that an individual geared to that level of close could be matched properly with the specific job.

LEAD PRODUCTION

It is also important to understand where leads come from. It is a far more difficult sale when cold-calling is required. The cold-caller must, out of necessity, experience far more frequent rejection, often of a far more abrupt, even nasty, kind, than the individual who follows up leads that have been furnished. The warmth of those leads also determines, in large measure, who can or cannot be successful in their conversions of prospects to customers. Thus a very clear definition of the job must be made internally and presented honestly to the candidate about the nature of customer conversion, cold leads, cool leads, well-screened leads, and so on. Very different people will be successful depending on an accurate definition of this aspect of the sales role.

NATURE OF CUSTOMER

It is also extremely important to thoroughly understand the nature of the potential customers. Many people would be highly successful at selling individual consumers a tangible product but would fail totally if faced with the necessity of making a full-scale, well-developed presentation to a committee or a board of directors. Others could deal extraordinarily well at connecting with purchasing agents, branch managers, or office managers but would find it extremely difficult to make presentations on the board room or CEO level. Still others would be effective at selling to one person but would lose effectiveness if they had to work their way up the chain of command to get the final sign-off. Thus it is critical to know not only to whom we are selling (companies, individuals, etc.) but also on what level the sale is initially made and on what level the final purchase can be approved.

TECHNICAL BACKGROUND

The technical background required for a specific sales job relates closely to the question of who plays the final part in the decision to purchase. If microcomputers are being sold to office managers who know little about the technical aspects of the machine, somewhat less technical proficiency probably will be sufficient for the salesperson as long as that salesperson can speak accurately about the machine's capabilities and its potential benefits to the customer. On the other hand, if the buyers are engineers or heads of data-processing divisions, the salesperson had better be exceptionally proficient in the technology, or his or her credibility and the credibility of the product will quickly be lost.

SUPPORT

There are many salespeople who relish their positions because they are able to function in a totally independent manner. This is one of the great attractions of the sales profession to many people. They like winning on their own.

On the other hand, there are equally successful salespeople who like and, in fact, enjoy the camaraderie of working with other experts collaboratively. They want to know that, if needed, they have all the technical support needed to make the sale. Such salespeople also may like to have their sales manager step into close a critical deal. And they feel better prepared knowing that they have a team of writers and researchers who can help to develop their all-important presentations. These are team players. They derive gratification by being part of a group that connects with each other, relies on each other, and succeeds together.

There are a number of other key aspects to be considered in a valid job description:

- How much travel is needed?

- Does the job require working from a home office, or is there a great deal of individual field work?

- To whom does the salesperson report?

- Does the salesperson have any administrative help?

- What is the compensation plan—salary, salary plus bonus, commission only, etc.?

- What is the career path of the position?

- Are we dealing with tangible or intangible sales?

- Are we dealing with small-ticket or big-ticket items?

- Are sales cyclic or consistent through the year?

- On average, how many contacts does it take to close a sale?

- Is the job in a big city, suburb, town, or rural area?

- How large is the sales force?

- Is the company known in the market, or is part of the sale selling the company name?

There are certainly more questions to consider. But if companies and sales managers do no more than develop their job description using the questions outlined here, they will have taken a major step toward achieving the job match that is the key to sales success.

The exercise of putting together such a job description for their own edification will substantially improve their ability to make judgments concerning who can fill the job. In addition, presenting a job description of this kind to individuals in line for promotion or to applicants will help these individuals immeasurably to determine whether they really want the particular sales position given a clear description of all its aspects.

Alisa Barry, chef and creator of Bell Cucina Artful Food, offers a word of caution and advice: "One of the things I've found most important is to create the job description first. To be clear about what I'm looking for. And to use it as a barometer for selecting the top candidate. Because I've found that small-business owners, especially, can just intuitively know they need to bring somebody on, to fill a space, and they start moving in that direction. But creating the job description first, then searching for the person that fits that description, is a much more effective way of making sure you are bringing on the right talent."

CHAPTER 10

Hunters
and Farmers

In virtually every study we have conducted of successful salespeople, we have found that the best succeed when they have a combination of the three qualities we've been discussing so far—ego-drive, empathy, and ego-strength. By way of example, when we combine all our studies of salespeople, we find that the mean score of the top performers is at the sixty-eighth percentile of ego-drive. Simply put, top salespeople have more ego-drive than 68 percent of the population at large.

This does, however, pose an interesting question: How do some successful salespeople thrive when their ego-drive is in the midrange or even lower? What we have found is that it depends on the nature of the sales position. Our research points to two broad categories—hunters and farmers.

On a very simplistic level, *hunters* are the classically driven, highly persuasive, fast-closing salespeople. Then there are the *farmers*, who slowly cultivate clients, build long-lasting relationships, and close less frequent but have larger sales. It would be easy to say that both these sales types succeed when they are matched to a product or service that requires such abilities.

But we have come across many situations in which hunters and farmers succeed side by side, selling the exact same product or service. If there is, in fact, one ideal profile of a top salesperson, how do we account for these two completely different types of salespeople succeeding together?

We have come to identify two very distinct personality profiles—both of which can be extremely successful in sales for entirely different reasons. Working side by side, these individuals succeed by playing to their core strengths. Allow us to share with you how hunters and farmers succeed in completely different ways by recounting the success stories of two top performers from competitive companies in the same industry.

HUNTERS

Hunters are more interested in going after new business. They create opportunities by initiating contact with prospects, often through cold-calling, in order to explain products or services. Once they build interest, they work to close the sale. Some of the titles commonly associated with hunters include account executive, outside sales, producer, agent, national account manager, sales representative, sales consultant, territory sales representative, and business development.

Beyond ego-drive, empathy, and ego-strength, an individual being assessed for a position as a hunter will be evaluated focusing on the following performance drivers: assertiveness, aggressiveness, energy, gregariousness, risk-taking, sociability, and urgency.

Job-related behaviors include contacting prospects and initiating relationships, maintaining existing relationships, confidently expressing ideas and opinions, persuading prospects and clients to make commitments, persevering to overcome obstacles, and bouncing back from sales rejection.

Unique position features include possessing sales and marketing knowledge, communicating with people outside the organization, engaging in cold-calling, creating impact, generating opportunities, influencing prospects' buying decisions, negotiating prices, and showing a competitive nature.

To give you a sense of how this all comes together, let us tell you about Karen, a consummate hunter. She was last year's account manager of the year for a leading manufacturer of computer software. Throughout the past three years, this recent college graduate has consistently surpassed her sales target. With no prior selling experience, we would describe Karen as "motivated to persuade and come through for clients."

She describes herself as "highly driven and very competitive." Karen started off doing 40 cold-calls each day. She now has brought in over 250 accounts.

She says that her greatest thrill comes from converting a brand new or dormant account into an active one. She particularly gets a kick out of getting a really big order, "especially," as she says, "when the effort is solely attributable to my own efforts." Preferring to work as a solo performer, she admits to getting frustrated when customers call on other people to help make the final decision.

Karen adds that it is "vital to establish and build relationships." She says that she hates losing a sale. When it happens, she says, "It is usually because I haven't grasped the opportunity quickly enough."

One of the things she likes about her company is that "a healthy competition is encouraged within the team, and our compensation is based on individual achievement." In fact, she has just returned from Greece, a trip she won for being account manager of the year.

What were the results when we assessed Karen's personality strengths? It is hard to describe Karen without using such words as *very*. Exemplary of the composite profile of hunters, she is very persuasive, extremely confident, definitely willing to take risks when necessary, and very assertive, disciplined, and gregarious.

Karen comes across as a truly outgoing, engaging individual who genuinely enjoys opportunities to meet new people and to transfer her knowledge. She enjoys persuading others or "guiding" them to what she believes is the best solution for them. And because of her confidence and assertiveness, she won't hesitate to share her point of view—which, because of her discipline and focus, is usually very well considered. Underlying all these qualities is a fundamental urgency or a need to get things done "now." This sense of urgency enables her to capitalize on opportunities and not allow commitments to go unfulfilled.

Karen's approach impresses customers because she conveys a definite perspective, in a confident manner, and wants to make sure that her solution is thorough and, ideally, delivered before it is even expected.

FARMERS

Farmers are focused on expanding a current book of business. They create opportunities by building relationships within existing client organizations, identifying the needs of clients, and matching those needs to solutions they can provide. Some of the titles commonly associated with hunters include account manager, sales associate, and inside sales.

Beyond ego-drive, empathy, and ego-strength, an individual being assessed for a position as a farmer will be evaluated focusing on the same performance drivers as a hunter (just with a more tempered style and approach): assertiveness, aggressiveness, energy, gregariousness, risk-taking, sociability, and urgency.

The job-related behaviors and unique position features for farmers are similar to what is expected of hunters, just, again, in a style and approach that are more moderated. And, as you can see by reviewing the lists in the next two paragraphs, for hunters, there is more of an emphasis on maintaining and building business from current customers than there is on developing new business from prospects.

Job-related behaviors include contacting prospects and initiating relationships, maintaining existing relationships, confidently expressing ideas and opinions, persuading clients to make commitments, persevering to overcome obstacles, and bouncing back from sales rejection.

Unique position features include possessing sales and marketing knowledge, communicating with people outside the organization, engaging in warm interactions, creating opportunities, influencing customers' buying decisions, negotiating prices, and showing a competitive nature.

To give you a sense of how this all comes together, let us tell you about Paul, a consummate farmer. Paul conveys a completely different demeanor and approach to selling than Karen. Being true to his inherent strengths has enabled him to be very successful for a computer software company that is in the same city where Karen works. He used to work in the company's customer-service department, so he brings a thorough knowledge and understanding of the needs of his 85 accounts.

In one particular instance, after only six months in his new position as a salesperson, Paul turned a negative situation into a growth opportunity, and the company involved has gone on to become one of the firm's largest clients.

Paul has maintained and grown his business by keeping close to customers and understanding their business. As he says, "Succeeding in sales starts with demonstrating awareness and understanding of each customer's needs." In order to do this, he "has to build trust and deliver on each and every promise."

Paul's personality profile is exemplary of the composite profile of farmers. He is quite sociable, highly engaging, enormously accommodating, with a consistently conscientious approach toward servicing his clients' needs. Not a risk-taker, Paul is the kind of individual who worries about whether or not his clients are satisfied. Clearly, this results in customer loyalty, account retention, and a client base that continually refers new opportunities.

Paul is, above all else, a service-oriented salesperson. His motivation to come through for others comes across loud and clear. He works with his customers as a partner—seeking to provide the best solutions possible. He has a need to "come through." Two terms—*conscientious* and *service-minded*—best describe Paul's character and behavior.

THE BEST OF BOTH WORLDS

These stories of how Karen and Paul are both succeeding in very similar positions pose an interesting dilemma for owners and sales managers who are trying to hire salespeople with the potential to build their business. Do you bring on hard-driven salespeople to convert sales quickly? Or do you invest the time necessary to hire salespeople with more of a consultant's demeanor, who will not necessarily bring in new business immediately but may, in time, create a solid foundation of loyal clients?

If you lean toward the more thorough and accommodating model, how do you know that such individuals will be able to survive through the first several years that it typically takes for them to build their base of business? Or if you are looking for the more classically driven salesperson, you have to ask yourself, Will this potential top performer be able to come across as a consultant and build long-lasting business relationships?

The ideal would be to find someone who is a combination of these two profiles—a hunter and a farmer. The perfect applicant would be empathic, driven to persuade, assertive, and able to bounce back from rejection while also being thorough, conscientious, sociable, and accommodating. Such an individual would be able to close sales early on and know how to build long-term relationships.

But we are rarely in a position to take advantage of the best of both worlds—particularly when trying to make quick hiring decisions. Usually, some tradeoffs are necessary.

So, while you might set your sights on finding individuals who are a combination of these two ideal profiles, the truth of the matter is that individuals who have all those talents, abilities, and attributes are very, very rare. If you do find such an individual, hire him or her on the spot. Then pinch yourself to make sure that you are not dreaming. In most instances, you will have to decide on someone who tips toward either the more consultative or the more driven profile. The question is, How do you decide which profile is best for your situation?

Coming up with just the right mix of sales talent depends on first determining the specific needs of your company and then assessing the potential of your sales candidates. You can start out by asking yourself what is most important. Selling more units? Increasing profit? Satisfying customers? Or bringing in repeat business? The answers to these questions and the order in which you prioritize them will point the way toward defining the profile of the next salesperson you are seeking.

Other questions to consider are: Does the location of your company require an enormous amount of prospecting? Are you trying to alter the public's perception of your company? Are you more concerned about your clients or your competition? And what is the mix of salespeople currently on your staff?

From a practical matter, tradeoffs are necessary more often than not. We may find a candidate for a sales job who possesses the requisite amount of empathy, ego-drive, and ego-strength but who lacks self-discipline. Do you hire this candidate? The answer might be *yes* if it's determined that he or she can be managed tightly enough to impose sufficient structure externally to overcome that particular lack of self-discipline. Similarly, another driven individual might lack self-discipline. Is he or she worth hiring? Perhaps, if there is a sufficiently well-organized service function in the company to provide the needed ongoing service. And so it goes.

As one of our clients put it so well, "Especially in sales, which is very much a people game, there is no one answer to what will work and what will not work. We have a very diverse group of salespeople, some who are more persuasive, others who are more service-oriented, and everywhere in between. You need that mix to keep your organization running."

We have worked with clients who have all hunters, others with all farmers, some with a mixture of both, and some who try to blend hunters and farmers into one individual. What works for one might not work for another. What matters is a clear understanding of the needs of your clients—the type of salesperson who will best be able to connect with them, to help them uncover their needs, and to come through with just the right solutions. Let us share with you what some of our clients have told us about how they've approached the equation between hunters and farmers.

Mark Nechita, senior director of international human resources at Callaway Golf, told us, "We quickly came to realize that they were completely separate roles for us. Farmers will never be hunters, and vice versa. You don't want to waste your time trying to focus hunters on farming-type accounts—because they just don't have the patience and the mind-set to unwearyingly work on a longer lead time or a more relationship-type sale."

How did Callaway, known for continually stretching the boundaries of technology in the golf industry, come to terms with this reality?

"In instances where we had salespeople who had been crossing over, trying to farm current accounts and hunt for new ones, we had to change our model."

For Callaway, it is about creating a sales culture that acknowledges and reflects inherent qualities of top-performing salespeople. It is a sales model built on recognizing that the strengths, limitations, and potential of hunters and farmers are very different. And purposefully playing to each of those strengths.

Peter Smith, executive vice president of Hearts On Fire, the premiere diamond company, likes to have a mix of one hunter for every two farmers in each of the independent retail jewelers that sell his diamonds, which have defined a new industry standard for perfection.

"Over the course of time, my philosophy has evolved," he shared with us. "Twenty years ago, I considered all sales jobs, and therefore all salespeople to be the same. So I kept trying to have hunters farm more and farmers hunt more. But I've come to realize that I was trying to defy gravity. Now I celebrate the differences and encourage the store owners to actually shape their compensation system, their training, and even their scheduling around recognizing the clear distinctions between hunters and farmers."

Would he want all the salespeople representing Hearts On Fire to be hunters?

"They are the ones who give you what you can fold and put in your pocket. But if I had all hunters, I'd have problems, because I'd have an atmosphere in the store that would have an edge to it. And that's not what you as a customer want to encounter when you are making a significant, sophisticated purchase. So I like to have a blend. If a store has six salespeople, I'd like two of them to be hunters and the rest farmers. That's an ideal blend. If there are too many hunters, you can have too much tension, too much individualism. So I like to shape that. But if I had all farmers, I might have an easier-going atmosphere, but I also would be losing business because I wouldn't be closing as many sales, not doing add-on sales and things of that nature."

Can the hunters light a fire under the farmers?

"I'm not sure of that. It's just recognizing that different customers want different experiences. There are certainly some farmers who will kick into another gear on Saturdays, when there are more customers, or when Christmas comes. But the hunters don't need a weekend or a holiday to step it up. They are always hunting."

For Ron Rubin, Minister of Tea (owner) at The Republic of Tea, the leading purveyor of premium teas, the focus is on growing current accounts.

Bringing in new accounts isn't a concern?

"We do bring in some new accounts," he told us. "But that's not currently our focus. We want to expand business with the accounts we already have. Our salespeople, we call them Ambassadors, start with a real passion for tea. They are extremely knowledgeable, and they are motivated to teach others about the quality and benefits that distinguish us."

So how does the selling occur?

"The Republic of Tea bottled ice teas appear in America's finest restaurants. In restaurants, we teach a new server how to introduce the teas, the quality of the product, how the teas are organic and the flavors all-natural. The Mango Ceylon bottled ice tea, for example, would complement a crab salad and our Republic Darjeeling is light and would go very nicely with a mild fish. Then we can also share from an economic point of view, the server can increase the average check size, and therefore his or her tip. All of this while creating a better, more refined experience for your customer."

Teaching is one way a farmer can sell.

Paulo Nascentes, vice president of Tigre Brazil, cautions that it often can be difficult to determine whether someone who is sociable, outgoing, and adept at developing relationships also has the persuasive drive to be a salesperson.

Tigre is a leading manufacturer of PVC pipes and fittings in the South American market. So, understandably, most of the firm's salespeople have an engineering background. Paulo shares with us that when they come across an engineer who is sociable and outgoing, there is a tendency to think that he or she might be able to sell. But, he says, more often than not, this is not the case.

"There is a real difference between liking people and liking to persuade people," he shared with us. "While someone might have a real strength in developing relationships, that doesn't mean that he or she will have an inner drive to persuade others."

It is important to keep this cautionary note in mind when considering an applicant for a farming sales position. Particularly in technical roles, such as engineering, it can be tempting to think that someone who is outgoing also might be able to sell. But keep in mind that being outgoing and being driven to persuade others are completely separate qualities.

When hiring a farmer, you need to make sure that he or she has an inner need to persuade others. Otherwise, you could have an excellent customer-service representative instead of a top-performing salesperson.

At the other end of the spectrum is Dan Sheridan, president and chief operating officer of Extensis, a comprehensive outsourced human resources firm, who "looks for pure hunters," as he told us.

In an article in the *Wall Street Journal*, he said that when he originally joined Extensis, "The first thing I could tell was that we didn't have the right salespeople." He turned things around by working with Caliper to identify applicants who were assertive, organized, could listen well, were able to stay focused and follow-through on a long sales cycle, and could pitch intangible products. Then, once selected, he had them all trained in a systematic approach to identifying needs, asking difficult questions, and uncovering opportunities. In less than two years, he was able to improve their closing rate from 18 to 26 percent.

"Our salespeople thrive on finding new customers and persuading them to bring us onboard," he explains. They are prospecting machines. That's the most fundamental and important aspect of our sale. They win by generating new opportunities. Constantly."

Interestingly, in the *Journal* article, he mentioned that when he started, the salespeople were referred to as "account managers." "That was a little misleading," he says, and it attracted applicants who weren't focused enough on generating and closing sales. Now his salespeople are called "sales representatives," a simpler and more accurate description of their duties.

We are often amused by some of the titles that companies will come up with to camouflage the title salesperson—account manager, account representative, director of account management, client representative. Anything but the dreaded word *salesperson*.

So what does Dan look for when hiring a hunter, a salesperson who will go after new business?

"We're looking for someone who is competitive and money motivated. These things are important when you're in a hunting position. Also, we're dealing with small-business owners, asking them to rethink how they are conducting their day-to-day operations. So we're looking for someone who is credible and trustworthy. These business owners are placing their faith in us. So our salespeople need to be strategic and consultative. Our sales process is long, and there are many moving parts. So, basically, they need to be willing to do things that I'd say 90 percent of most salespeople aren't willing to do. A lot of that has to do with keeping up with the activity, sticking to a structured sales process, putting in the extra hours before nine o'clock and after five o'clock. Our sales team actually has the Yabba Dabba Doo song on their computers, and if anyone leaves at five o'clock, they'll play that song to rib each other."

The guiding rule is to create a sales organization that reflects the predominant needs of your customer base. What experience are your customers looking for? The answer to this question will start to tell you whether you need hunters, farmers, or both.

From Transactional to Consultative

There are basically two ways to sell—to be consultative or to be transactional. And which approach is most appropriate will depend on several factors, including the nature of the product or service you are providing and the needs of your prospects and clients. By way of a quick example, if a company is selling a data warehousing software, it is more of a strategic sale than someone who is providing off-the-shelf software security software for a home computer.

But it is often not just this simple.

Jim Dickie, managing partner at CSO Insights, explains, "We were just working with a paper company. So that seems like a straightforward transactional sale, right? They're providing 24 pound white recyclable paper. So where is their product edge? Any of their competitors can make the same quality paper. But they changed the game and went from being a transactional supplier to a strategic partner by going to their clients and saying, 'If you continue buying at current levels, we will share all of the information we are aware of that could possibly impact the price of paper so that you have a six-month warning to adjust your budget.'"

This is an example of how you can change the relationship from transactional to consulting. Jim describes five levels of a sales relationship—from approved vendor to trusted partner—that define the depth of the relationship your organization can have with your clients.

As an approved vendor, you're nothing special. You've made the list. The company can buy from you. At the end of the day, though, there's no real difference between you and anybody else. "Sales at this level can be as automatic as my purchasing computer talking to your selling computer," Jim told us.

Then you can move up to being a preferred supplier, where, based on your marketplace reputation and past dealings with your customers, you will, in all likelihood, get more than your fair share of business with that client.

The next level is to be a solutions consultant. This is where, based on a specific set of product-related value-added knowledge or services that you offer, your customers see you as more than a vendor. This is where you also start to become a consulting resource on how to best use your products or services.

The fourth level of the sales relationship is where you become a strategic contributor to your client. At this level, you are not just taking the products and services you provide and applying them to a specific problem. As a strategic contributor, you are viewed by your clients as an expert they turn to for help dealing with broader-based challenges they are currently facing.

Then, at the highest level, as a trusted partner, you are seen as a long-term partner whose contributions are key to your client's long-term success. This is where conversations focus on preparing for what may be going on three, four, or five years out.

"So, for instance, somebody at Boeing is not just thinking about what United Airlines needs this year. They're thinking about the possible design of a plane five years from now. And they are working with other partners, such as General Electric (GE), who make the aircraft engines and collaborating on the future," Jim explains.

So, at each level of the sales relationship—from approved vendor to trusted partner—as you can see, it takes a different level of sales professional.

"It's like a pharmaceutical rep who drops by a doctor's office with a pizza on Friday versus a sales executive who is selling a quarter-of-a-million-dollar blood chemistry analyzer to doctors," Jim adds. "The second decision is not going to be made because you bought a pizza."

At the heart of these different levels of sales, along this sliding scale, companies need different types of salespeople to move up the relationship food chain.

As a sales leader, you must be able to identify the DNA your sales-people need, not just the skill set they may have learned. Do they have the basic built-in dynamics to change the conversations with your clients? To move the relationship from a vendor to a strategic partner?

If you are selling network security software, for instance, and have, in fact, improved the network substantially for your client, can you advance the conversation to move the relationship above and beyond the current success? Can an introduction to the chief information officer be arranged? And can that conversation advance beyond solving a specific security problem to other vulnerabilities within the organization. Is your salesperson ready to engage in a different level of discussion about strategic goals, not just for a department, but for the company? And can that conversation evolve to looking over the horizon to how the strategy needs to evolve over the next five years? And how your organization can have a significant voice in that evolution?

Let us share with you some specific examples of how some of our clients are focusing on selling consultatively—and the types of sales-people who are making that happen.

Steve Bohnenkamp, vice president of sales and marketing at Plymouth Tube Company, told us, "One of my most important responsibilities is to coach a new salesperson to understand the many levels of a client's needs and then to discover how to connect with that client in ways that transcend how they may have thought of us before."

Plymouth Tube is a family-owned company with fourth-generation leadership that customizes the production of steel and titanium products that, for instance, are used in aircraft to withstand four times the burst pressure of previous tubing.

How does Steve change the conversation from "You use tubing? We've got tubing" to understanding the needs of the client and delivering a solution that far exceeds expectations?

"Much of our old sales force was calling on purchasing agents for the most part. They were 'skimming' accounts, not taking a deep dive into understanding the business of their customers. So, at that point, you're always competing on price because the customer doesn't see any other value. I started bringing in more technical salespeople, sales professionals that just so happened to have a technical education or engineering degree. And I am not saying an engineer who wants to take a stab at being a salesperson. Quite the opposite. I'm saying a sales pro who just so happened to have a technical background. Big difference. Such individuals are intrigued by walking through a plant, looking at the processes a customer has, and asking some really good technical questions. Then maybe making some astute technical recommendations. The goal is to call on multiple levels at the account, not just purchasing. We want to include our customer's engineers because they are there to help solve problems—so that they can understand the value we can really bring."

How do their salespeople change their contacts inside the customer's company so that they can change the conversation?

"It starts with where your connection is. Perhaps your only point of contact is in purchasing. Then, by showing that you understand the nuances of the business and that you have ways of customizing solutions, you change the conversation. Then, when trust is established, you can request to be introduced to plant engineers, the head of engineering, and eventually, the chief financial officer and even chief executive officer."

Some of the most impressive salespeople we have come across can be in a meeting with the head of technology, the head of global operations, and the head of finance and speak to all of them in their language, addressing their needs—while not making any of them feel like they're missing a beat.

"Exactly. It is a matter of understanding the needs and interests of everyone in the room and then being able to ask enough probing questions and provide enough insights to engender the trust that is needed to be thought of as a strategic partner. Once that trust is established, the game changes completely."

Does someone need industry experience to succeed in selling consultatively?

"If I had to choose between hiring somebody from my industry who did not understand the selling process and someone else who understand how to sell consultatively but did not have knowledge of our products, I'd go with the person who understood the consultative selling process. No question. Consultative selling is a lot harder to teach than product knowledge. Such an individual will be able to ask the right questions, to tease out information, and to identify problems and needs that the customers probably didn't even realize they had. Someone with only product knowledge will just try to push products. This is all they'll know how to do. The difference between these two different types of salespeople becomes a competitive advantage."

Alyson Brandt, executive vice president, general manager Americas for Forum, said that from her perspective, "Consultative selling is a unique combination of four distinct skills. And they all need to be equally strong and to blend into each other seamlessly. It starts with being able to build relationships, to connect with your clients, to establish trust, and to create new openings and new possibilities."

Trust is the most basic part of credibility. It is all about whether you believe that what I'm telling you is true.

"That has to be the starting place. Otherwise, there is no place to go. The best salespeople then combine their relationship skills with consulting capabilities. Information needs to be leveraged, experience shared, and insights imparted. Clients are looking for someone who can quickly and clearly convey value."

This is a lot to convey quickly. But first impressions last.

"Exactly. There is no starting over. Then the third skill needed is the ability to navigate the sales process. It is a unique ability to connect with your client's various decision makers and influencers, to understand the subtle buying signals, and to be able to respond in such a way that drives performance."

Understanding how to navigate the sales process is a two-way street—often with a lot of traffic. It has to do with understanding and blending your sales process with your client's. And managing expectations. It is a lot to balance.

"And finally, although, as I said, these are all needed, so the order isn't to be thought of sequentially, one of the key skills a consultative salesperson brings is the ability to collaborate and work as part of a team."

And that team changes with each client. So the team becomes a unique blend of the resources at your company and at your client's company.

"That's so true. It's about recognizing how you fit into the team, keeping everyone on your team and your client's team energized and inspired, being able to bring resources to bear to solve the client's need, and ultimately, building firm and lasting relationships with each client."

Consultative selling is taken to an entirely new level by Vascular Solutions, a medical device company committed to providing superior clinical solutions for diagnostic and interventional vascular procedures. Heather Bergmann, director of human resources, shares with us that her company began its search for consultative salespeople in the very shallow pool of professionals who already had an extensive clinical background.

"For instance, we would be interested in someone who was a cardiac catheterization lab technician. So these are people who hand the physician the equipment when they're conducting diagnostic procedures, such as angiograms and angioplasties."

You wouldn't typically think that someone who had pursued such a background would have a proclivity for sales.

"That's right. But some of our most successful salespeople have come right out of that environment. Because of the work they've done previously, they're comfortable advising a doctor on how to use a product for the first time. And they understand the way to communicate with doctors, particularly when it comes to life-and-death situations, such as a heart attack. Their clinical background and experience with doctors give them the confidence to suggest to a doctor that he or she try something new, something that would be a vast improvement."

How does the sale occur? Does the doctor make the final decision?

"Depending on the hospital, the process can be different. But, for the most part, our salespeople will meet with the doctors or the technicians in the labs and, by demonstrating the benefits of our products, engage them to become advocates. Then it can mean having the doctor convey to a purchasing manager the importance of using our product. This can lead to a committee, which might be evaluating five such products. So, getting a doctor to recognize the value of our new product is just the starting point."

This consultative sales approach gives multiple levels a new meaning. It clearly takes a consultative approach, selling every step of the way, creating an advocate in the doctor, and then being able to navigate through each hospital's purchasing procedures.

From transactional to consultative, from being a vendor to being a strategic partner, the path is one of refinement and relevance. Are you one of many? Or one of a kind? Do you bring a product or a solution?

In the future there will be somewhere between very little and no need for transactional salespeople. None of us wants them. Or needs them. We can purchase whatever they offer online—and have it delivered without ever having to talk with an annoying salesperson who is trying to convince us to be doing something else with it that we really don't want.

The future belongs to those who sell consultatively. To those professionals who are intrigued by working with their clients, on getting them to open up and helping them to solve problems—problems that sometimes they may not have even realized they had before.

Not only are the best consultative salespeople solving problems for their clients today, but they are also looking for things that their clients are not worried about right now that they should be.

The best consultative salespeople get a special invitation. They are invited to look at their client's organization with new eyes. And that view is truly welcome.

CHAPTER 12

Job Matching:
The Bottom Line

O nce you have the information about a job and you have an applicant for that job, the actual job-matching process can begin. As we discussed earlier, the first step of this process is to define the job. What is needed here is an understanding of the day-in and day-out functional requirements of the job, the competencies needed for success, which will enable the holder of that job to attain the goals and objectives set by management. In other words, what is needed here is not simply a job description but rather a thorough understanding of what the job holder needs to do to achieve success in the job.

The next step is to determine what qualities are needed by an individual to perform effectively in that job. Completing the kind of job analysis we discussed earlier should permit management to determine the qualities an individual must have to excel in a particular position.

The third step of the job-matching process is to look at the individual being considered and determine whether he or she has the qualities needed for the job.

The fourth step needs to be taken only if there is such a match—if the strengths of the individual match the strengths required by the job. This step involves determining whether there is a *knockout factor*.

THE KNOCKOUT FACTOR

All human beings are made up of an enormous package of motivations, abilities, and attributes. All of us are in the top 10 percent of people possessing certain specific qualities or abilities. But then we are all also in the bottom 10 percent for certain other qualities. And we are more likely somewhere in the middle for other qualities. No human being is or can be all things.

There is a great myth represented by the following statements: "You can be anything you want to be," "All you have to do is work hard enough, and you can do it," and "There is nothing you cannot achieve."

All these phrases add up to the idea that because winners work so hard, anything they touch turns to gold. On the other hand, losers fail at anything they attempt. At the risk of sounding irreverent, we must say that statements such as those we quoted, as well as the entire concept of the winner/loser, are nothing but rank destructive nonsense.

We have found that the winners in this world all share one thing in common: They are lucky enough or perceptive enough to be doing a job for which they are ideally suited. Winners play to their strengths. They do not attempt to work at jobs for which they are unsuited.

On the other hand, losers are trying desperately to do something totally alien to their basic personality. In sales, losers account for those who are trying to defy gravity by becoming what they are not. If those losers in sales, however, were to play to their strengths and change professions, becoming administrators, teachers, lawyers, engineers, accountants, or whatever they were ideally suited to, they quickly might become winners.

The key to success in selling, as in all other professions, is playing to your strengths, being the best at what you are, and staying away from weaker areas. We think that this is a very important point to understand as we look at ourselves, as we look at people we are currently supervising, and as we look at those whom we are considering hiring.

So we go back to the central job match and to the knockout factor. One tradeoff that cannot be made is the match between the functional job requirements and the key strengths possessed by the person who must fill that job. The knockout factor comes in when we look at the weaknesses of an individual and determine whether those weaknesses would, in fact, make it difficult for the person to do the job successfully.

The word *nontrainable* is extremely important to understand as we look at knockout factors.

There are some weaknesses, as we said, that are simply a basic part of an individual and, regardless of training or motivation, really cannot be expected to be substantially altered. For example, if people simply do not enjoy the persuasive process—if they seriously lack ego-drive—they can learn all the technical aspects of sales in terms of tools and techniques, but you will never really make them enjoy selling. As a result, you will never really make them effective salespeople. Nor should you. That lack of ego-drive is simply too basic to their personality, so the reality is that such individuals simply should not be selling.

On the other hand, if someone has some weakness in time planning, that person might be helped through a good time-planning program. A bit more difficult but still possible is a situation where an individual is inconsistently assertive. In instances where such an individual has enough intelligence, openness, and willingness to learn, such a weakness can be improved.

Thus, if we focus on the fact that all people have strengths and weaknesses, that nobody is everything, and we look to match appropriate strengths with the real requirements of a job and make certain that there are no nontrainable knockout factors among the individual's limitations, then we have a job match, with the resulting likelihood that, given training and proper supervision, the individual will perform at a high level of productivity.

RESULTS OF JOB MATCHING

Earlier we said that the existence of so many inappropriate people in sales jobs is traceable, in part, to the fact that people are hired for the wrong reasons. We mentioned that despite legal issues, age, gender, race, experience, and formal education are frequently used as hiring criteria—and our studies have found that these criteria are invalid. It is appropriate here to describe the most comprehensive of these studies not only to debunk these invalid criteria but also to show how the job-matching process, if substituted for these invalid criteria, indeed could go a long way toward solving the poor productivity and high turnover that plagues many organizations.

JOB MATCHING FOR BETTER SALES PERFORMANCE

The results of our comprehensive 14-industry study were published in the September–October 1980 issue of the *Harvard Business Review*. With the permission of the *Harvard Business Review*, we present excerpts from that article.* The findings we report are based on our study of more than 360,000 individuals in the United States, Canada, and Western Europe since 1961.

The study covered 14 industries:

Automobiles	Banking and finance
Chemical manufacture	Business forms manufacture
Life insurance	Data processing
Media and publishing	Farm equipment
Pharmaceutical manufacture	Heavy manufacturing
Real estate	Printing
Stock brokerage and mutual funds	Property and casualty insurance

The seven industries in the first column characteristically have a high turnover of salespeople, whereas those in the second column have a lower turnover.

A random sample of individuals who were hired after testing was selected from each of these industries, and performance data were gathered. The members of the sample then were compared on the basis of

---

* Jeanne Greenberg and Herbert Greenberg, "Job Matching for Better Sales Performance." *Harvard Business Review*, September–October 1980. Copyright 1980 by the President and Fellows of Harvard College. Reprinted by permission; all rights reserved.

industry, age, gender, race, experience, and education. Finally, they were compared as to whether or not they had been recommended for hire on the basis of their possession of appropriate dynamics for their specific sales job. In other words, they were compared in regard to whether or not they were appropriately job-matched.

Author's note: Our consulting firm, Caliper, up to the present has evaluated more than 3 million individuals.

AGE

The worship of youth has long been recognized as a feature of the American culture. The myths relating to the value and attributes of youth have done wonders for clothing designers and cosmeticians. Few others, however, have benefited from our obsession with youth.

When it comes to hiring, we have found no statistically significant difference when comparing the job performance of people over age 40 with that of their under-40 counterparts. Nearly the same percentage of individuals in the older and the younger groups performed in the top quartile of their sales forces after 6- and 14-month periods. Even in turnover rate, the two groups remained extremely close, although the older group did turn over at a slightly lower rate.

GENDER

How well do women perform in sales in comparison with their male counterparts? The results show, beyond statistical question, no performance difference between men and women, even in industries such as stock brokerage and auto sales, which until recently were considered exclusively male bastions. Virtually the same percentage of women and men performed in the top quartile of their sales forces after 6 and 14 months.

RACE

The law and a sense of justice tell us that we cannot discriminate against individuals because of race. The data indicate clearly that it is also not good business to do so, if for no reason other than self-interest. People of color performed on the job as well as their white associates, and turnover rates were virtually identical.

From our sales force data, we conclude that sales performance has absolutely nothing to do with race.

EXPERIENCE

Experience is usually a principal criterion for making hiring decisions. Someone with experience enjoys a great advantage in applying for a sales position. Yet we found little difference in performance between experienced individuals and those with no experience. The person with no experience, given training and supervision, is as likely to succeed as the person with two or more years of experience.

There is an old saying that 20 years of experience can reflect one year's bad experience repeated 20 times. Our findings confirm that this is often the case. Too many people cling tenaciously to their unsuitable jobs and do just well enough not to be fired. These are the individuals who can contribute to a negative reputation for sales.

EDUCATION

During the 30 years between publication of our *Harvard Business Review* article and publication of this book, much has occurred pointing toward additional emphasis on education. The emphasis on more and more high-technology products and the increasing emphasis on the consultative rather than the hard sell have geared the sales profession toward the better-educated individual, especially at the highest levels. With this said, however, our more recent studies continue to show that degrees per se or number of years of education per se are not a good predictor of sales success. Where education really is essential, the necessary level obviously must be a requirement, but using education itself as an absolute criterion for predicting sales success continues to be a fallacy.

As a value to be cherished and encouraged in our society, education cannot be challenged. The use of formal degrees as an absolute criterion for judging someone's potential effectiveness in a sales or a sales management job, however, must be challenged.

Obviously, in certain specialized fields, complex technological knowledge is required. A computer salesperson must know the technology necessary to deal with the specialist in the company who may purchase a new system. Of course, intimate knowledge of the product or service is necessary in all sales situations. For many sales situations, though, such knowledge can be obtained through the company's training program.

Unlike the four other criteria discussed earlier, we found some industry-to-industry variations according to levels of education. College graduates and multidegree recipients slightly outperformed their less educated competitors in industries characterized by big-ticket, highly technical sales and by sales requiring lengthy follow-up.

JOB-MATCHING APPROACH

In view of these findings, an obvious question arises: If these long-used criteria are invalid, what criteria can industry use that would better predict job performance? The answer is criteria that make a better match between the person and the job.

The experience of companies that have tried to match applicants with their sales openings shows distinct differences in performance. A final aspect of this study was a comparison of new hires in terms of whether they were job-matched.

People who had been job-matched in the first six months with appropriate sales positions outperformed, to a statistically significant degree, those who had not been job-matched. Moreover, the differences widened after 14 months. Finally, the turnover rates of job-matched individuals were much lower in all cases.

For the purposes of clarity, we reformulated the data from the study so that performance could be compared among individuals still on the job after 14 months. We compared the performance of individuals whose personality dynamics matched the job for which they were being considered against those who were not recommended but were hired because they met the traditional criteria—relying on factors such as age, gender, race, experience, and education.

Tables 12-1 and 12-2 illustrate the performance of job-matched individuals compared with those who were not job-matched for both high- and low-turnover industries.

Table 12.1 Performance of Those in High Turnover Industries Who Were "Job Matched" Compared to Those Who Were "Not Job Matched"

Measurement Period after Hiring: 14 months	Top Half
Job Matched	85%
Not Job Matched	17%

Note: Sample sizes—4,362 people who were job matched and 8,740 who were not job matched.

Table 12.2 Performance of Those in Low Turnover Industries Who Were "Job Matched" Compared to Those Who Were "Not Job Matched"

Measurement Period after Hiring: 14 months	Top Half
Job Matched	76%
Not Job Matched	21%

Note: Sample sizes—1,800 people who were job matched and 3,961 who were not job matched.

It can be seen from these tables that in the high-turnover industries, 85 percent of individuals recommended for hire on the basis of their appropriate personality dynamics were performing in the top half of their sales force after 14 months, whereas only 17 percent of individuals hired who were not job-matched were performing at that satisfactory level. In the low-turnover industries, 76 percent of those recommended for hire on the basis of their appropriate personality dynamics were performing at that high level, whereas only 21 percent of those not job-matched were doing as well.

The study reveals another important difference: In the high-turnover industries, 57 percent of individuals hired by the old criteria were no longer on the job after 14 months, whereas only 28 percent of those who were hired on the basis of job matching quit or were fired. The turnover difference was even more dramatic in low-turnover industries, where only 8 percent of the individuals for hire on the basis of their appropriate personality dynamics quit or were fired, whereas 34 percent of the non-job-matched group was no longer with their companies after 14 months.

As we wrote in the *Harvard Business Review*, "While error-free personnel selection will remain an impossible dream, this study points out a direction business can take to reduce such errors." We are convinced from this study, and many other smaller studies that we have conducted within individual industries and across industry, that when job matching replaces the old invalid hiring criteria, the sales profession, because of the quality of its people, will indeed achieve the level of productivity and professionalism to which it is entitled. There is no doubt in our minds that if management moves toward job matching in its hiring of salespeople, the sales profession will be characterized by the quality of what is now only the top 20 percent.

PART 4

SELECTING AND HIRING TOP TALENT

Up to this point, we have been focusing on the qualities that distinguish top-performing salespeople, the need to accurately define the unique requirements of the sales position you are seeking to fill, and the importance of establishing a match between the requirements and the qualities you are seeking.

Now we will turn to how you can identify applicants with the potential to be one of your next top performers. We will explore how to recruit, how to screen out those who don't measure up, the importance of incorporating psychological testing into you hiring process, tips for interviewing, and how to make the final decision.

CHAPTER 13

Your Top Performers Are Your Blueprint for Success

When the leaders at SAP unveiled the company's innovative vision for the year 2014, they knew what they had to do to accomplish their goals. They had to accelerate the development of their current top performers and redouble their efforts to identify people who had the potential to become their next top performers.

According to Paul Orelman, director of top management for SAP, the company, which has been renowned for its innovative technology since its founding in 1972, was now intent on also becoming known for developing great talent.

But how does one of the world's largest companies become an incubator for finding and keeping talent, particularly when its key competitors, with very deep pockets, are doing everything they can to pirate that talent away?

SAP is taking a five-tiered approach to building on its innovative and competitive culture. For our purposes here, we'll focus on how the company is identifying and developing top sales talent.

Paul told us that while you certainly want to start out by hiring salespeople who have innate ability, that is only the beginning. The first step is to identify the qualities, strengths, and potential that distinguish the organization's best salespeople from the rest of the salespeople. Then you can use your best as your model for developing your midrange performers and for hiring new people who have the potential to be top performers.

For example, are your top salespeople more assertive or more consultative? Do they have a need for fast results, or are they patient enough to handle a longer sales cycle? Do they need a structured sales process, or are they comfortable setting their own schedule? And how do these traits compare with the people in the middle and those who are not measuring up at all? All these traits, depending on the product and service being sold, can be strengths or derailers.

To determine the answers to these questions, SAP administered in-depth personality profiles to its current top performers and high-potential employees—"to gain objective insights into their individual and collective strengths," Paul says. "So we wanted to be as clear and accurate as possible about exactly what those strengths were. And we recognized, of course, that we could not objectively evaluate ourselves. So we turned to outside experts in this area."

In this way, the organization's best salespeople provided a blueprint for the future. By identifying the distinguishing qualities of its top talent, the company knew exactly what to look for in its next employees.

Thus SAP's five-step approach to building, identifying, and developing top sales talent starts off with assessing the strengths and growth opportunities of the company's top talent. This certainly includes using a valid personality assessment to find out what sets those individuals apart.

Second is to develop growth plans for each of those key individuals. As Paul told us, "This starts with understanding the individual goals of each of these highly talented people and letting them know that the leadership of the company is committed to their futures. Our philosophy of high-potential development includes having them work on real strategic issues that are vital to them and to our organization."

Next is to recognize the gaps that exist between the current level of talent in the organization and the organization's future needs.

Fourth is looking deeper inside the organization to recognize future talent that can be developed. In this case, it is identifying people who have the ability to move into sales. As Paul says, "Talent development is building the skills of the entire workforce for current and future success."

And the fifth step of this process is to hire new individuals who have the potential to flourish in the company's culture. That potential will have been assessed by comparing them with the blueprint of top performers, which was created in the first step by assessing the qualities that distinguish the organization's top performers.

Using this process can provide a model for identifying sales applicants who share the distinguishing qualities of your top performers. And from a developmental standpoint, it can provide guidelines for setting individual goals and can become the basis for performance reviews of your current employees.

Without revealing trade secrets, it was established that SAP's most talented individuals are all extremely bright, very independent thinkers with a strong goal orientation. They are adept at thinking on their feet, don't get mired in details, and are very comfortable taking initiative. While you might expect top performers in a software development company to be somewhat rules-driven, they were the exact opposite. Certainly, there are many individuals inside the organization who maintain policies and procedures. But to continually create innovative solutions, top performers at SAP need to be independent thinkers and perform well under first-time challenging conditions.

As a result, these top performers have helped to define SAP's unique culture—which is action-oriented, highly competitive, and driven by quality.

And therein lies the solution and the challenge.

To remain innovative and to keep its competitive edge, it is vital for SAP to find and develop individuals who share these qualities, who can thrive in this unique culture, and who have the potential to be top performers and future leaders of the organization.

This same approach can give you a clear picture of the strengths of all your top performers and provide you with a blueprint for future hiring.

The process we suggest, for medium to large companies, is to identify a sample of your company's top, marginal, and bottom performers. It is crucial to use objective data to identify who your top, marginal, and bottom performers really are. In sales, this is relatively easy because you can look at such metrics as which people continually miss, hit, or exceed quota. Analyzing the data makes certain that you are getting the best information and that sales managers are not merely identifying as top performers individuals whom they personally like the most. However, identifying top, marginal, and bottom performers is just the first step. Using a validated personality assessment will give you the information you need to identify the traits that set your top performers apart from the rest. The idea is to develop a composite profile of the personality strengths and motivations of this top group. In other words, the group is combined statistically as though it were one individual—thus the top group might average, for example, in the seventieth percentile of ego-drive, the eighty-fifth percentile of assertiveness, and so on.

For instance, one company might see its top-producing salespeople being in the eighty-third percentile of urgency, whereas another company, in a different industry, might see its urgency mean score at the fiftieth percentile level. The differences in sales situations create the differences required for each characteristic. In addition to looking at your top performers, by studying marginal and bottom performers, you can compare results and see how they differ. The result of this comparison is usually quite telling, highlighting the key qualities that sharply distinguish one group from another.

For example, the top-producing group might have a mean of 85 for assertiveness compared with the marginal group, whose urgency is at the thirty-third percentile level. This difference, then, points to one critical characteristic beyond the key sales characteristics that should be looked at in making a hiring decision. The hiring manager in this case would want to think long and hard the next time a promising candidate was interviewed who was low on assertiveness if this quality is determined to be a key factor for success for this particular sales job.

This exercise allows management to do two things. First, if psychological testing or a similar assessment technique is used, it allows management to compare a job applicant's assessment with the profiles of top performers to determine how closely the applicant's profile matches the ideal. This will provide a clear picture of whether an applicant who interviews well truly matches the job.

The second benefit of this approach is that it allows management to see where the deficiencies are in the marginal performers and to start to bridge those gaps with very targeted training and coaching. A vice president of sales at a major car rental company had a composite profile developed of his most successful salespeople and discovered, as he said, "that the make-or-break quality for succeeding with us is the ability to listen closely enough." He added, "While salespeople have been glibly described as having golden tongues, we have found that our very best salespeople have golden ears. What we need to know is whether a promising applicant is empathic enough to be able to truly listen and understand where our prospects are coming from."

And the training development coordinator for a major graphic communications company in Chicago, who has adopted this approach to hiring and developing top performers, said, "I know to look for five qualities in new employees: attitude, attitude, attitude, attitude, and then skill."

We have found that the distinguishing qualities of the best employees are centered on their personalities—who they are (Figure 13-1). You can always provide technical training, but some things just can't be taught.

At smaller companies, there may not be a sample size large enough to study. It is only slightly useful for a company with six salespeople to attempt a benchmark using their top two people. This exercise could be interesting, but it is likely to produce erroneous results because two employees are simply not enough of a sample to be valuable from a statistical perspective. What, then, can a smaller company do? First, it would be useful to assess the sales force both as a means of upgrading individual productivity and as a way to get a sense of the team's overall strengths and limitations. In hiring for smaller companies, however, we feel that it is most appropriate for them to use industry norms as the benchmark for judging promising applicants. Clearly, this cannot be as customized and well targeted as it is when a company can use its own personnel as the benchmark.

However, comparing an applicant with industry norms provides far better and more precise criteria than simply depending on the sales dynamics. Even as this benchmark approach is used, it must be understood that tradeoffs will continue to be necessary. As a practical matter, it is often difficult to find enough candidates who match your ideal profile, who possess the highest levels of every key quality you are seeking. However, the ideal profile can serve as your roadmap for future hiring. It will allow you to make informed decisions about which tradeoffs

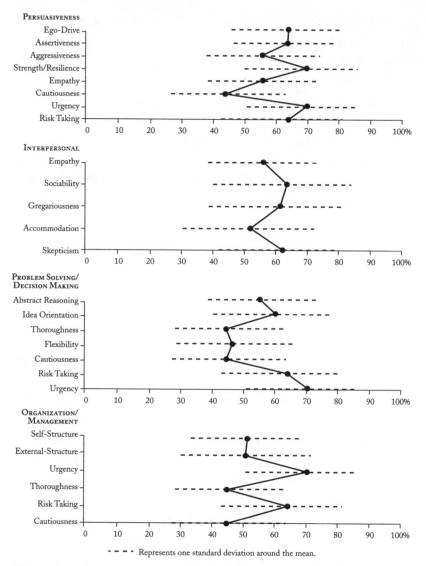

Figure 13-1 Top salesperson benchmark.

in a particular candidate might be acceptable and what kind of training or coaching would be appropriate to address any particular weakness from the beginning.

Thus, while some compromises inevitably will have to be made, the overall result of this approach is most likely to be a substantial increase in your hiring batting average, with a resulting sales force that more closely approaches the ideal, more closely represents the composite of your top producers.

With this new information in mind, you can now look deeper within your organization to identify employees who have the ability to move into sales. And when you do hire from the outside, you can select only individuals who have the potential to flourish in your culture. Creating a blueprint of your top performers actually increases objectivity during the hiring process by ranking job candidates based on the known requirements for success. This also aids in selecting individuals with strong potential for fast tracking and for succession planning.

As you look to the future, the most successful companies will be those who create effective, long-term strategies for investing in the growth of each individual, their teams, and their company as a whole. The approach we're suggesting combines precise assessments with expert advice to provide you with specific solutions. This will allow you to select the right people, develop productive teams, and bridge the gap between where your company is and where you want it to be.

Let us share with you how Avis Budget Group has developed a benchmark of its top performers to gain a clear understanding of the potential of all the organization's entire sales force. Tom Gartland, president, North America of Avis Budget Group, made sure that the organization's entire sales force of over 600 individuals had an in-depth psychological profile matched to their performance reviews and their career aspirations.

As Tom explains, "We had in-depth personality profiles conducted for everyone in our sales organization. That gave us a baseline view of each individual's potential, strengths, and limitations. When we match to their current performance, we are able to view them from where they are now, how we can help them meet their goals, and where we see them moving next, with an eye even further down the road."

This is an extremely comprehensive view—and an enormous commitment. It sends a very clear message to everyone inside the organization of how committed Avis Budget Group is to their success. And it creates an extremely attractive culture for attracting top talent when the company is hiring.

"Through these comprehensive personality assessments, we have developed a thorough understanding of the unique qualities that distinguish our top performers. Those unique qualities create a pattern that has become our blueprint for bringing new people into the organization. If a promising applicant shares similar personality dynamics with our top performers, then we become very interested," Tom explains.

Anyone being hired into such an organization certainly would have a clear understanding of the commitment that is being made to them. They would know that they are entering an organization that is interested in hiring them now, as well as hiring them for the future—a future that will tap into their real potential.

CHAPTER 14

Recruiting Productive Talent

Entire books have been written on how to recruit top talent. Social networking has opened up new possibilities, and virtually all our clients have human resources departments. So we're not going to go through a step-by-step process on how to create a rigorous recruitment approach right here. What we'll do instead is just mention a few important things to remember when you are recruiting.

The best advice is to be constantly looking. Bill Eckstrom, president of EcSELL Institute, told us, "One of the biggest challenges sales leaders talk about is how difficult it is to find top talent. And a huge part of that problem is because they are reactive rather than proactive about seeking talent."

When someone leaves, there is an opening that needs to be filled, and a scrambling often takes place.

"It baffles me as to why sales leaders put themselves in that position. The single item that distinguishes top sales leaders from the rest is their ability to identify, develop, and retain top talent."

If this is the biggest issue, then it needs to be woven into the fabric of the organization. There should be a constant search for talent.

"Exactly. The talent is there. It is just hard to find when you search for it in small windows with the pressure of a deadline. It is hard to find talent in an isolated search. It is easier to find it when you are always looking for it."

Thus, keeping a talent pool, keeping in touch with individuals you'd like to bring on board, letting them know that you're interested, and letting them know that you'll be working with them when something opens up, they may be working with you.

"It's like a prospect list. You teach your salespeople to keep a constant prospect list. So why shouldn't you, as a sales leader, have a constant prospect list of the talent you'd like to add to your team when the time is right."

A prospect list. That's a great way of putting it.

In addition, our advice is to look inside before you look outside. But before we get to that advice, let us pose a question: Have you ever hired someone based on your gut feeling?

A lot of leaders will confidently say, "I'm going to go with my gut on this one."

Let's just pause and consider your gut for a moment. Your gut is basically your intestines and stomach. That's not a very appealing way to go about making a decision. Not to mention it is a very circuitous route.

So that got us wondering, why in the world do we use our guts to help us make important decisions?

The nerve cells in our gut, it turns out, are stimulated when the brain releases stress hormones in response to an uncomfortable or frightening situation. It causes a physical reaction. This is the old "fight of flight" mechanism that has enabled us to survive since prehistoric times.

So it makes sense that if your gut is saying that something is wrong, you should, by all means, listen to it.

However, what doesn't make any sense is to decide that you're going to make an important personal or business decision based solely on your gut telling you that this just "feels right."

Your gut is not the body part you want to call on for making a refined decision.

Such a decision is where our hearts and minds can synthesize all the information we've gleaned, reflect possibilities, seek wise counsel, sleep on it—and then call on our intuition.

So here's our simple note of caution: If your gut is saying, "I don't know exactly why, but I know this person is right for this job," then it is time to put your gut on hold and consider what is really going on.

Does the job candidate you're enthused about remind you of someone you're very fond of? (Yourself, perhaps?) Or does the applicant share similar interests that make you very comfortable with him or her?

If your gut says, "Forget it," then, by all means, listen.

But to make well-informed hiring decisions, you need to start with an approach to recruiting that places the odds in your favor—especially when you consider, as we've said, that over half the people currently working in sales would be doing themselves, their company, and certainly those of us who are unfortunate enough to come in contract with them a favor if they just gracefully bowed out and pursued an entirely different profession.

Consider this: We surveyed over 500 executives and asked them, "How long does it take to realize you've hired the wrong person?"

In other words, after you've gone through the rigors of your hiring process and brought on someone who you believe has what it takes to succeed, how long does it take to realize you've made a colossal mistake?

Over half the executives we surveyed said that they could tell if someone wasn't going to make it within the first week on the job.

The first week.

That's after taking three months, in some cases longer, to fill an important position.

What's wrong with this picture?

Add to this that most companies give new employees a standard 90-day trial period.

Therefore, as managers, we have no choice but to spend our time, energy, effort, money, and whatever other resources we have—hoping against hope that we can somehow turn the situation around. And we're obliged to do this, knowing the likelihood of the outcome—which is that we are going to have to let the person go and start the process all over again.

Just add it all up.

If the wrong person is hired, let's be conservative and say that it took three months to bring that individual on board. Then another three months to try to correct the mistake. Then another three months to find someone else. That's nine months—wasted!

Therefore, as you look to recruit productive talent, we want to first tell you some of the things you absolutely should *not* do when it comes to hiring. These mistakes have become woven into the fabric of many hiring processes for many companies.

THE MOST CLASSIC HIRING MISTAKE

The most common hiring mistake is to hire someone who has the right experience. We know that this sounds counterintuitive, but hear us out.

When you're putting together a help-wanted ad, what's the first thing you write?

"Needed, a salesperson with at least one year of experience." No. Wait a minute. This is a much more important job. Let's say, "Needed, five years' experience."

Experience is what we look for in job candidates.

If two candidates seem equally qualified for a position, and one has slightly more experience, the decision seems easy. Experience wins. Some executives even will look in their competitors' backyards for individuals who are ready to make a move. Conventional wisdom is that an experienced individual will hit the ground running.

But how many times have you come across someone who has five years of experience that adds up to just one year's bad experience repeated five times?

Our advice is not to hire from your competitors—unless you want to do them a favor.

Don't fall into the trap of relying too heavily on experience. It is an easy approach, but it can be very costly. Let your competitors steal from each other.

Instead of focusing on what someone has done, look, instead, to what they can do—to their potential.

Andrew Marshall, the former director of corporate sector and SMB at Virgin Media, told us: "We learned to avoid hiring from our main competitors. There are two other key competitors in our space, and some of our biggest failures have come from hiring from them. Because we are the third largest telecommunications firm in the United Kingdom, when we hire from our competitors, we find that they are not used to truly being competitive. They've come from much larger organizations and, we found, have succeeded based on the brand they were representing, not because of their particular skills. In addition, they just don't fit into our corporate culture, which is very agile and where we expect people to take on a lot of ownership for their own decisions. When we've hired salespeople from our competitors, they're more used to going through a lengthy bureaucratic process to arrive at a decision. So they have a difficult time adapting to the agility of our organization."

Mark Dennis, vice president of sales and marketing at Veolia Environmental Services, put it succinctly: "I have finally come to the point where I could care less whether somebody has industry experience. I've had way too many instances of hiring people who have industry experience who just get in their own way because they are set in their ways. They believe they know it all. And they are not open, willing or flexible enough to want to change, to look at the industry from our perspective. So training them can become an absolute nightmare."

Mark told us: "I've learned the hard way that often when we bring in somebody who has 'industry experience,' we're just recycling inept salespeople through organizations—just because they have experience. It can be appealing to the sales manager who is under pressure to bring new people up to speed faster. But it can be very deceptive. Because whatever they did at their prior company—good, bad, or indifferent—whatever they did there, they're going to do at your company, whether you like it or not."

And your competitor is probably thanking you. Immensely.

Experience, it turns out, often can keep you where you are rather than helping you to move forward and see new possibilities.

LOOK INSIDE

Instead of turning to the outside, we strongly suggest that you look inside your own company first.

Andrew Marshall adds: "Recruitment is the hardest part of the hiring process because you're making a decision based upon a snapshot in time, typically around an individual that you've never met before. And that becomes really difficult. That's why I have become a strong believer in trying to develop from within and to create what we call the life cycle of a salesperson. Because if you have someone already in your company, you're taking far less of a risk promoting them than you are by recruiting externally. Additionally, you are sending a strong, positive message to everyone inside the company about their possible futures." Pausing, he continues: "That's why it has become extremely important to have a very scientific approach to hiring. Otherwise, you can be easily fooled, because, as it turns out, some of the worst salespeople in the world have the gift of gab. And that makes it quite easy to make a mistake."

We work with many insurance agencies, for instance, who find their new producers from among the executive assistants, underwriters, or customer-service representatives already on board. Likewise, many auto dealers we work with are able to find excellent salespeople among their service writers and mechanics. Many production people in printing firms, given the opportunity, have proven to be the company's best salespeople. And some of our larger clients have been able to recruit top salespeople from their accounting departments, engineers, and even factory personnel.

Before turning to the outside, we strongly suggest that you take a hard look at your existing people to see if someone who is currently performing in a job that is not sales-related might have the persuasive drive, empathy, and resilience needed to succeed in sales. Such individuals will bring many key advantages. For starters, you know them, their values, and their work habits. And they know your company, your values, and your work habits. So there is already a cultural match. In addition, there is a strong morale factor to be gained by giving people an opportunity to better themselves within your company: Top performers in your company want to know that they have a place to grow.

REFERRALS

Now if you don't have people on board who might be interested and have the potential to succeed in sales, the next best thing is to reward your employees for being recruiters themselves. Provide them with a finder's fee of $500 for anyone they recommend who is hired. The benefits are many-fold. People will gladly recommend friends whom they feel will be a fit for your company, and they will, in all likelihood, share many of the same values. In addition, you are helping to create a culture in which people connect on a real level.

BANK OF APPLICANTS

Having a bank of applicants with whom you stay in touch, who are interested in your company and whom you are interested in, is extremely important. When we ask our clients how long it takes to hire someone, we get answers that range from two to three weeks to three months or more.

Companies that take the longest are the ones that have to start from scratch whenever a key employee leaves. They don't have a succession plan, let alone a backup plan. As a result, when someone leaves, they have to scramble. And by the time they place ads, cull through the résumés, narrow down the pool, conduct initial interviews, narrow down again to final, often multiple interviews, check references, make an offer, negotiate and wait for the candidate to give a two-week notice, three months can go by easily.

On the other hand are companies that have an applicant bank that they keep current and active. This is a list of attractive applicants who may have expressed interest when there wasn't an opening, as well as applicants who were among the final two or three candidates for a previous position but weren't selected at that time. This can become an extremely valuable list for your company. We have clients who stay in touch with such candidates every few months, just checking in, letting them know that there is still interest, and updating any news about potential openings. Then, when the right opportunity for that applicant appears, they can be called immediately. And the opening can be filled without missing a beat.

NONTRADITIONAL SOURCES OF TALENT

Our underlying message is that in order to look for potential rather than experience, you have to change the way you look at recruiting. Before closing this chapter, we want to reemphasize that what you should be looking for is an individual's potential. And potential often has very little to do with experience.

Allow us to tell you a story that brings this point to life. In the late 1960s, we undertook two major programs—one in Puerto Rico and one in New York City—that provided conclusive evidence that the unemployed and underemployed are an untapped and exceptionally rich source of talent. Suffice it to say that in these two programs, when people's personalities were job-matched to a specific job, those people succeeded. Not only did people become highly productive and remain in their jobs, but many were promoted and moved on to managerial positions. In all, more than 3,000 people were placed in some 70 companies. Nearly half of them filled sales positions, and the remainder were placed in more than 50 other job categories. And in follow-up after two years, it was found that fewer than 3 percent had been terminated because of their inability to do the job.

To reemphasize the importance of this figure, few, if any, of these individuals had sold before or had filled jobs similar to the ones in which they were placed. What they had was the potential, the basic ability to do the job in which they were placed, and of course, they also were given the necessary training to do the job effectively.

These programs put our hypothesis—that sales ability exists across the population, regardless of what individuals have or have not done in the past—to the test. Literally hundreds of cases could be presented in which individuals totally lacked any of the typical criteria that would encourage management to hire them, and yet, given their inherent core strengths, they were able to perform brilliantly. Let us cite just a few in order to underscore this important point.

In the project in Puerto Rico, anyone earning more than $1,800 a year was not eligible. This project was funded by the then-existing Office of Economic Opportunity and was cosponsored by Sales & Marketing International of San Juan. Maria was a 42-year-old woman whose earnings were well under the required $1,800 per year figure. Testing indicated that she had sales and even sales management ability, so she went through two weeks of job readiness training and then entered a sales training program that was conducted by a large mutual fund sales organization. She became the first woman to be licensed to sell mutual funds in Puerto Rico, and six months after her initial training, she came back to the program to hire five people to work for her.

The New York program was under the auspices of the National Alliance of Business and was funded by the U.S. Department of Labor. Participating in the program were 52 New York–area companies that offered 55 job categories to the so-called hard-core unemployed. One of those hard-core unemployed was a 22-year-old man from Harlem. The only work he had ever done was some deliveries and other scattered odd jobs. When he was tested, it was discovered, as his counselor put it, "that Georgie could sell sand in the Sahara Desert." The plan was to refer Georgie to a life insurance company that was participating in the program. When he was approached with this idea, Georgie literally laughed and asked, "What's life insurance?" He totally ridiculed the idea of being a salesperson, particularly the idea of attempting to learn a profession about which he had absolutely no knowledge. It took several counseling sessions to finally get Georgie to laughingly admit that maybe he did have some sales ability. "I guess I can sell," he said, as he realized how he would convince his friends to go along with him. Georgie went for the interview and was given the job.

Now, to understand what followed, two premises of life insurance sales must be stated. First, you need a market. Georgie obviously had no market. Second, you cannot sell ordinary life insurance door to door. However, Georgie had no other way to do it. The result? Georgie was a member of the "Million Dollar Roundtable" within two years of acquiring his license.

A third example is perhaps closest to Herb Greenberg's heart. A young man, let's call him Ralph, fell asleep while taking a test early one morning. There was fear that drugs were involved, but as it turned out, Ralph had tended bar until 2 a.m. that morning and was simply exhausted at 7:30 a.m. In any case, his test indicated that he not only had enormous sales potential but also possessed even better management ability. There was one problem, however. He had a rap sheet, and it was a rather extensive one. There were no violent crimes, but there were enough arrests and even convictions to block him from consideration by most companies. Gimbels Department Store, however, had some very good experiences with a number of people that we had placed with them, so the company took a chance on Ralph. He received five promotions in two years. Like Maria, he hired some people from within the program, and when Herb Greenberg's daughter was born, he received a dozen roses from Ralph, with a note saying, "To a new life, from a life you saved."

That spirit of identifying potential is very much alive at United Rentals, Inc., where Craig Pintoff, senior vice president of human resources, told us: "We have recognized the leadership value and work ethic that military veterans can bring to our company. We are very focused on recruiting returning veterans. It is not just that they've given so much to their country, and we want to recognize that. They bring enormous talent and have a strong sense of pride, discipline, and commitment, which is very much a part of who we are. Our company's values are closely aligned with those of veterans and reservists, including strong leadership, teamwork, discipline, diversity, and work ethic. In addition, there are many transferable skills that fit in perfectly with our company—from drivers to mechanics to sales professionals to managers. We are very proud to have been named for the third year in a row by *G.I. Jobs* magazine as one of the hundred most military friendly employers in America."

In short, there is no shortage of candidates with the potential to succeed. The good news is that recruiting top talent actually may be easier than you realize. Our very strong advice is to keep in mind, as you look to someone's potential, that you cannot give someone the right attitude. An applicant who possesses a positive attitude is bringing you an enormous gift. Whenever you come across an applicant with the right attitude and with the potential to succeed, you have found someone worth investing in because they possess the essential foundation on which you can develop your next top performer.

CHAPTER 15

Screening Out
the Inappropriate

The dilemma of the selection process that we've just outlined is that you have to cast a very broad net to attract individuals who have sales potential rather than just past sales experience. So how do you narrow down your pool of candidates?

We suggest a pyramid approach to the selection process, starting with the broadest base of applicants that can be created by good recruiting, and then narrowing, step by step, to the peak of the pyramid, from which the finalists are evaluated and from which the individual or individuals are selected to fill the position. Broadly speaking, this pyramid process is divided into the screening-out segment, narrowing the base to manageable numbers, and then a final screening in process, designed to make the best possible selection from among those under consideration. In this chapter we will look at the process by which inappropriate people are screened out, while the next chapters will deal in depth with each component by which the screening in takes place and the final hiring decision is made.

REVIEW OF RÉSUMÉ

The first step in screening out the obviously inappropriate is the résumé review. This typically can be done quickly and yet accomplish a great deal toward reducing the sheer numbers of applicants with whom time must be taken. We should insert a word of caution here that applies to any step in the screening-out process: In dealing with the practical necessity of screening out large numbers of people, a few diamonds in the rough could be eliminated from this group. This should be kept in mind as résumés are reviewed so that where there is some doubt, if numbers permit, the benefit of the doubt should go to the applicant, at least by carrying him or her to the next step. Résumés should be reviewed to ascertain the degree to which applicants possess the essential job requirements. To this end, applicants who have submitted résumés can be separated into three distinct groups: those having most of the requirements, those possessing some of the important requirements, and those clearly not qualified to assume the job responsibilities.

The third group obviously will be screened out immediately. In doing this, management should be certain that it is not screening out on the basis of invalid criteria but that it really is screening out on the basis of clear objective facts that would preclude the individual from being effective on the job. While it is absolutely necessary as a practical matter to screen out people on the basis of their résumés, some care should be taken to avoid being trapped by the superficial. In reviewing a résumé, it is important to get an overview in order to ascertain an applicant's complete job history and then read between the lines to assess not only the information stated on the résumé but also the story behind the job changes: periods of unemployment, seeming inconsistencies in dates, and other information.

On the positive side, above and beyond sales experience, which, as we have repeatedly emphasized, may be totally irrelevant, management should look at job and life experiences that indicate specific accomplishments and obstacles that have been overcome.

Another obvious positive is a pattern of job changes, all of which move in the direction of enhancing the individual's career. On the negative side of this coin is the job hopper who explains each change by indicating poor environment, little opportunity, and so on. In essence, reviewing a résumé permits management to eliminate obviously inappropriate people from further consideration. In no sense, however, does it allow management to make a positive hiring decision. All that a review of a résumé can be expected to do is to narrow the pyramid and to point to the individuals who are worth further exploration.

A QUICK PERSONALITY ASSESSMENT AS A SCREENER

For applicants who may have potential, a quick personality assessment can serve as a screener to determine if they are obviously lacking in one or more of the fundament qualities needed to succeed in the sales position you are seeking to fill. If, for instance, the applicant does not possess enough empathy to tune into the needs of a prospect, or if the applicant is not driven to persuade others, then you no longer have to pursue him or her. You know all you need to know.

These insights will not tell you whether the individual has all the qualities needed to succeed in your sales position. That review comes a bit further in the recruitment process. But the insights from a screener can tell you whether the individual is obviously missing one or more of the key qualities you are seeking in an ideal candidate.

THE TELEPHONE SCREEN

The next step we recommend is a telephone screening. While there can be no doubt that an in-person interview will yield more data than a telephone conversation, as a practical matter, if the number of applicants demands it, the telephone screen becomes a valuable tool as a less time-consuming next step in the screening-out process.

What we are suggesting is that the individuals who have most of the requirements should be given a telephone call. This telephone call should be relatively short, between 10 and 15 minutes, because its purpose is not to make a positive hiring decision but rather simply to screen out clearly inappropriate people. If, for example, someone's demeanor is less than professional, then you should screen that person out. What the telephone interview is designed to do is simply determine whether or not the applicant is worth pursuing further.

To accomplish this, you should straighten out any discrepancies in the résumé, briefly explain the job, and permit the applicant to quickly sell you on why he or she is a viable candidate. So, while this method is not foolproof, if the applicant does not leave a favorable first impression with you on the phone, this could be a good indication that the screening process should stop right there.

If, on the other hand, a decision is made to bring the applicant in for the next step, then schedule a brief initial interview at that time. It is important that the brevity of this interview be spelled out on the telephone when the interview is being scheduled so that the applicant does not feel that he or she is being pushed out in too short a time. This in-person interview is not designed to produce a positive hiring decision, Again, you are in the screening-out phase, so you are looking to examine additional factors in a little more depth, allowing you to screen out still more people. While the applicant is there, we would suggest having him or her fill out an in-depth personality assessment. We will discuss the role of this in-depth personality assessment later, but suffice it to say here that if the applicant takes the test the same day and is screened out later, then the test does not have to be evaluated and so will not cost the company any money or time.

REFERENCE CHECKS

The next step is to check references. While we strongly suggest that reference checks be done, it is important to be aware of their limitations. First, the applicant is certainly going to provide references with which he or she is totally comfortable. No one is going to knowingly give a potential employer names of people who will say negative things about them. This is why it is important to ask for at least one additional reference beyond the initial two so that the applicant will have to dig a little bit deeper, and the references will not just be completely glowing.

The second problem relates to the pervasive guilt that may exist among managers who have fired people. If the references are from a company where the applicant was let go, the manager may give a glowing reference as a means of alleviating his or her own guilt.

The third major problem relates to people's fear of litigation. No one wants to be accused of unfairly damaging someone, and as we are all well aware, fighting a lawsuit, even one we win, is extremely costly. Thus people are going to tend to say noncommittal, nonthreatening, nondamaging things, even about employees whom they felt did harm to their company.

What we recommend is to have the hiring manager or a human resources manager make the reference calls himself or herself. We emphasize here, make the call. When form letters are sent to references, we can guarantee that you will not get very useful information beyond dates and job titles. When a manager makes the call, it is important to tune in carefully to the tone of the person called, as well as to the content of what is said. If the manager uses his or her empathy, then the pauses, inflections and things that are not said often can provide more valuable information than the glib words that might be expected. If a company truly cares about who is hired, then the responsible manager should make the call himself or herself and should use all his or her listening skills when doing so.

The key to the actual discussion with the reference is to find ways to give that person permission to say negative things. Ways must be found to alleviate the fear of litigation and to allow the person to indicate negatives without feeling that he or she is hurting the applicant. One of the things that can be done is to preface your questions with a compliment. For example, "I found Joe to be extremely personable, but have you noticed that he seems somewhat impatient?" or "From our interviews and from other references, we certainly agree with you about his presentation skills, but this job involves a minimum of four solid hours a day of being on the phone and cold-calling. If he is uncomfortable with that, he'll fail within a week. How do you feel he'll react to that, and what do you think we can do to help him?" A summary kind of probing question could be something like this: "I'm really pleased to hear all these things, and frankly, I'm not surprised because she comes across as a very impressive person. Now that I've told you something about the job, can you suggest ways that we can help her? Is there anything you can tell us about the training or supervision she might need? What I'm asking is, how can we help her achieve her top potential?" What you're doing in asking for these suggestions is allowing the former manager to at least touch on some possible weaknesses without asking directly, "What are her weaknesses?"

At the end of the reference check, management will have screened out a substantial majority of the broad base of applicants the recruiting process had brought in. True, as we have said before, a few potentially good people might be screened out, but as a practical matter, this narrowing pyramid process is designed to minimize management's time spent screening in applicants.

Although the screening-out process is time-consuming and certainly not a perfect approach, it is hoped at least in the vast majority of cases that inappropriate people have been eliminated. Then you can focus on those who have a real chance of succeeding. Those are the applicants who deserve your full attention. By putting them through a rigorous and comprehensive screening process, your final hiring decision will be extremely well considered and poised for success.

CHAPTER 16

Psychological Testing: Gaining Objective Insights

I n Chapter 15 we dealt with means by which job applicants can be screened out. We stressed, and this is worth repeating, that neither the résumé review, the telephone interview, the quick personality assessment as a screener, the short initial in-person interview, nor the reference checks can or should serve as the sole basis on which to make a positive hiring decision. Each of these steps is designed to trigger red flags that allow management to narrow the applicant pool to a manageable degree. In other words, by the time we have reached the screening-in process, we should be dealing with only candidates who are worthy of in-depth consideration.

The reason that a definitive hiring decision cannot be made on the basis of the earlier steps is simple. All these steps involve subjective, not objective, feedback. The résumé, as we discussed, may be professionally prepared and may or may not really reflect what the applicant has accomplished. The telephone interview can, at most, provide management with a subjective impression, which may be good enough to screen out people but is certainly not sufficient to make the enormous commitment involved in offering someone a job. The quick personality assessment can tell you who you should *not* consider any further because they don't possess the essential qualities you are seeking. Similarly, the in-person interview can create impressions that, if sufficiently negative, could knock out someone but still does not provide objective input into the dynamics of the individual. And finally, reference checking has so many built-in flaws. Even when conducted properly, it is still so subjective that only negative factors may be usable, but certainly all the praise in the world should not convince management to make a job offer.

After all these subjective knockouts have reduced the applicant pyramid to a manageable size, what is needed is objective information about the individuals obtained through use of a valid psychological test and the confirmatory input of an in-depth interview. The need for this objective input has, in a large sense, been recognized by the industry at least since the end of World War II. By the late 1950s, when our work really began, tests, structured interview guides, and demographic scales had proliferated. As we mentioned earlier, this proliferation actually began our involvement in the business of testing and evaluating personnel. We were asked to review many of the then-available assessment instruments to help a company decide the most effective way to reduce its sales turnover. Even back in the 1950s, companies were groping for some objectivity to help them make more balanced, sound, and correct hiring decisions. In their attempt to reach objectivity, they would set up arbitrary cutoff scores on invalid tests, use tests developed for one purpose for a totally unrelated purpose, and in short, flounder through the jungle of available instruments and procedures, often making matters worse instead of really infusing the objectivity they sought into their hiring.

While we state emphatically that the use of valid psychological testing is critical to effective hiring, we should begin our discussion of testing by examining why so many of the tests offered are totally invalid, inappropriate, and ineffective as an aid in making objective hiring decisions by management.

WHY TESTS MISFIRE

It was our in-depth study of why so many tests misfire that led us to develop our own testing instruments. At the time, we discovered that there are seven basic reasons that most tests fail to produce the accurate results that industry seeks.

1. Tests Have Been Looking for Interest, Not Ability

The idea that a person's interest can be equated with that person's ability is an important cause of test failure. Tests have been developed by asking questions of applicants, with the assumption that if an applicant expresses the same kind of interest pattern as a successful performer, he or she too would be a successful performer. This assumption is wrong. Psychologically, interest does not equal aptitude, and this is quite simple to illustrate. Someone may have exactly the same interests as Michael Jordan or Wayne Gretzky but may be entirely lacking in athletic skills. By the same token, an individual might have the same interest pattern as a successful salesperson or manager but have little talent for selling or managing. Even if the person wanted to sell or manage, it does not mean that he or she could.

2. Tests Have Been Eminently "Fakable"

Anyone applying for a job will attempt to give answers that he or she thinks the potential employer wants to hear. An intelligent applicant knows enough to say that he or she would "rather be a manager of people than a librarian," "rather be with people than at home reading a book," "rather lead a group discussion than be a forest ranger," or "prefer talking at a public meeting to listening to good music."

Much has been written on how to beat aptitude tests, but even without such help, a person of average intelligence can quickly see what is being sought and then provide the "correct" answers. Thus the tests simply may succeed in screening out the notably unintelligent or the conspicuously naive.

Perhaps an example of two test formats might serve to illustrate this point of "fakability." Figure 16-1 demonstrates an easily "fakable" test.

Obviously, the test taker wanting to get the job will know how to answer the questions in this test. He or she undoubtedly will answer "TRUE" for all the items.

The group below contains four statements expressing personal characteristics.

Examine each statement. If the statement accurately describes you, indicate "TRUE." If the statement does not accurately describe you, indicate "FALSE."

	TRUE	FALSE
I am a good leader.	_____	_____
I am a responsible person.	_____	_____
I get along with people.	_____	_____
I am emotionally stable.	_____	_____

Figure 16-1

The second example, shown in Figure 16-2, illustrates a more sophisticated, valid test design that is much more difficult to fake. Applicants who look at the four items shown in the figure will realize that there is simply no way to claim everything good or reject everything bad. They may try to convey a more positive image of themselves, but in the end, what they leave out can be just as important as what they select to describe themselves.

As you can start to see, an entire test filled with such questions can penetrate the facade that individuals work hard to build. Such a valid

The group below contains four statements expressing personal characteristics.

Select the one statement that is most like you and fill in the "MOST" circle on your answer sheet. From the remaining choices, select the one statement that is least like you and fill in the "LEAST" circle on your answer sheet. Be sure that for each set of four statements, you fill in only one "MOST" circle and one "LEAST" circle on your answer sheet.

	MOST	LEAST
I am a good leader.	O	O
I am a responsible person.	O	O
I get along with people.	O	O
I am emotionally stable.	O	O

Figure 16-2

test can assess the basic strengths, weaknesses, and motivations of an individual. An effective test literally can use the manner in which an individual projects himself or herself as a means of understanding who that individual really is. Such a test in the hands of business-oriented individuals capable of proper evaluation not only can help management to directly determine the potential of an individual but also can help management to determine how that individual will perform in a specific job. In this way, management can use the test to help determine whether there is a job match. The test results can help to determine whether the central qualities and motivations of an individual match the functional requirements of the job while also helping to determine whether the individual has any qualities that might preclude him or her from succeeding in that job. If used properly, the same test results can help to guide management toward the best ways to manage and motivate promising applicants to maximize their productivity, should they be hired.

3. Tests Have Favored Group Conformity, Not Individual Creativity

Recent critics of psychological testing have decried tests that seek conformist and standardized approaches to judging salespeople, managers, and other applicants. This criticism is all too valid. The creative thinker, the impulsive free spirit, the original, imaginative, hard-driving individual is often screened out by tests that demand rigid adherence to convention—an adherence, in fact, that borders on passive acceptance of authority and a fear of anything that might upset the bureaucratic apple cart.

Paradoxically, while this fearful, cautious, authoritarian conformist might make a good civil servant, a reasonably effective controller, or a rule book executive, he or she would never be a successful salesperson, a dynamic sales manager, or an assertive administrator.

Many of these tests not only fail to select good salespeople or managers but possibly screen out top producers because of their creativity, impulsiveness, or originality—characteristics that most tests downgrade as evidence of weakness or even instability.

4. Tests Have Tried to Isolate Fractional Traits Rather than Reveal the Whole Dynamics of the Person

Most personality and aptitude tests, in their construction and approach, see personality as a series or bundle of piecemeal traits. Thus someone might be high in sociability while being low in self-sufficiency and dominance. Someone else might be high in personal relations but low in cooperativeness. Somehow, the whole (or the *gestalt*) gets lost. The dynamic interaction that is personality, as viewed by most modern-day psychologists, is buried in a series of fractionalized, separable traits.

It is said that the salesperson, like the Boy Scout, should be very sociable, dominant, friendly, responsible, honest, and loyal. But these qualities don't really convey anything meaningful—without being woven together in a meaningful way to provide insights into an individual. The totality—the dynamics within the person that will permit him or her to sell successfully—is lost sight of through such tests. Clearly, someone might be sociable, responsible, and so on but still be a poor salesperson or manager.

5. Tests Have Depended Heavily on Past Experience as a Prime Qualification

We have emphasized that most of the people currently earning their living in sales should not be—or, at least, certainly should not be in their specific sales job. Given this fact, any test that favors persons already holding sales jobs can only serve to perpetuate inappropriate typecasting.

Some sales aptitude tests use vocabulary and/or the understanding of sales or management situations to measure an applicant's potential sales or management ability. These techniques seek to ascertain experience rather than real ability. Anyone who has ever sold or who has been exposed to selling, even academically, may do well on such tests, whether or not he or she has any inherent sales ability. Terms such as *close*, *cold calling*, and *prospecting* will be familiar. The test taker will be able to rattle off appropriate responses, even if this person's dynamics guarantee him or her far better prospects as an engineer or manager than as a salesperson. On the other hand, the inexperienced but potentially strong salesperson is not likely to know these terms. If judged by experience-oriented techniques, his or her appraisal will be unfavorable. By the same token, an individual who has served as a manager for a number of years would be extremely familiar with such terms as *line versus staff*, *management by objectives*, and *goal setting* and, as a result, would have an unfair advantage over an inexperienced person applying for a managerial position.

6. Many Tests Are Used for Purposes for Which They Were Not Originally Designed

A very well-known test that dates back to the late 1930s in its original form was designed to study the psychotic behavior of patients at mental hospitals. The test was developed using the patients of hospitals as the study group and people visiting them as the control group against which the study group could be compared, item by item. This test, like a number of others in this category, has value in clinical use but goes completely astray when it is inappropriately used for personnel evaluation and selection.

We like to cite the example of an individual applying for a large life insurance policy. Can one imagine the applicant, while being examined by the life insurance company's physician, pointing to a place on her chest and saying, "Doc, can you tell me if this lump might be a problem?" Or can one imagine a 50-year-old man saying to the insurance physician, "I have these pains in my chest. Do you think they are a problem?" Obviously, the applicant will not do anything of the sort but rather will hope that the insurance physician discovers nothing and clears him or her for the policy. Perhaps the very next day those individuals might go to their own physician and point out the lump or talk about the chest pain. The difference here is exactly what the difference is when a test designed for purely clinical purposes is used for sales or management selection. When people are in psychological pain or looking for vocational guidance, they will answer a test truthfully or reveal themselves as fully as they can within their own personal limitations in an interview in order to get the help they seek. On the other hand, when those same people are applying for a job, looking for a promotion, or in any way taking a test for their company, they are going to cover up their weaknesses and work to sell their strengths just as surely as the two-pack-a-day smoker will present himself to the life insurance company as a nonsmoker or the woman with a pain will reveal nothing of the sort to the company's physician.

Thus a test may be perfectly useful when a fundamental assumption can be made that people will, at least as far as they can, attempt to tell the truth and yet be totally invalid as an instrument designed to really uncover an individual's sales potential. However, since many of these tests have famous names, have been around for a long time, and were studied by psychologists in school, they continue to be used as part of a company's selection procedures, with the doubtful results.

7. Many Tests Produce General Results without Relating to the Specific Job Match

Some tests may, with some validity, describe the personality of an individual. These are among the relatively few tests that have avoided all the pitfalls we have just discussed. Yet even some of these fail to provide management with the in-depth information it needs to make a correct hiring decisions. The key to this problem is the job match. Even if a test accurately describes the level of assertiveness, dominance, or sociability possessed by an individual, the question still remains as to how those levels relate to the specific requirements of the job in question. It is certainly easy to say that management wants the most assertive person possible, or the most social, but as we have seen, there definitely can be too much of a quality—even ego-drive—for a specific job, and balances of many qualities are required for other jobs. These tests, which are often spit out by computers, with the results presented in a neat graph, fail in any sense to relate their results to the functional requirements of the specific company's job. It is really left to the manager to decide whether the particular applicant is assertive enough, energetic enough, or driven enough to do the job, and although these tests can be useful, they often fall short in providing the precise information the manager really needs to make the best hiring decision.

If tests in this category are indeed accurate in their description of an individual's traits, this provides an important plus in that it offers management input that it can get in no other way. However, the potential misuse, misunderstanding, and failure to job-match the data can lead to incorrect and costly hiring decisions.

CHOOSING THE RIGHT TESTS

Still, it is clear that valid, job-related psychological testing can provide an objective method of penetrating the superficial facade that applicants present in their résumés, in the interview, and even through their references. An effective test, in the hands of business-oriented consultants capable of proper evaluation, can help management to directly determine the strengths, limitations, motivations, and potential of an individual applicant. In addition, the test can help to determine whether the central qualities and motivations of the individual match the functional requirements of the job while also helping to determine whether the individual presents any concerns that might preclude him or her from doing the job. If used properly, the same test results can help to guide management about the best ways to manage and motivate promising applicants to maximize their productivity should they be hired.

But how can management select a valid test?

Literally thousands of tests are on the market, ranging from score-it-yourself versions for a few dollars to batteries of tests in assessment centers costing thousands of dollars. As we have said, a vast majority of these tests, regardless of price, are not job-related, valid predictors of success. Thus, as important as the use of a psychological test is to the selection process, it is even more important for management to be certain that the test selected is valid and effectively assesses the particular qualities needed to succeed on the job.

With thousands of tests available, many looking quite similar, how can a test be selected that is legal and will help to predict whether an applicant can really do a specific job? To help you with this decision, we've developed a series of questions that you should ask about any test before deciding to use it. If the answer provided by the test publisher to any of these questions is no or noncommittal, that test should not be used under any circumstances.

1. Is the test specifically job-related? Does it measure qualities required for your particular job?

2. Does the publisher of the test provide published proof that the test does not discriminate against individuals by sex, age, race, color, religion, or national origin?

3. Does the publisher provide published proof that the test has a high level of predictive validity across the industry and specifically in a situation at least closely related to the position for which the test is being given? Is there proof that people actually do perform as the test predicts they will?

4. Is the database from which the test is developed and on which the test's reliability and validity are measured large enough and compiled over enough years to provide dependable evidence of the test's reliability and validity? In other words, has the test publisher tested enough people and followed actual performance over enough years to prove that the test works?

5. Does the publisher provide you with a list of customers you can contact who have used the test long enough to judge the results?

6. Are the test results related specifically to a company, or are they generalized results? The key here is whether the test is evaluated against a company's particular requirements, that is, job description.

7. Are results of the test provided promptly so that management will not lose good applicants as a result of waiting?

8. Does the company provide a trained test evaluator who is a specialist in your field? Will the evaluator discuss the test

results with you and provide assistance in relating those results to the other steps of the assessment process?

9. Will the testing company provide ongoing help if problems or questions arise relating to poor initial performance, slumps, future promotions, training, and management issues?

10. Are the qualities measured by the test those which are essential to performance in the job for which the test is to be used? If, for example, the test does not measure ego-drive (persuasive motivation), it probably would not be appropriate for use in sales selection. It is important that the test clearly measures exactly the qualities that management wants to assess in its developmental, promotion, or hiring decisions.

With these concerns in mind, a valid psychological test that uncovers an individual's basic occupational motivations can go a long way toward reducing costly mistakes.

WHAT CAN A VALID TEST DO?

A valid test will be able to penetrate an individual's facade and provide management with objective insights into the applicant's basic personality and motivations. The results of such an assessment also will help, ultimately, to make a job match. By way of example, our psychological test can provide answers to such questions as

- Does the individual have persuasive motivation?

- Can he or she listen effectively?

- Can he or she take rejection?

- Does the individual have a service motivation?

- Is the individual assertive enough to ask for an order and tenacious enough to follow through?

- Is the individual a good self-starter?

- Can the individual organize his or her work and time and follow up on the work of others?

- Can he or she make decisions?

- Does the individual have the potential to grow on the job, or can he or she only be expected to perform at the entry level?

- Is he or she intensely competitive or laid back?

- Can the individual cope with detail sufficiently?

- Is the individual shrewd in judging situations as well as people?

- Is the individual an original, innovative, creative thinker, or is he or she tradition-bound?

There are, of course, many more questions. But whether we talk about our test or any other valid test that is used for the evaluation of sales and sales management personnel, these questions and many others related to the sales job should be answered reliably. The right test can provide data that in no way can be objectively provided by the earlier steps in the screening process. The information you really need can only be provided by penetrating the individual's facade and getting at the reality of who that individual is.

In addition to being a vital part of the decision-making process, the test results also can play an important role in structuring the final step of the process—the in-depth interview. By integrating the data provided by all the earlier steps into the insights provided by the test, the interviewer can structure the interview in such a way as to probe discrepancies and apparent weaknesses and to move the interview away from the superficial and toward specifics.

For example, if the test shows some concerns about the applicant's persuasive ability, this can be explored in the interview and the applicant's reaction studied carefully. Questions can be asked, such as:

Tell me about a presentation that you were particularly proud of. Why was it effective in winning others to your point of view?

Tell me about a situation when you really wanted to win in an argument or discussion but were not successful because you used the wrong approach.

Tell me about a time when being firm and forthright made the difference in closing the sale.

Describe your approach to selling your ideas.

The answers to these questions will help you consider the applicant's self-awareness and ability to connect with others – and with you.

Before closing this section, allow us to provide a cautionary note about applicants who come across as sincere, open, and outgoing. It is natural that such applicants will impress you because they are very likeable. And it is also natural to confuse your favorable impression with believing that such applicants have the potential to be a top performing farmer for your sales organization. While that individual's strength may be in developing relationships, you also need to make sure that the applicant has an inner drive to persuade. If the applicant is all about building relationships, he or she may be great at servicing an account. But if servicing is all the applicant is about, if he or she is not willing to take the relationship further, to propose new products, new ideas, and new solutions—if the individual is not about getting an order—then you can have that account handled by a customer-service representative rather than a salesperson. When hiring a salesperson who will serve as a farmer, you need to make sure that he or she has an inner need to persuade others. And, in particular, since that talent is more subtle in farmers, it can be very difficult to detect in a hiring interview alone. This is where an in-depth personality profile can delve below the surface and provide the insights you need to make the best possible hiring decision. In short, the test results, as well as all the previous information, form the basis for a more effective interview.

In addition to its use in the selection process, an in-depth psychological test can be used to develop appropriate prescriptive training programs designed to strengthen an individual in areas where he or she is weak. Rather than waste valuable training dollars, management can use the test results to pinpoint specific areas in which training is most needed and gear supervision toward providing the specific support the salesperson requires.

Similarly, a test should provide important insights into how to effectively manage each person currently on staff. It can point to who might be promotable and into what positions.

A valid test, in short, is vital as part of an effective selection process and can be equally important as a tool in upgrading the productivity of an entire organization.

How much can an in-depth personality assessment really help you to make the best possible hiring decision? Curt Nelson, president and chief executive officer of Entrepreneurial Development Center, told us, "If you really want to know how you're going to feel about somebody 12 months from now, there is only one way to do it: Have them assessed before you hire them."

17

The In-Depth Interview

Here are some of the funniest things anyone ever said during a hiring interview.

These are true stories, shared with us by some of our clients.

One applicant said: "I will definitely work harder for you than I did for my last employer." Another one said: "My résumé might make it look like I'm a job hopper. But I want you to know that I never left any of those jobs voluntarily." One of our favorites is: "I don't think I'm capable of doing this job, but I sure would like the money." And someone actually said, "What job am I applying for, anyway?"

It would be great if every applicant who wasn't right for the job automatically raised such red flags. But they don't.

This is why the thorough process we are describing is so essential to selecting candidates who have the potential to be your next top performers.

As you prepare for the in-depth interviews, using the approach we are describing, you will have done everything to eliminate all but the finalists, those who deserve your full attention. The use of a valid psychological test should give some clear indications that the remaining people have some of the important attributes for a potentially good job match. What remains now is to bring together all the information that has been gathered by all the steps in the screening process, to use the in-depth interview or interviews to integrate the information, and to use every technique available to confirm, in as absolute a way as possible, the efficacy of the hiring decision.

These final interviews should be as long as necessary to help make that all-important final hiring decision. A further purpose of these in-depth interviews is to make certain not only that management wants to hire the candidate but also that the candidate fully knows and understands the opportunities that the job offers and also is aware of all its negatives. In this way, both parties enter the relationship with all the facts in hand and any potential concerns jointly worked through together. For example, it is far better to know that the amount of travel involved would create an impossible burden on a salesperson's family life before making the hiring decision than to find this out a month or two later after time, money, and effort have been invested in the individual. It is not management's job to sell the position to the applicant. Rather, management should arrive, with the applicant, at the best joint decision—whether negative or positive. If the proper screening has been carried through, by the time you reach the stage of the final in-depth interviews, you are dealing with people who clearly possess the potential to do the job.

And now it is your and the applicant's responsibility to see if that potential can be translated into a practical on-the-job reality. This is why an oversell or a lack of honesty in presenting all aspects of the job can serve to defeat all the work that has gone before and ultimately contribute to an inappropriate decision.

As with every other stage of the selection process, the in-depth interview, while of great importance as the final step in making the hiring decision, is still flawed; its flaws must be thoroughly understood and worked through to get the most out of this step.

Just as a review of résumés leaves much to be desired, a telephone screen can easily fool the interviewer, reference checks have serious built-in problems, and even the best psychological tests are not perfect. Similarly, the in-depth interview has many built-in problems, After all, how often after hiring someone who does not work out have you thought to yourself, "But he looked so good in the interview"?

Part of the problem is the inherent limitation of the interviewing process. Very few of us can conduct an interview with the skill, depth, and finesse of a Charlie Rose. And even if we could, that would not completely solve the problem. More often than not, instead of lending insight, interviews become a form of theater in which all the actors are tripping over one another, trying to put their best foot forward. The employers are busy trying to create a favorable impression of themselves and their company, while the applicants are trying to mold themselves into whatever they perceive is desired.

Meanwhile, it must be kept in mind that any bookstore worth its salt has a shelf full of guides for playing this game to the hilt. Anyone serious about applying for a job has read at least one of these guides. Thus job interviews are replete with people trying to leave the best first impression. The result, all too often, is what we call *interview stars*, individuals whose best performance occurs during the interview. These stars are able to convey a favorable first impression, but that impression bears no relationship to their eventual performance. Even for a sales position, it must be kept in mind that although some applicants can sell themselves in an interview, it does not necessarily imply an ability to sell a product or a service.

One of our senior consultants relates an incident that illustrates this situation well.

Some time ago, our consultant relates, "I recommended that a client not hire an applicant. There was a moment of long pause, and after experiencing thousands of these situations, I was not at all surprised at what came next. The client, as I expected, said, 'But that's impossible. This person came across so strong and was such a pleasure to talk to.' I replied that I was not at all surprised by his comment because the applicant was extremely intelligent, had good empathy, and was strongly motivated to make people like him. In fact, his strongest single motivation was to be liked—to receive approval from anyone with whom he comes in contact. I added that in addition to the overall good conversation, I would guess that the applicant told the manager how impressed he was with the company, how much he would enjoy the job, and that if I did not miss my guess, the manager probably had received or would receive a letter thanking him for his courtesy and for the time he took in the interview. The manager hesitated briefly and said, 'You hit it right on the head, including the letter, which I received this morning. So what's wrong?' I explained that what was wrong was exactly what the manager liked so much in the applicant. I went on to explain that the applicant made his impression because of his intensely strong motivation to please, to be liked, but given his lack of assertiveness and lack of strong persuasive motivation, ego-drive, this desire to be liked could act as an important negative in relation to his ability to do the sales job. I explained that once the individual got past making the impression, he would find it extremely difficult to risk that impression—to risk the disapproval of the prospect—by pushing strongly for the order." Our consultant concluded his comment by telling us that he finally convinced the client by asking him if at any time the applicant really pushed him toward a decision. Yes, he thanked him for the interview; yes, he spoke interestingly; and yes, he wrote that very nice thank-you letter, but did he ask for the job? If he wasn't even going to ask for the sale at that point, how do you think he will ask for a sale day in and day out? At that point, my client understood that he was dealing with an interview star, not someone who had the potential to be a star performer.

Interview stars, it turns out, are overly concerned with making a favorable impression. It is fundamental to such an individual's sense of well-being to be liked, appreciated, and perceived in favorable terms. An individual with this motivation will work very hard to make a good impression in an interview and, with the help of a few guides, probably will succeed. Yet, while this motivation to be well liked is important for many jobs and can be helpful in many sales jobs, it will not, in and of itself, ensure success in sales. Sometimes, in fact, too much of a need to be liked can work against an individual's ability to make difficult decisions, let alone to risk rejection when the situation calls for it.

A tip-off provided by this case also can be helpful. The applicant did not try to get the employer to move a little closer toward offering him the job. One can suspect a definite lack of assertiveness and view the existence of ego-drive with suspicion if an applicant does not say something toward the end of the interview such as, "I like what I have heard. I am extremely interested in the being part of your organization. Will you give me an opportunity?" Even if these or similar words are said, by no means is this proof that the individual is really assertive and/or ego-driven, but certainly the absence of these words provides a warning sign.

Here is a good example of how test results and this kind of interview feedback can be integrated. If the test, for example, indicated borderline ego-drive and gave some cause for concern about the applicant's assertiveness, the failure to make this minimum move toward closing the sale (or getting the job) would confirm any doubts. On the other hand, given this same marginal test result, a strong push on the part of the applicant might tip the balance toward the applicant. In any event, there cannot be a simple assumption that because the right words are said in this context, the individual is going to be effective. Keep in mind that there are many instruction manuals on how to interview. You have to keep your antenna up so as not to be taken in by an interview star.

It is in the process of penetrating the facade created by the interviewee that the information produced by the psychological test is of maximum value. The information provided by the test can be used to confirm impressions, explain them, or deny them; whatever the case, the interview can be carried forward more effectively with this information.

Before turning to a few specific how-tos, it might be useful to look at how not to. The following interview is admittedly extreme. We strongly suspect that few interviewers would really conduct such a totally incorrect interview, but we equally strongly suspect that many interviewers make at least some of these mistakes. By being extreme, we are able to make a number of points that more moderate words or admonitions might not achieve as well.

THE INTERVIEW

"Good morning, Ms. Moore," you say. "It's a pleasure to meet you."

She says the pleasure is all hers and then comments on the attractive view from your window. While you settle behind your desk, the applicant sits across from you. A friendly smile offsets her intense eyes.

"First off," you say, scanning some papers on your desk, "I was very impressed with your résumé. It was clear and concise. And your background is particularly well suited to this new opening we have in our sales department. In fact, this is an exciting time to be coming on board with us because things are really booming. But more on that later." You quickly add, "I took the liberty of checking some of the references you provided me with, and they were all glowing," Actually, one reference disclosed that she left under curious circumstances, but you decide to wait until later to delve into that.

"Enough of me talking about you," you say. "Why don't you tell me about yourself? Let's see, how long ago did you start your current position?"

"The exact date is on my résumé, but it has been over two years." Ms. Moore goes on to say that she's been selling advertising space for a local newspaper, which she likes but finds limiting. Although the job has enabled her to meet various clients in numerous settings, she would like to find a job that would allow her to be on the road more, with one-on-one contact.

"I'm sorry. I didn't realize that you had somebody in your office," one of your salespeople says, sticking his head inside the door you left slightly ajar. "I'll check back later. Please excuse the interruption."

"That's all right," you say. "Now, where were we? Oh, yes. Well, I'm sure you have a lot of questions about the company and the job. Let me try to anticipate some of them for you. Since the company was founded a little over a decade ago, we've been on the right path, and that road is now smoother than ever. Of course, the owners keep their hands in things, which can get a little sticky at times. As a matter of fact—well, let me just tell you this one quick story to illustrate what I mean," you say, leaning across your desk, lowering your voice in confidence. "It happened just the other day, so it's still fresh in my mind, but it's a classic example of what I go through. I had been after the three owners to get an estimate out to a prospective client for the last two weeks. Because they must have their imprint on everything that goes out of here, the estimate was getting delayed for this reason, then for that reason. Yesterday, when I asked about it, I was told that it was being reviewed. So I had to do handsprings to get all three of the owners to drop everything else they were doing and concentrate on this proposal. Not only was it aggravating, but it cost us a bundle to get it to its destination on time. But that wouldn't be a concern of yours should you come on board," you quickly insert. "But enough of me talking; you must have some questions."

"As a matter of fact, I was wondering if you could describe this sales position to me in more detail. If I accept this position, what would I be doing on a day-to-day basis?"

Pausing, you say, "As far as your job is concerned, you'll be constantly selling. Our product is known in the marketplace and highly regarded. So you'll have a solid base upon which to approach prospects. It depends upon how adept you are at persuading. But then, I wouldn't be overly concerned about that if I were you. I've always believed that if you can sell, you can sell. Excuse me," you apologize, as the phone rings. "No. I'm in the midst of an interview now. Tell her I'll get back in touch with her as soon as I can."

You continue, "One thing I wanted to ask you about was Harlequin. I see from your résumé that you used to work there. Do you remember a guy named Johnson, Robert Johnson?"

"Yes, he used to work in accounting, I believe. I didn't get a chance to know him well," she says.

"Oh, Bob and I go way back. We graduated together from Pitt. Those were some times. The things I could tell you about him back then. He was wild on the football field and even wilder off," you say, laughing at the memory. Then, you quickly add, "One thing you'll realize if you come on board with us, Ms. Moore, and all our salespeople will confirm this, is that as far as money is concerned, the sky is the limit. Since we work on a commission basis, after your brief training period, your income is only limited by your ability."

"That was something I was meaning to ask you. Just to give me an idea of where I might stand, what is the average take-home pay for a salesperson on your force?"

"Oh, the average is nothing you should concern yourself with, Ms. Moore, because I'm sure you'll do much better than average." Smiling, you remember another question you wanted to ask. "One thing I always like to ask is what is the one thing you like least about your current job."

"That's a tough question," she says. "I mean, I don't want to incriminate myself. But let's see. I'd have to say that the job is needlessly bogged down in detail. I completely understand the importance of management knowing what is going on with each of our accounts. But there is a tendency to waste salespeople's time with paperwork that could be completed more efficiently with a more effective CRM [customer resource management] system or by someone in a clerical position."

"I'm sorry to hear you say that," you respond, "Too many salespeople think of detail as something that simply slows them down in the achievement of their goals. That impatience can be fatal when it comes to satisfying customers. That's the very attitude that can erode the success we've worked so long to build here." Leaning back in your chair, you stare at the applicant, searching for her response to one of you steadfast beliefs.

Recoiling slightly, she says, "I don't believe I have any problems handling detail. It's just that I think the operation where I'm currently working could be run more smoothly if salespeople could concentrate more on meeting clients and following up on prospects and the other more essential parts of selling."

You could pursue this train of thought, but glancing at your watch, you realize that you're already late for an important strategy session with the owners of the company. "I'm sorry. The time has just shot right by. I wish we could talk longer, but I'm already late for a meeting, and the owners probably will have my head." Rising from your seat and gathering a few papers from your desk, you add, "Listen, it was really a pleasure. I'm not sure how long it will take us to come to a final decision on this hire, but it shouldn't be more than a few weeks or so. If you have any questions concerning anything we didn't cover, please don't hesitate to call." Opening the door to your office, you add, "My secretary will be glad to direct you to the parking lot. Thanks again."

THE 10 ERRORS

The 10 basic interviewing errors are as follows:

1. *Don't be afraid to ask tough questions.* The first mistake occurs almost immediately, when the interviewer does not pursue why the applicant was dismissed from a previous job. If you uncover anything during the reference check or employment history review process that warrants tough questioning, do not be afraid to ask about it during the interview. It is important that you begin your relationship with a new hire on a frank basis.

2. *Don't oversell your company.* The interviewer makes his second mistake by bragging about how things are booming while not giving specifics to back up the claim. He follows this up with pat statements such as, "Since the company was founded a

little over a decade ago, we've been on the right path, and that road is now smoother than ever." An adept interviewer will lay out the strengths and weaknesses of the firm, putting them in perspective. Do not paint an unrealistic picture of your company in order to lure an applicant on board.

3. *Don't ask for information you already have.* The interviewer asks, "Why don't you tell me about yourself? Let's see, how long ago did you start your current position?" This shows a lack of interest in the candidate because this information was obtained earlier. The interview should be used to obtain new information or to confirm or reject tentative information already acquired.

4. *Don't allow yourself to be interrupted unless there is an emergency.* The interview is interrupted twice, first by a salesperson sticking his head in the door and then by a telephone call. Too many interviewers allow the interview to become disjointed by not taking steps to prevent interruptions. Your office door should be closed. Put calls and messages on hold.

5. *Don't talk too much.* The interviewer tells the applicant, "Well, I'm sure you have a lot of questions about the company and the job. Let me try to anticipate some of them for you." This is a classic case of an interviewer who loves to hear his own voice. At the most, an interviewer should say one word for every ten spoken by the person being interviewed.

6. *Don't use the interview as your therapy.* As part of his need to hear himself talk, the interviewer told a confidential story about some of the problems he encounters in his position. Too many interviewers use their sessions to spout out their concerns about the company. When an interviewer vents emotions in an interview, he or she may feel better but may lose a prospective employee in the bargain.

7. *Don't be afraid to spell out in detail the requirements of the position.* When the applicant got a word in edgewise and asked about the specific requirements of the job, she was brushed

off with the pat answer, "But then, I wouldn't be concerned about that if I were you. I've always believed that if you can sell, you can sell." It is imperative that people know what is required of them before beginning a job. The interview is the time to outline the job's requirements, as well as your criteria for evaluating success in the role.

8. *Don't gossip or swap war stories.* Many interviewers try to find familiar ground they can tread over with the applicant. Although this might seem like a comfortable way to get an interview under way, inquiring about friends and relatives can get things sidetracked, wasting a huge amount of time. The interview should be devoted to obtaining as much information as possible in order to make a sound hiring decision.

9. *Don't put the applicant on the defensive.* There is no point in creating unnecessary tension during the interview. Knowing an applicant's personality strengths and weaknesses is vital to making the best hiring decision. Openly discussing Ms. Moore's statement about detail on her former job might provide valuable insight, particularly if the test results provided evidence that there was indeed a sufficiently strong dislike of detail to create concern. A speech embodying a long-held philosophy is inappropriate, but a frank discussion of the importance of detail in the job and how Ms. Moore might deal with the detail aspect of the job would be constructive and would allow both people to make a more reasoned decision.

10. *Don't be afraid to make the interview as long or as short as you deem necessary.* The final mistake was that the interview was concluded in an unnecessary rush. As the interviewer noticed the time, he realized that he was late for another appointment and excused himself hurriedly. To be effective, the interview should make the fullest use of everyone's valuable time. There are no set guidelines on length as long as you clearly spell out the anticipated length of the interview and as long as the time is spent wisely.

ADDITIONAL MISTAKES TO AVOID

It may be difficult after reviewing this dreadful interview to imagine that there are even more common mistakes that somehow were not included in this example—but there are. They include the following:

- *Don't ask questions that can only be answered by a simple yes or no.* Instead, try to ask questions that must be answered at some length and with some explanation. The key to a good question is not only to get a specific answer but to get that answer by listening to the interviewee's response.

- *Don't simply indulge in generalized conversation as though nothing had occurred prior to the interview.* Although this was done to some degree in the interview of Ms. Moore, the point should be further elaborated here. The interviewer should have a great deal of information in hand relating to the applicant's past experience, feedback from references, early impressions from the telephone interview, and of course, the data provided by the psychological test. All these impressions should be checked throughout the interview, and conflicts should be resolved. If, for example, the résumé speaks about a previous position as a "division manager" and the reference check reveals that the applicant managed no one and the title was simply another name for a salesperson with a territory, that apparent discrepancy should be discussed: "Tell me specifically what you did on the job. Do the best you can to tell me how you functioned on a day-by-day basis." If after this explanation the discrepancy is still not resolved, the interviewer should not hesitate to confront the applicant with the evident discrepancy and ask the applicant to discuss it. Obviously, this discrepancy might be more or less important depending on the nature of the job for which the applicant is being considered.

  Similarly, if the applicant described his or her previous job as involving hard, frequent closes, and the test indicates some doubt about the applicant's level of ego-drive, questions could be raised about the discrepancy, giving the applicant plenty of opportunity to sell the interviewer on the fact that he or she was able to close despite what the test says—and getting the applicant to explain precisely how he or she accomplished this. What we are saying here simply is to try to avoid general conversations and home in as precisely as possible on specifics.

- *Don't ramble.* Although there is no precise ideal length of an interview, it is important to show the interviewee that there is a respect for time, not only the time of the manager but also the time of the interviewee. While being friendly, stay on course, and keep the interview moving in a clearly defined direction. Finally, unless by the end of the interview you have ruled out the individual, don't leave him or her with a generalized, "We will be in touch." Rather, spell out what the next steps will be, even if those steps simply involve a management decision and notification to the applicant. If future interviews are going to be requested, say so, and if group interviews, spouse interviews, and the like are to be part of the process, spell out these as well. In other words, the applicant should leave the interview knowing, with relative precision, when a decision is going to be made, on what basis it might be made, and what other steps, if any, may be required in the decision-making process.

AVOID HIRING IN YOUR OWN IMAGE

There is just one more common error that many managers are prone to during the interviewing process. They understand completely that they are trying to delve below the surface. But where do they start? One of the most natural places for many managers to start is with themselves. It seems obvious. After all, they're driven to succeed. So all they need to do is hire someone who has their same drive. Right?

The truth is that nothing could be more wrong.

What we all need to keep in mind is that it is only natural for us to want to work with people who we like. And we all tend to like people who are most like ourselves. It's just human nature. Therefore, without being conscious of it, we often end up hiring people who remind us of ourselves or, at least, with whom we have much in common.

Then we end us saying something such as, "There's something about that person I really like. I'm not quite sure exactly what it is. But she reminds me of somebody I'm very fond of. Hmmmmm. Oh, yeah, it's me."

Of course, we don't want to surround ourselves with people who get on our nerves. However, if we hire an entire staff of people just like ourselves, we will inevitably create an unbalanced organization. We have to remember that a staff with all of our strengths and virtues also will share our faults and shortcomings. So they will help us to stay right where we are—not help us grow where we need to be.

This is a tough mistake to avoid because it is often unconscious.

Instead, we want to underscore the importance of focusing on the competencies and personality qualities that distinguish our top performers. This will become your ideal profile—and you can use it to measure your most promising candidates to see if they have what it takes to be your next top performers.

STRUCTURING THE INTERVIEW: INTERVIEW STRATEGY

So now let's focus on the interview strategy. As we said earlier, all too often the interview is, by its very nature, a form of theater, with the participants performing an adversarial dance. The applicant is trying to make the best impression and in that effort is working to psyche out the interviewer, looking to say precisely what the interviewer wants to hear. Similarly, the interviewer is trying to penetrate the facade of the applicant to ascertain what is really there, what his or her real motives and the like are.

In this ritual, the interviewer does begin with some important advantages, which all too often are not used. First, and of most importance, the interviewer enters the situation armed with a good deal of knowledge about the applicant. As subjective as some of this knowledge is, it still provides a body of data on which a strategy for the interview can be laid out. Add to this the more objective input of the test and potential discrepancies between various elements of information produced prior to the interview, and the interviewer really has tools with which to probe the facade with good effectiveness.

Using these tools, however, does require planning. Before the interview begins, the interviewer should have firmly in mind, or even in writing, a series of questions to ask—and the answers that are being sought. The final interview should not simply be another place in which to gain an impression but should be the mechanism by which everything else in the process is confirmed, denied, or left ambiguous. Thus any discrepancies, problems, and/or doubts created in prior parts of the process must be probed in the interview, along the lines we discussed. Such probing must be well planned, and the strategy for such probing must be developed. If the applicant has survived all the steps in the screening process, the odds are that there are not too many weaknesses or discrepancies, but the ones that exist must be dealt with if the proper decision is to be made.

Apropos of this point, and also to be fair to both the applicant and the company, it is important in this interview to fully describe the job in terms of its functional requirements, performance expectations, and potential upward mobility. If elements of job expectations happen to fly in the face of certain motivations or weaknesses of the applicant, being aware of them could lead the applicant toward making a negative decision, which, in the long run, would be positive for the company. It is better for everyone concerned that the job be presented honestly, with its opportunities and problems, so that the interviewer and the applicant can face the issues, discuss the problems, and arrive together at the most informed and mutually beneficial employment decision.

In short, if most of the pitfalls we have outlined can be avoided, and if you are certain and clear about the information you want to obtain, the interview can be extremely important in the final hiring decision.

Before concluding this section, allow us to share with you some insights from a few of our clients that might help you to become an even more effective interviewer.

Curt Nelson, president and CEO of Entrepreneurial Development Center, told us, "I ask every candidate exactly the same questions, and I score every question based on their answers. For salespeople, I might ask them to sell me a pencil. What are the first three questions they would ask me? I also might ask them to describe the most important part of the selling process. (Invariably, they will all say, 'the relationship.' But they better also say, 'understanding the customer's needs.') I get very particular about what I really want to know. And I build interview score sheets for each individual so that I can compare them fairly afterward."

Chris DesRoches, vice president of customer service at Casella Waste Systems, started out as vice president of sales at Casella in 1996. After nine years in that role, he became vice president of selection and training, helping people to raise their game in selection and also coordinating leadership and sales training. Then he was asked to head up customer service for the company.

In essence, he was spending so much time helping people in the organization bring on the right people in all kinds of different roles that his boss came to him one day and said, "Look, Chris, you can't keep going in two directions. I'm perfectly happy with you going in either direction. But we're going to bring somebody into the company to spearhead selection. So I need you to know that, but you've got to pick a path because you can't walk both of them." And it took Chris a fraction of a second to go the selection route because, as he said, "It was like my dream job."

What is one of his favorite questions to ask in a hiring interview?

"I like to ask, 'If you could write the script, and it was totally up to you, what would be the perfect job for you?' It's just an innocuous question. But it always tells you something. And then we go onto the best job you ever had and why. And then the worst. And that tells you a lot about the applicant."

It's all about getting at their strengths, their limitations, their potential, and how much they really know themselves.

"The real question is, how well do you know yourself? And the answer to these questions, along with the in-depth personality profile analysis, will tell you how self-aware someone really is. I would say about 30 to 40 percent of the applicants know themselves well. But the rest of them really struggle with it. Either they haven't stopped to think about themselves in a reflective way before, or they are concerned that they may reveal something about themselves that they don't want you to know. Either way, your antennae go up. Listen. Because you're probably picking up on something that could be a real concern later."

Those questions, at the end of a thorough and rigorous selection process, can tell you an enormous amount, if you are listening well.

"There's one more I like. I also ask them to share with me one story, a real situation they've been in that they believe they handled particularly well. Their answer will provide me with a lot of insight into how they think about themselves and others."

Those are great questions.

"They are. But what is revealed is all in the answers. You have to listen. I tell everyone, 'If you catch yourself doing any more than 15 percent of the talking in an interview, please go find anything else to do, but don't interview people for hiring situations because you're going to be terrible at it.'"

Greg Mayer, chief people officer at Snagajob.com, has introduced his organization to a very thorough and comprehensive methodology for interviewing. After narrowing down the top choices through the approach we've described here, he has developed an interview guide for every position. He told us, "We have developed behavioral questions, organized in three categories. We're looking for what applicants can do, what they will do, and will they fit."

Can do, will do, and will fit?

"Exactly. In the 'can do,' we're looking for, Do they have the knowledge, do they have the skills, do they have the qualities, do they have the competencies, and do they have the experience that would say that they should be able to do this job? In the 'will do,' we're looking for, Do they have the drive and motivation to do the job? And in the 'will fit,' we're looking for, Will they fit our culture at SnagAJob? We have a very defined culture here, with three core values: We're collaborative, accountable, and passionate. So the questions we ask in the 'will fit' category are around these three core values. We are looking to hire people who have natural tendencies in each of these three areas. Collaboration, in particular, becomes important for salespeople because it isn't a word that traditionally is associated with sales. For us, though, it is really important. We are a very collaborative organization, working together as a team, supporting each other, and being built that way is extremely important to us—for every position here."

Who decides on the best candidates, the human resources manager or the hiring manager?

"After the in-depth personality profile is evaluated and the results considered, the finalists go on to a panel. We have a very thorough process. So our recruiter will conduct the initial screen and determine the slate of candidates that the hiring manager will want to consider. Then, in addition to the hiring manager, we will have peer salespeople also interview the candidates. So we have five or six people interview a promising candidate. And it becomes a collective judgment on the part of the people who conducted the interviews as to how well they believe the applicant measured up."

With such a thorough process, and with everybody weighing in, and everyone's vote counting, can you think of a situation where everybody was in favor of an individual, and then one person saw something different that everybody else was not getting?

"Absolutely. And that is the beauty of our approach. It is extremely collaborative. And everyone involved weighs in, and their voice counts."

Can you give us some examples of the behavioral interview questions you like to ask?

"For the 'can do' part, we'll ask questions like: 'Tell me about the toughest objections you have had to address' or 'What would you say if a customer told you, *it's too expensive?* For the 'will do' part, we'll ask questions like: 'What are some of the things you find difficult to do?' or 'How do you plan your day? Describe your typical day to me.' And for the 'will fit' part, we'll ask, 'What do you think of your current boss?' or 'What three character traits most define you?'"

Those are great questions—because the answers will tell you an enormous amount about the candidate. How open is the candidate? How self-reflective? And none of it has to do with the candidate pretending to have the right answers to your questions. You are simply looking for honest, open responses and then seeing if they match your expectations for the position and the culture.

We leave you with a few of our favorite interview questions. As Peter Drucker says, "The best leaders ask the best questions." And they know what to listen for. What you want to get at is: Does the applicant have a moonshot? A purpose? A driving ambition to achieve something meaningful? Listen for how clearly the applicant expresses what he or she really wants to do—their dreams, what he or she wants to accomplish.

Certainly you want to know why the applicant is interested in leaving his or her current job. But what you're really listening for is the applicant's tone and his or her take on reality. Do they blame things on others? Have they realized something about themselves? Or are they just looking for another opportunity to make the same mistakes?

"Tell me about a time when you failed or were rejected. How did you deal with it? The answer will provide you with insights into how well the applicant knows himself or herself and whether he or she takes rejection a bit too personally—or can bounce back with an "I'll show you attitude."

"What is the most significant achievement you've accomplished in your present job?" If the applicant can't come up with anything, that will tell you a lot. When the applicant has to select one thing, it can be very revealing about what he or she thinks is important. Then you can decide whether it is also important to you.

"What is your favorite part of your current job?" Then ask, "What is your least favorite part of your current job?" Each of these answers will tell you how well the applicant knows himself or herself. And if in the telling the applicant shares with you that he particularly dislikes one of the most important parts of the job for which he is applying— that will tell you everything you need to know.

The answers to these questions won't definitively tell you who you should hire, but they can absolutely tell you who you should avoid.

18

The Final Decision

We have been focusing on how a company should best go about building a winning sales team. It is our purpose in this chapter to wrap up and summarize our suggested pyramid process of recruiting, screening, and selecting productive salespeople. We will also deal, to some degree, with the other side of the decision-making process—the applicant, who has to make his or her decision as well

As we look at the final decision and attempt to summarize how it is made, let us emphasize that the right decision must be a joint decision by the company and the applicant. There cannot be a winner and a loser in the hiring decision. If the hiring decision is a correct one, it must be a positive one for both the applicant and the employer.

THE COMPANY'S DECISION

Let us bring together all the various facets of the hiring process. To quickly review, the recruiting and screening processes have now been completed. The company has conducted an effective search among its existing employees to determine whether some of its salespeople could be made more productive and to see whether there may be hidden sales talent among individuals doing other, nonsales jobs for the company. After completing this at-home talent search, the company has put out the broadest possible net, attracting every potential available source of talent. It has screened out people who clearly lack educational or background factors that are absolutely essential to selling the company's product or service. A brief personality profile at this point can screen out individuals who absolutely do not possess the essential personality qualities needed to succeed in sales. This base is then further narrowed by means of a brief telephone interview. Those who go onto the next stage are scheduled for a brief in-person interview. Then reference checks will complete the screening-out process.

It is at this point that the remaining candidates should be few enough in number to permit the company to focus a great deal of attention on them in order to make that final, all-important hiring decision. The first step in the screening-in process is the use of an in-depth psychological test to uncover an individual's real potential—his or her strengths, limitations, motivations, and potential—and to provide further insights into the final job match. In all probability, some additional individuals will be screened out after the test results are reviewed. The consultants interpreting the assessment will be able to provide insights into how each applicant could do the job, as well as questions to pursue during the final interview, tips for how the manager could work most effectively with each individual, and how he or she will fit in with the rest of the team.

With all the weaknesses of the interview process, the final interview is still the step that integrates all the other steps, paving the way for the most effective final decision. It is during the final interview that discrepancies in information gathered by all the other steps can be reconciled, final impressions confirmed, and doubts alleviated. It is here that no effort is too great, no interview is too long, and no further checks are too detailed, given the importance of the final hiring decision.

We are certainly not saying that even with all these admonitions and even with this pyramid approach to narrowing your search there will not be hiring mistakes. The process of recruitment and selection still remains as much an art as a science; and when it comes down to it, it still depends a good deal on the skill of the individual doing the recruitment and selection. However, even the most skilled interviewer, using the finest, most valid, most reliable, most job-related psychological test and checking references in the most meticulous way, still will make hiring mistakes. This being said, it should be emphasized that by making hiring decisions in the way described in this book, your batting average will improve significantly.

THE CANDIDATE'S DECISION

One thing to keep in mind, however, is that most managers tend to forget that the candidate is involved in an equally difficult decision-making process. It is as critical for the applicant as it is for the company to make the right decision.

Each step, then, in the pyramid process can be thought of by the candidate as part of his or her own information-gathering process. The decision is a two-way street. The hiring process should be viewed not just as the company's opportunity to ask questions and draw out information from the applicant but also as the applicant's opportunity to find out more about the company. A few probing questions can help the individual to determine whether he or she would want to sell the product or service the company offers, work for the manager involved, and fit into the organization's culture.

For the applicant, this should not be viewed as an opportunity to be accepted or to win a contest. It is a vitally important decision about how he or she is going to pursue his or her professional life. And it also will affect the applicant's personal life as well, enormously.

THE CRITICAL DECISION

What we are saying, in short, is that the hiring decision is an extremely critical one—for both the individual and the organization. Suffice it say that the costs are far too high for everyone involved to make mistakes.

Allow us to share a final bit of advice from Alisa Barry, chef and creator of Bella Cucina Artful Food. As you consider making the final offer, review the list of qualifiers or qualities that you determined essential for an individual to possess. "If your applicant only has three of the five qualifiers, keep looking," she advises. "Because, unless they meet and have all the qualities you know are necessary, that individual is never going to operate at the stellar level that you want them to. And, particularly if you only have a few people on your team, you want them all to be stellar."

We are convinced, and we have seen in our work with thousands of clients, that when a company and an individual together make an effort to determine whether a match exists between the individual and the job, both profit enormously. Sometimes the best thing that can happen to an individual is to be turned down for a sales job for which he or she is not appropriate. Conversely, some of the greatest sales success stories we have come across are people who never dreamed of sales but who are now numbered among the top performers. The opportunities are exciting, and the final decision is critical. If done systematically, the final decision can be ideal—for the company and for the individual.

PART 5

BUILDING
A WINNING
SALES TEAM

Up to this point we have been focusing on the psychology of a successful salesperson. We discussed sales as a profession, dealt with some of the reasons most salespeople don't achieve their full potential, and explored the central dynamics needed by an individual to succeed in sales. We then concentrated on the job-matching process, highlighting a clear-cut, step-by-step approach to hiring top performers.

In this part we will explore how an effective sales team starts with the manager, how to get new employees up to speed faster, how to coach more effectively, how to improve the productivity of marginal performers, and the connection between sales and sports.

Our focus will be on how to tap into the potential of the individual you've just hired and blend his or her talents into your top-performing team.

A Winning Team Starts with the Manager

How many coaches, general managers, or owners of professional sports teams spend time fantasizing about how wonderful it would be if they could replace their entire team with one of the greatest teams in the league? What a wonderful fantasy to suddenly have your basketball team, which has not made the playoffs in years, replaced person by person by the roster of the playoff finalists. A wonderful fantasy though this may be, such dreams really do not come true. What is true is that the only way a cellar dweller, a team perpetually at the bottom of the league, can be turned into a championship team is through painstakingly building the team into a winner. Since you cannot suddenly replace 12 basketball players, 25 baseball players, or 49 football players with an equal number of better players, the first key step is to make the best use of the talent you have on hand.

There are, in fact, as all sports fans well know, many teams that perform far beyond what their individual talent level would indicate because they are able to totally maximize the talent that exists as a team. On the other side, many talented teams fall short throughout the years because they are not able to maximize their existing talent.

So the first step in building a winning team, whether in sports or in business, is to get the most out of what you have and then add to or start to change the roster. In sports, this is done through trading and the draft; in business, it is done through recruiting and selecting productive people.

To build a great sales team, we suggest starting with the manager.

THE MANAGER

For the purpose of this discussion, let us look at the sales team as one unit, led by a sales manager. In a large organization, there may be many of these teams divided into districts and regions, but each of these teams really must be viewed and worked with separately if real progress is to be made.

A team must be viewed as a totality and not simply as individual elements. Every team has particular strengths and weaknesses. We should start, however, with the team leader—the sales manager.

The sales manager's primary responsibilities are to motivate and supervise his or her sales team. Sales managers assign territories to salespeople, set targets, and connect with other managers in such departments as marketing, production, and customer service.

The best sales managers, we have found, are bright, creative, accommodating, assertive, driven to persuade, view setbacks as learning experiences, are adept at structuring their own and others' activities, and have a strong sense of urgency. They are able to recognize problems, issues, and opportunities; establish goals, objectives, and priorities for their team; persevere to overcome obstacles; and work directly with their salespeople to monitor performance and provide appropriate coaching. Mike Ferguson, CEO at VXI Corporation, told us, "I've always thought of sales management as, in part, a teaching position. The fun part about sales management is connecting with people who are motivated to succeed, realizing that everybody approaches sales from their own perspective, and helping them to realize their potential—a potential they might not have even known they had."

That's the fun part.

"The tough part is when someone is not making the grade, when they're not working hard, not giving it their all. And as I moved up the management ladder, I didn't have mentors who helped me with that part. So a lot of my lessons were self-taught. And it meant a lot of sleepless nights. I had to realize that I had to reach people where they were. Not everyone was going to do it my way. Finally, I realized that if they had the potential and would give it their all, most of the time we could find a way to succeed. But if they weren't going to give it their all, then I had to let them go."

The fun part and the tough part of sales management exist side by side, constantly. There are the huge successes—and the enormous disappointments. Sometimes in the same day.

"Salespeople become successful more rapidly. And they can fail more rapidly. Then, as a sales manager, you also can be confounded by people who you just can't figure out because they succeed one month, then the next they're down. Why is he or she inconsistent?"

Those are the banes of a sales manager. And it is knowing that every personnel decision is visible, high-profile, and affects the entire company.

"Regardless of whether there are 5 salespeople in a company, 50, or 500, there are basically 10 people per sales rep in that company, whose continuing employment rests on the shoulders of the sales team, saying, 'If this salesperson doesn't do his or her job, I could lose my job.' So in sales it is knowing that your success means that other people keep their job. There is the constant pressure. This, I believe, is part of why salespeople fail faster or succeed faster. Everything is under a microscope, with a greater sense of urgency."

Ultimately, Mike reminds us, "The real world can get in the way of your expectations, understanding, and belief in people. The biggest concern a sales manager has is, 'Did I hire the right person? Do they have the skill sets? Have I provided the best training and coaching? Have I put them in a place where they can win?' If the sales manager has done all that, then he or she has done all he or she can do. The rest has to do with the salesperson working hard enough, seeing enough customers, opening up opportunities, and making things happen."

TWO TYPES OF SALES MANAGERS

For a sales team to be successful, the first thing that needs to be done is to really understand the strengths and limitations of the individual leading the team. Most managers fall into one of two broad categories. The first category is typified by an outstanding salesperson who was promoted to the position of sales manager. He or she is replete with empathy, ego-drive, and ego-strength but often lacks some key management attributes. Sales managers in this category need a group of self-reliant, well-disciplined, self-starting salespeople reporting to them. In all likelihood, such sales managers cannot be counted on to be highly effective at delegation or follow-up. They are, most likely, not very strong in structuring the work and time of subordinates.

On the other hand, such sales managers are likely to be extremely effective at going into the field with a salesperson and helping to close tough deals. Of course, one of the things that these highly driven sales managers might have to work on is the tendency to want to do too much themselves. Typically, they have difficulty delegating. Their motivation is often to show salespeople how to sell by outselling every one of them. In our work with such sales managers, we have to get them to literally sit on their drive if they are to be successful in developing the potential of their sales force.

The second category of sales manager is exemplified by those who possess strong administrative skills. Managers in this category help to plan and structure the work of a sales force, follow up effectively on the work of others, and are adept at analyzing data. They set goals and objectively evaluate performance; they certainly possess sales instincts, but they do not intensely need the close. Therefore, they can be effective delegators. Lacking a strong sales drive, they might not be helpful in closing deals and, in some cases, might even have some problems relating to the highly driven salespeople reporting to them.

By presenting these two broad categories of sales managers, we are trying to highlight the fact that in order to understand the dynamics of a team, it is essential to start out by understanding the strengths, weaknesses, and motivations of the sales manager. A team's productivity obviously is greatly affected from the top down.

One brief case history of the sales management relationship may illustrate this point. We were asked by the vice president of sales for an international computer firm to conduct a team analysis of one of the firm's regional offices in a major city. The primary purpose of the study was to explore the region's strengths and weaknesses and to make suggestions for improving sales productivity. The executive also wanted us to help increase morale and enthusiasm among managers and other sales personnel.

The region had recently experienced a change in top management. The previous regional manager was held in high regard by the branch managers and sales personnel. After a year under a new manager, the organization continued to grow, but not nearly at a level consistent with its previous record. We conducted interviews with the regional management staff and salespeople. During these sessions, our findings for each manager and his or her sales staff were reviewed. Suggestions were provided to the managers regarding methods of supervising the people who reported to them.

On the whole, there appeared to be a strong negative mind-set on the part of the region's management team. Part of the problem was identified by comparing the personality of the old manager with that of his replacement. The original manager was a strongly driven, dynamic individual who was a classic example of the so-called charismatic leader. On the other hand, his replacement was an individual who was superbly trained in the technical end of the business and possessed the personality dynamics of a process-oriented, highly capable manager.

Even a year later, it was not uncommon for members of the sales team to speak fondly of their previous charismatic leader. More important, however, was the fact that when the old leader would set goals or demand effort, the tendency of the team was to respond positively. On the other hand, the very same demands or goals put forward by the new manager were viewed as unrealistic and were resisted. A negative mind-set was established that served to erode confidence in management. If people feel that goals cannot be met, they will not, when push comes to shove, be met. Motivation in this case was a top-down activity. In other words, the new regional manager would have to embrace his goal with enthusiasm and project his optimism toward his staff, which, given his personality, was not natural for him to do.

What the original manager was able to accomplish through sheer leadership dynamics was to drive the team toward meeting tough quotas tied to compensation. He was also able to cover up, through sheer activity, two fundamental problems that became apparent when the new manager took over. There was limited formal sales training for the branch managers and an inefficient development program for the unit sales force.

One of our first suggestions was that the new manager reestablish more realistic sales quotas that could be attained. The fact that the old manager could, at least for a short term, drive the team toward the higher goals did not mean that over the long haul the team, led by the new manager, could hope to attain that consistent level of productivity. In interviews, even the strongest supporters of the old manager admitted that some of his projections were overly optimistic and contained certain inaccurate assumptions that, in the long run, could prevent the goals from being attained.

Establishing sales quotas that are realistic, achievable, and challenging at the same time is essential to creating a positive, high-energy environment. We strongly recommend that quota-setting activities be carefully reviewed and given sufficient attention that the goals were challenging rather than defeating. In addition, we felt that it was important for the new manager to recognize his role in creating an environment that was energizing, optimistic, and results-oriented. Moreover, he must convey these values to his organization with great concern for the welfare and success of the sales staff, his branch managers, and his own personal gain. Further, as mentioned, by and large we found that the branch managers were poorly prepared for their role as sales managers. None had direct selling experience, and formal sales management training had not been provided. It was strongly recommended that all these managers participate in a formal sales management training program. By sharing the experience together and acquiring a common language, the branch managers would gain a great team orientation.

The existing sales force was next broken down into three groups, organized around individual specific areas in need of improvement. Once these targeted needs were established, trainers were brought in from corporate headquarters to design and implement programs geared to the specific needs of each group.

In addition, we developed composite profiles of the most successful sales representatives, which then were used to assist managers in evaluating new applicants. These profiles helped managers to identify strengths and weaknesses in relation to successful employees and improved management's ability to identify applicants with the greatest chance of success.

As can be easily seen from the foregoing, this sales team needed assistance on every level, from the regional manager who needed specialized assistance in setting realistic goals and motivating his subordinates, to the branch managers who needed hands-on training in the sales field, to the sales force who were divided into three groups, with each group receiving training targeted to meet its specific needs.

What can be readily seen from this case is how differently a team will perform depending on the nature of its leadership. At least in the short run, this particular team was producing as a result of the sheer intensity, dynamism, and leadership of the old manager. When that force was removed, however, the real quality of the group found its true level. Very different techniques had to be applied, and specific solutions to each problem had to be found in order to improve productivity.

HIRING IN ONE'S OWN IMAGE

One of the most common problems we've encountered in studying sales teams is that they reflect many of the manager's particular strengths as well as his or her weaknesses. This is so because very often people are hired in the image of the manager. The problems stemming from this kind of imbalance can be myriad.

We have seen many situations over the years in which a sales force with this kind of imbalance has literally come across to the public as a bunch of animals. There is little or no cooperation among the salespeople themselves. Rather than viewing one another as colleagues, salespeople in such situations view each other as direct competitors. We have seen situations where a salesperson will work harder to thwart his or her colleagues to grab sales out from under them rather than fight the company's competition. The issue of who is first in this month's sales report can become more important to the members of the sales team than the level of overall productivity for the company. The manager in this scenario is unable to control this jungle atmosphere because he or she is essentially cut from the same cloth and so tends to exacerbate the problem rather than to cure it.

What finally happens is that people who might tend to balance the group will not come aboard because they do not like the climate, so the people who are brought in often tend to be essentially the same personality types, thus compounding the problem.

At the other end of the spectrum are teams we have evaluated where the existing salespeople almost entirely lack ego-drive. Typically, they survive by providing excellent service and being exceptionally committed to ongoing relationship building. In most cases, such companies are well known, so the salespeople are doing adequate business despite a total lack of dynamism. Still, twice as much business would result if such companies had real salespeople. The problem here is that strongly driven, dynamic salespeople generally are not attracted to teams with such sleepy atmospheres.

The majority of sales forces are not representative of either of these extremes but rather consist of people with a range of abilities and personality attributes. Most, however, suffer from some imbalance, and all have to deal with the realities involved in the strengths and weaknesses, motivations, and differing personality dynamics of all their team members.

USING CHEMISTRY TO BUILD A CHAMPIONSHIP TEAM

Another thing to consider is the chemistry that exists between management and salespeople, as well as among the salespeople themselves. That chemistry will strongly impact whether a company's goals will be achieved.

There are, indeed, some companies that see each salesperson as a totally independent island who makes or breaks it for himself or herself with no relationship to other people on the team. If their product is also a small-ticket item involving a quick, hard one-time close, perhaps their vision would be realized by having a team of animals. There may even be some companies that are so convinced that the salesperson's only job is that of an order taker and servicer that the sleepy climate we discussed would be totally congruent with their vision. Although neither of these extremes normally fits with a corporate vision, our point is that the vision must define the qualities needed and the chemistry of the team. We suggest that management meet first by themselves and then bring in an outside consultant to determine their corporate vision and define their goals.

They should consider such questions as

- How much do we need our team to sell during the next fiscal year? Over the next five years?

- Who are the targets for these sales?

- Ideally, how should the sales be made?

- What is the relationship between acquiring brand-new business and expanding and maintaining existing accounts?

- How much of a gap are we willing to tolerate between the productivity of the top and bottom performers on the sales force?

- Will we earmark funds to further develop our sales team?

- What kind of climate do we want within the sales team? Cooperative? Competitive?

Once a core provision is defined, a plan then can be developed to reach the goals prescribed by that vision.

The next step is to define the tasks needed to achieve those goals, communicate the goals and required tasks, and analyze members of the existing sales team to see if they have the abilities needed to get the job done. Each person must be evaluated to determine whether he or she has the ability to do the job as defined or whether through training or a shift in responsibilities that ability can be developed. The relationship between the sales manager and his or her people has to be understood. Then it has to be determined how that relationship acts positively or negatively toward achieving corporate goals. And, of course, the chemistry of the team itself has to be studied to see how its dynamics affect the likelihood of reaching those goals.

There are many excellent tools available to help management move the company forward. Objective measurement of performance, geared at developing people in areas of deficiency, can go a long way toward increasing productivity and achieving goals. Attitude studies, in-depth psychological tests, employee productivity workshops, and team-building activities are just a few approaches worth noting. Whatever approach is taken, it is most critical to have a thorough understanding of both the company's sales team and the way that team meshes with the company's goals if there is to be any hope of developing a strategy to improve the productivity of the team.

UPGRADE PRODUCTIVITY

Let us share with you now just a few of the approaches that our clients have undertaken to upgrade productivity.

- Many clients start off by conducting team-building sessions among the salespeople and between salespeople and management to increase morale and productivity. Others have developed a team selling system that allows the strengths of one salesperson to augment the weaknesses of another.

- There is also providing training to enrich the product knowledge and technical know-how of salespeople, as well as offering developmental programs for specific areas such as assertiveness training, time management, listening skills, closing techniques, presentation skills, and approaches to prospecting, just to name a few.

- We've also worked with companies to reorganize their compensation plans so that they connect the dynamics of the sales team with the goals of the organization.

- Another approach is to divide sales responsibilities between those capable of new business acquisition and those more suited to maintenance and expansion of existing accounts.

- We also have found instances where reassigning salespeople to managers with whom their chemistry is more effective can have significant results.

- Coaching managers on how to deal more effectively with certain individuals on their teams can help an average performer move ahead of the pack. It also can be vital to install objective performance measurement systems to make sure that a salesperson's success is tied directly to the success of the company.

Which of these activities, or a combination of these activities, is appropriate for a particular company again depends on that all-important understanding of the gaps that exist between the team and the company's vision of the future.

CHAPTER 20

Getting New Employees Up to Speed Faster

We all know that first impressions can be lasting. As a result, most new employees fall into one of two categories. Some are overly concerned with making a mistake, so they hold back. They are frozen in time, waiting, overanalyzing every situation. Others dive in quickly and, because they haven't read the situation correctly, make a mistake that characterizes them as "not quite fitting in." Often they're just plowing forward with what worked for them in the past rather than taking the time to accurately assess the current situation, and as a result, they never really become part of the team.

The first few days of a new job are what you might call the "Goldilocks time." New employees are trying to be not too hot and not too cold. So how can they come across as "just right"?

New employees are keenly aware that they are being evaluated by their new colleagues. In fact, nearly 20 percent of the executives surveyed recently by Caliper said that they could tell within the first week if they had made a hiring mistake. The first week. This is after going through the time-consuming rigors of hiring, including posting ads; combing through countless résumés; narrowing down a pool of top candidates; assessing their potential; conducting multiple interviews; conferring with colleagues or a consultant; and then making that final decision.

To make sure that the investment is worth it, executives need to help new employees set the right tone in those first few crucial days on the job.

"I always think that going into a new organization is like the ball that gets launched in a pinball machine, quickly shooting around—going ping, ping, trying to find its way," says Helen Slaven, Ph.D., chief learning officer for Montefiore Medical Center, the University Hospital for the Albert Einstein College of Medicine. "There has to be someone who can help them make sense of it all because there is just too much coming at them too fast. New employees need a solid understanding of how they can best contribute to their new environment," she told us.

A new employee can get lost in the shuffle unless there is someone to take him or her under their wing and introduce all the secret handshakes.

"People who have gone through the onboarding process have a stronger sense that they understand what is expected of them. And they're getting the opportunity to spend time with their manager on a regular basis. One of the things we hear from people who have been through this onboarding process is that they know there's a plan, and they're not guessing about what is going to happen next. So they are more secure and confident in knowing exactly how they can contribute and shine."

It says out loud to the new employee that the organization is committed to his or her success.

"That's so true. It allows for all kinds of thoughtful conversations. And it allows, very quickly, for a deep understanding of how the new employee can most effectively succeed."

We love that phrase *thoughtful conversations*. It can truly transform the relationship between the manager and the new employee.

One common reason new employees stumble at first is because they don't yet have a firm grasp of their new company's culture. There are cultures where you can be direct, others where you would not say anything at all, and some where you can get your point across if you do it subtly.

One client of ours recalled a new employee who correctly sized up a particular problem the organization was facing and offered what he felt was an ideal solution. But because his style was aggressive, overly direct, and forceful, it was like he was hitting everybody right between the eyes. So, while that employee may have been correct in his assessment of the problem, he ended up being wrong for the organization.

He turned people off because he came across as a strong, opinionated outsider. He was viewed as a critic rather than a collaborator. And he never quite recovered from misreading the first meeting he attended.

We've helped many companies in similar situations by providing the new employee with an independent coach who provides insights and an objective perspective on what he or she needs to do to succeed. And in the process, such a coach can send two very strong messages. First, new employees will know that the company is committed to their success and willing to invest in their future. Equally important, new employees will sense that they are truly valued. When given this coaching opportunity, new employees gain valuable insights into the company's culture, the team they are joining, and how their manager works. And equally important, they also become more aware of their own strengths, motivations, and areas they can focus on developing.

Mitchell Kauffman, owner of Kauffman Wealth Services, a financial management and advisory firm affiliated with Raymond James Financial Services, Inc., had us compare his style of management and expectations with those of a new employee he had hired.

"The coach helped me accelerate the getting-to-know-each-other curve," he told us. "As a result, we were able to understand each other better, avoid conflicts, and be very open about our different approaches to succeeding." He added that the coach helped them to improve their working relationship on two levels. "First, we were able to set our own patterns of expectations rather than just allowing patterns to develop between us and then trying to adjust them afterwards. Equally important, the coach was able to reinforce my model of open communication, which is an essential ingredient of our culture here."

THE FOUR BENEFITS OF EARLY COACHING

Employees who are coached at the beginning of their new job are able to contribute more to the team and reach their peak potential sooner. The benefits of early coaching can be broken down into four categories: First, employees acclimate to the company's culture much faster. Second, employees obtain straightforward insights that will help them to work more effectively. Third, employees have a clear understanding of their manager's work style, so they can work better together. And fourth, employees help to create their own action plan with measurable goals to give them a roadmap for success.

So what are these coaching sessions like? Typically, the coach starts off by sharing the results of the new employee's in-depth personality profile with him or her. This assessment, which is typically taken as part of the hiring process, now can serve the purpose of providing the new employee with insights into his or her motivational strengths, as well as areas for developmental opportunity.

For instance, a newly hired salesperson might be competitive and persuasive and have a strong need for autonomy. These qualities can go a long way toward helping the new employees succeed as long as they are nurtured and the individual works on developing other areas. However, this particular individual might not be adept at cooperating with others, maintaining accuracy, and adapting to feedback. So the coach might help the new employee recognize that while his or her strengths may be excellent for networking, moving an agenda forward, keeping others up to date, and succeeding with minimal supervision, he or she may want to ask others to double-check his or her work and go out of their way to elicit advice and input from others. The coach then will help the new employee to create a personalized action plan tied into specific goals and deadlines. In addition, the coach will share insights into how the new team member can work most effectively with his or her new manager, fit in with the new team, and understand the culture of the company.

We came across one situation where the new salesperson was gregarious, outgoing, and loved to tell stories. However, his sales manager was direct and was looking for someone to get to the point. We were able to help the new salesperson become more effective by conveying that he had, in fact, succeeded in closing a new deal before telling a long and winding story about how he got there. Without knowing the ending, the manager would lose patience with this salesperson's long wind-up and pitch, which could go anywhere. By adapting his style, however, this new salesperson was able to better relate to his manager.

Coaching, then, can lead to a thorough understanding and appreciation of the manager's and new employee's strengths and similarities and how they can complement each other.

If new employees receive coaching as soon as they start their new jobs, they will get up to speed faster because they understand how to avoid potential clashes and can adapt their work style to fit in with the organization's culture. Ultimately, new hires will feel immediately more engaged when they realize that their employers are willing to invest time and money into their personal development during their first few weeks on the job.

The final result is everyone's goal. Employees who are coached at the beginning of a job will be able to contribute more to the team and reach their peak potential sooner.

CHAPTER 21

Sales and Sports: The Psychological Connection

M any executives are drawn to watching professional sports. In fact, which sports you like can say a lot about you. Do you follow rugby or tennis? Are you into aggressive team sports with few rules or individual sports that test an individual athlete's endurance? This is probably why so many sports analogies are commonly used in business settings: "The deal was a slam dunk." "We need a new game plan." "That was a home run." "We need to put on a full court press." "We better punt."

When we asked Roger Staubach, legendary quarterback who led the Dallas Cowboys to two Super Bowl victories and founder of The Staubach Company, an enormously successful commercial real estate enterprise, which sports analogies make the most sense to him in the corporate world, he told us: "Competition is certainly important. Being clear about your goals is crucial. But for me, the key to developing a successful organization is all about team building. It's all about the people you surround yourself with. Succeeding in business, in sports, in your life, is a matter of pulling together people you can trust; who are honest; who have their priorities in line; who have the talent, ambition, and desire to reach beyond themselves and make something really big happen—particularly when the pressure is on."

With that in mind, allow us to share with you some of our work assisting sports teams in the selection and development of professional athletes and explain what it can mean for sales.

In the mid-seventies, we developed the theory that the job-matching process discussed in the previous chapters could be applied in the sports arena. We had a first opportunity to test this theory with the Rutgers University football team. But it wasn't until 1984 that we were able to test our concepts on the professional level with the then Minnesota North Stars hockey team and the NBA's Cleveland Cavaliers. Since these initial trials, we have worked with 23 major league sports teams and 6 colleges in five sports and have developed a substantial body of data validating the fact that job matching can be as effective in sports as in business.

In sports, we started with the assumption that virtually all players seriously considered by scouts and coaches have a great deal of talent. Yet a vast majority don't live up to their scholarships in college and don't make it to the major leagues. So talent alone cannot be the predictor of success. The fact that a player dominates in college because of talent simply does not mean that he or she could dominate on the professional level when going up against people of equal or better talent. More often than not, it comes down to what is in the head and the heart that make the difference. This is where the psychological job match proves to be effective: to separate the players who simply have talent from the players who are able to transport their talent to the next level.

Let's take a moment to examine the psychology of sports and sales so that we can understand why they are so strikingly similar.

COMPETITIVENESS

Competitiveness is obviously the starting place for anyone who succeeds in sports, and that same competitive drive we have found is one of the distinguishing qualities in the best salespeople. Defined succinctly, *competitiveness* is that burning need to win with all your heart and soul. It's not just the desire to win the game, which every athlete has, but it's also that instinct to compete with every move you make on the field or the court. For instance, if someone comes dribbling the ball down the court, you want to block him or her, stop him or her, get the ball out of his or her hands—whatever you need to do to win at that moment.

Now, in the case of the salesperson, that drive to win is very specific: It's the desire to get the "Yes." It is not just a matter of making a lot of money. Making money to a salesperson is like winning the game is to an athlete. Sure, you want to make a lot of money, but the key to the successfully competitive salesperson is that need to get it done now. He or she wants to get the "Yes" immediately. The money, then, becomes not the drive but the symbol of that success.

EGO-STRENGTH

The next quality shared by top-performing athletes and salespeople is ego-strength. All top performers must know how to face rejection and even failure if they want to succeed. The ability to move beyond life's inevitable rejections will determine success much better than talent alone. In baseball, a Hall of Fame hitter might bat .333 over his career. But if he does bat .333, this means that for every three times he comes up to bat, two of those times he doesn't get a hit. He fails two out of every three attempts.

Similarly, even the best salespeople are rejected more frequently than they are accepted. With one of our stockbroker clients, the hope is that out of a hundred cold calls a salesperson will get three appointments and close one sale. And this is being enormously successful. So, whether it's in selling or in sports, the way someone deals with failure is as critical to their success as their talent.

An all too frequent story is the phenomenon in baseball—the hot rookie who comes to camp batting .400 or striking out everybody in sight. Everything seems golden. Then he encounters an inevitable slump—and doesn't know what to do. He starts changing his swing, holding the bat differently, but nothing works, and within a few months, he's out of the game, never to be heard from again.

With two salespeople of roughly equal ability, the difference between short- and long-term success is often determined by self-esteem. Self-esteem is one of the most critical attributes to success, and a lack of self-esteem is probably the single most common characteristic that defeats good athletes and good salespeople.

As with athletes, no matter how successful salespeople are, they are going to experience slumps and rejections, and no matter how strong their ego-drive, they are not going to want to face that next rejection.

To move beyond feelings of vulnerability and rejection, you've got to have a sense of self-esteem. This characteristic is what enables a successful salesperson to say, "Okay, I know I'm going to get four turndowns before I get to a yes." It basically comes down to not taking the rejections personally, not having to disappear for a three-hour lunch or do anything else just to avoid facing more rejections.

Athletes, we have found, may manifest a lack of ego-strength or self-esteem by getting injured frequently—if you're not playing, you can't fail. Without good self-esteem, an athlete is likely to freeze in the clutch by missing that critical foul shot, or dropping that winning touchdown pass, or striking out with the bases loaded.

SELF-DISCIPLINE

Along with competitiveness and self-esteem, self-discipline is critical to success in both sales and sports. In essence, *self-discipline* is that internal taskmaster—that voice inside of a top performer that says, "I want to practice because it will make me better." It is this self-discipline that distinguishes an athlete who comes to camp in better shape than last season from an athlete who arrives overweight. It is that same self-discipline that enables top-performing salespeople to continually improve their presentation skills, to constantly get better at managing their time, and to continually develop stronger and closer relationships with their clients.

The tables that follow present data from studies conducted in baseball and basketball. In these studies, the performance of players recommended for drafting because of their psychological match to their sport and their position is compared with the performance of players drafted in the same rounds who were felt to be not matched. (*Talent played no role in these assessments. The only data we had were the psychological test results.*)

It can be seen from Table 21-1 that in baseball the young men who were psychologically job-matched had significantly more hits, walks, home runs, and so on than their peers who were drafted, again, in the same rounds but who were not psychologically job-matched. Similarly, Table 21-2 shows that in basketball the job-matched players outperformed their non-job-matched competitors better than 2:1 in most statistical areas, such as average points scored, assists, steals,

Table 21.1   Baseball Statistics

Average per Player per Season Overall		
	Recommended	**Not Recommended**
Number of hits	145.78	70.96
Home runs	9.53	4.83
Total bases	208.86	102.57
Runs scored	80.1	38.48
Runs batted in	68.94	34.7
Walks	65.25	32.84
Stolen bases	23.75	9.99
Pitcher ERA	3.76	4.21
Major League Statistics—Players Who Reach Majors		
	28%	17%
Major League Statistics—Average per Player per Season		
Number of hits	125.64	51.81
Home runs	14.96	4.86
Runs scored	66.39	27.48
Runs batted in	62.75	26.86
Walks	52.29	20.29
Stolen bases	5.7	3.67
Batting average	0.24	0.2
Batting average (pitchers omitted)	0.273	0.237

Table 21.2   Basketball Statistics

Average per Player per Season Overall		
	Recommended	**Not Recommended**
Points per season	909	376
Rebounds	320	160
Blocked shots	51	23
Assists	207	91
Steals	77	33
Minutes played	1,919	1,004

rebounds, and so on. The only difference between the two groups was the job matching.

OTHER ATTRIBUTES FOR THE JOB MATCH

As we discussed previously, it is insufficient to make a judgment about the effectiveness of a salesperson simply by looking at his or her empathy, ego-drive, and ego-strength. These traits are the essentials, so we start there. Then, if an individual has these three qualities, we look for many other attributes to determine not simply if the individual can sell but, more important, can the individual sell the specific product or service for the particular company in question.

In the same way, while we start looking at athletes in terms of their competitiveness, self-esteem, and self-discipline, we also must look at a number of other qualities to help determine whether they match the team and the position for which they're being considered.

On a number of occasions, just as we've suggested shifts of salespeople to other sales roles or even to nonsales roles within the same company to make a better job match, we have suggested shifts in position within a team to achieve better performance. For example, on several occasions we have suggested that a catcher not be kept in that position but rather be moved to first base, third base, or left field if he's physically capable of playing those positions. We've suggested moves from point guard to shooting guard, from middle linebacker to defensive end, from offensive line to defensive line, and even in a very recent case from running back to wide receiver. These suggestions were not based on any knowledge of the athlete's particular talent. Those decisions, obviously, had to be made by the coaches and managers. Our suggestions were based purely on psychological issues—matching individuals to positions based on their intrinsic abilities and motivations.

Some examples here might make this point clear and also will demonstrate the strikingly similar issues that must be dealt with in sales and in sports. Take, for instance, a good quarterback, a good catcher, and a good point guard. All of them must possess several additional attributes, talent aside, if they hope to perform at the very top level of their position. They must be intelligent so that they will make astute judgment calls in the middle of a game. They must be willing to be wrong occasionally in order to get the job done. They must possess leadership qualities, and they need to be team-oriented so that they can maximize the abilities of the players around them.

We could, of course, go on, position by position, describing the specific qualities required for top performance. But we hope the foregoing is sufficient to make two points. First, there is a striking similarity between building a sales team and building a sports team from a psychological perspective. And second, as a team is built, consideration must be given to the interactions of that team. The best quarterback who ever lived will fail if he does not have the offensive line to protect him and the receivers to catch the passes he throws. Many great basketball teams with five all-stars have not won because "there were not enough basketballs for each of the players." Even in baseball, where there's more individuality than in basketball or football, great teams, loaded with great players, have failed to win the pennant because they didn't work as a "team."

So, as we look at building a sales team, we must look not simply at what each person can or cannot do but also at how each individual fits into the team—and fits into the team's game plan.

This is why Sean Sweeney, president and chief operating officer for the Philadelphia Insurance Company, told us he prefers to hire only athletes.

"What I try to do is hire Division 2 or Division 3 athletes. The reason I generally don't hire Division 1 athletes is because I find that they are often coddled, genetically gifted, and if they are applying for a job with us, I know that in the back of their minds is always that unfulfilled dream of making it to the pros. So taking a job with us would be a substitute for that dream. On the other hand, Division 2 and 3 athletes, I find, are grinders. They understand that they have to practice and to give it their all to win. They are competitive, self-disciplined, and resilient. They know how to come back from a setback. And they're not looking to be a superstar. They just want to show up every day, deliver a quality job over a long period of time, and be part of a winning team. And they bring that winning attitude to everything they do. That's an attitude I understand and can work with. It's knowing that success is a long race."

This is an interesting notion. The idea that a Division 1 athlete could bring a bit of a prima donna attitude, as well as the notion that in the back of their minds is always that lingering idea that they never quite made the pros. So you might be dealing with someone who was essentially disappointed because he or she hadn't quite reached his or her dream—and working in business could be less than fulfilling.

Sean actually has competed in an ironman race himself, which is a 2.4-mile swim, followed by a 112-mile bike ride, and a marathon, raced in that order and without a break. The grueling race starts at 7:00 a.m., and all finishers must complete the marathon by midnight. (Sean told the president of the ironman competition that if he moved the business to Philadelphia Insurance, he would start training the next day.) With a coach and eight months of daily training, he finished in the top 10 percent of those racing that day.

"I attribute my finishing time to being diligent, to preparing, to training, and to giving it my all. There are a lot of parallels to that in selling insurance—to making quota, hitting objective, and being accountable for an outcome."

It also positions him as a leader who can take on a real challenge.

"I say to my team, 'When we get a goal, it may sound impossible, but if you break down the process, and you are disciplined, and you adhere to the practice, you will be successful.' And I assure them that I am here to provide an environment for them to be successful. And together we will succeed, so long as they bring their competitive spirit, their resilience, and their self-discipline."

Mike Nagel, president and chief executive officer of Vomaris Innovations, has done several triathlon competitions. "I have a rep in Sacramento that I just hired who is a triathlete, I have another rep who has done several ironmen competitions, and I just hired someone who finished the Leadville 100 Mile Bike Race. So, for me, keeping yourself fit and active is part of an attitude. It doesn't automatically get you hired, but it moves you up in the ranks. It shows that you are good at planning, you can follow a schedule, you can handle going out of your comfort zone, and you are willing to put in long hours for something that is meaningful. It's an attitude that you can't give somebody. And I like my top performers to have a passion for something outside of work, as well."

Paul Knee, managing director at Verathon, said: "I find top-performing salespeople are often athletic. There is a common link. There is the competiveness, the enthusiasm, and the desire to always improve, to become better, continually. There is a desire to take on challenges for the sake of the challenge rather than for what they'll get out of it. It is a part of their makeup. And whenever I am involved in recruiting, I always want to look at what someone is doing in their spare time to get a glimpse of who they really are."

That competitive spirit is something that either is there or is not. You can't give it to someone. You just want to know that it is there—as a starting place.

Mark Nechita, senior director of international human resources at Callaway Golf, told us that his salespeople actually can find themselves in unusual situations where they are playing golf (competing on some level) with their clients. Do they let them win? Go for the burn?

"It's about wanting to show your client that you know what you're doing," Mark says. "You want them to have a great experience. So you're introducing them to the course and taking a new club out of your bag and demonstrating how it can improve your game and letting them try it. So it's all about enjoying the experience together. And the competition is always with yourself. So they may be thinking, 'Maybe if I use that club I can play like him.' And who knows? For our salespeople, it's creating a dynamic that can lead to a stronger connection. And that can happen on the golf course, when you're relaxing, enjoying the company and trying to play your best game."

It's a very unique dynamic, where the sport actually becomes part of the sale, not just an analogy or a pastime.

On a final note, we knew Mark Dennis a long time before he mentioned in passing that he tried out for the Miami Dolphins. "I was a free agent," he told us, with an undeniable sense of unpretentiousness. "Although I was in the pro camp, it didn't last long."

That is still impressive.

"People try to make it bigger than it was. And it's really not. The point is that I was close but didn't make it. And I realized at that point that I had to let go of that dream. What I did see when I was there were an incredible number of really good athletes—and there's a very small margin between the athletes who make it and those who don't make it. You realize the heart is a very hard thing to measure. But when you play against people who may not be the best of talent, they may not be the biggest or the fastest or the strongest, but their heart will not allow them to fail. And when you find that, you have a winner. In whatever they are pursuing," adds the vice president of sales and marketing for Veolia Environmental Services.

It would be an interesting study to see how many athletes in school went on to become successful at some other pursuit in life. Clearly, having the self-discipline, resilience, and competitive spirit can take you a long way if you're clear about where you want to go.

While we certainly recognize the strong connection between sports and business, allow us to leave you with an observation: In many ways, professional sports is much easier than business. We know that this might sound counterintuitive, but hear us out: In business, your competition can be on the other side of the world, awake while you are sleeping. So you can't study their game videos from the prior week. And you are not going to be seeing them face to face on the same playing field. There is also not a clock ticking that tells you when the game is over. There aren't four quarters or nine innings. And there are no referees with clearly defined and agreed-on rules. No one is calling penalties. And there are no time outs.

Perhaps this is why we all like to watch professional sports. We can root, from the sidelines, get our competitive juices flowing, without getting hurt, while watching the best of the best play on a level field.

CHAPTER 22

The Psychology of "A" Players

As leaders, one of our most important challenges is to make sure that our top performers and those who have the potential to be our top performers know how very important they are to us. We need to recognize them and keep them engaged, motivated, and enthused about their future with us. Nothing is more important than making sure that we keep our top talent because, at the end of the day, our top talent is ultimately what distinguishes us. Everything else can be copied by our competitors. To keep them, we have to make sure that our top performers understand that we are intent on creating a championship team—and that they are a vital part of that vision.

Many leaders mistakenly believe that top performers will inspire and raise the level of performance of everyone else around them. We have found, though, that this is not what happens. And it is, in fact, the opposite of what top performers are looking for.

One thing we've learned for certain about top performers is that they want to be connected with other top performers. They do not want to be working side by side with someone who will not complete their part of an important project on time. They get very upset by the behaviors and attitudes of mediocre performers. They do not want to be playing with someone from the junior varsity team. Top performers want to be part of a winning team. And they want to make a difference.

"'A' players are different psychologically," according to Kerry Sulkowicz, M.D., founder and managing principal of the Boswell

Group, a CEO advisory firm. He told us: "The 'A' players I view as naturals. They have interpersonal skills that are hard to mimic. That's certainly not to say that all 'A' players are alike. They can, in fact, be quite different. But their interpersonal skills come naturally. 'B' players, on the other hand, tend to try very hard—and, in some ways, the trying hard can get in their way. They can come across as trying too hard."

So they can trip over themselves and come across as less than sincere and not quite natural.

"I believe that's because a lot of times when they're trying so hard, they end up trying the wrong things."

And it can come across as a bit desperate.

"Exactly. The 'A' players, on the other hand, have a remarkable ability to relate to and connect with their customers. They have an intuitive ability to empathize with their customer, to get into the mind of their customer. The 'B' players, on the other hand, spend more time in their own mind—doing what they honestly believe is a lot of preparatory work. They are constantly preparing, studying, doing research. And my feeling is, while you certainly have to be prepared, at some point it becomes wheel spinning rather than going out there and taking a risk."

Their lack of confidence keeps them constantly preparing.

"They don't feel ready to just be in the moment with their customer and to create an opportunity together. That feels dangerous to them. The challenge for 'B' players is on an emotional level. It is behavioral, in the realm of the interpersonal. It is about being present for their customers, in the moment, in the here and now. That frame of mind is the difference between 'A' and 'B' players."

And it is not something that you can just give to somebody. Would that it were so.

Since it is not, though, it is extremely important to realize that your 'A' players are rare gems—and to treat them that way.

Ed Siciliano, chief sales officer at Marlin Leasing, told us that his 'A' players think about the business differently. "What separates them, in my mind, is that they are not just thinking about their next sale. They take a few steps back, on a regular basis, and analyze their business. They are constantly asking themselves, 'What could I do differently to achieve even higher growth?' Perhaps it's thinking about one of their top customers in a way they hadn't before. Or uncovering something that is common to each of their customers who are growing. They are constantly challenging themselves to do better. But also stepping back to look at their business from a higher perspective."

It is not just "There's the door. Now go run through it." Top performers take time to reflect on their clients and on themselves.

SPEND MORE TIME WITH YOUR TOP PERFORMERS

We recently asked over 500 managers who they spend most of their time with: Top performers? Average performers? Or poor performers?

Do you know what they answered? Any ideas?

Nearly half the managers said that they were spending most of their time with poor performers.

It begs the question: Who should you be spending most of your time with?

In essence, as managers, we have to ask ourselves, "If I'm spending most of my time with poor performers, what's the best I can hope for? To bring my worst employees up to being barely average at best?"

Many executives get trapped into spending their days dealing with problems—often caused by less-than-effective employees. None of us plan our days this way. It's not like we're driving to work thinking, "I know what I'll do, I'll get in, grab a cup of coffee, and spend my day solving one problem after another—and never get to the things I really want to do." But how often does this happen?

The truth is that if someone is not built for the job—if they don't have the empathy and desire to persuade that is needed for sales—then they are trying to defy gravity, climbing a steep hill, with a very slim chance of succeeding.

And if you're spending too much time with poor performers—or trying to resolve problems caused by underachieving employees—you're probably not focused on the future, on what your company can become.

Don't spend time trying to change people.

Spend time hiring and developing more people like your top performers.

And spend more time with your top performers.

One of our clients, John Beattie, former senior vice president of human resources for GMAC Insurance, told a very revealing story about recognizing and developing top performers.

He said that one day he got a call from one of his best performers who told him that she was quitting.

He was stunned and asked why.

She said, "John, I'm out here alone. I can't get any of your time. This just doesn't work for me anymore."

There was a half hour between the phone call and the time she got to his office. During that time, John said that he did a lot of soul searching. When she arrived, he was obviously shook up. He said to her that he understood what she was saying. Then he sincerely apologized. And he asked if she would stick in for another month and give him a chance to turn the situation around. And fortunately, she did.

He said that was his wake-up call. And now he spends much more time with his top performers . . . and much less time with his poor performers.

Take John's advice.

Spend less time with your poor performers and more time with your best employees—because your best employees want to hear from you. Focus on the people you want to stay—the ones who, if they left, would feel like a kick in the stomach. Your attention will keep them engaged, knowing that they're valued. And they'll be much less likely to start looking for greener pastures.

Spending more time with your "A" players will send several messages to your organization. First, it will affirm your values. It will be a physical reminder to everyone of who and what you value. Second, it will inspire you and keep you energized and enthused. Equally important, you'll gain insights into what is really working for your company. And you'll have a much clearer understanding of what to look for when it's time to hire your next top performer.

On top of that, as you get to know your top performers even better, you will also grow with them. You will recognize the distinguishing qualities that you all share and that make your organization so special.

Your day will be filled with optimism, resilience, empathy, persuasiveness, perseverance, the capacity to quickly analyze problems, the knack for arrving at solutions, and the ability to connect with people in a very real way.

And you'll know exactly what to look for in your next promising applicants. This is the potential you're looking for—in your employees and in your company.

Your "A" players will keep you focused on what works—and how to keep making what works even better.

CHAPTER 23

The Marginal Producer

Salespeople, broadly speaking, fall into three categories. There are those elusive few, typically the 20 percent of the firm's salespeople, who are highly productive, who sell most of what is sold. These individuals have precisely what it takes to sell in their particular situation. They can sense the desires of a prospect, are driven by a need to persuade, and can bounce back from the rejection that is an inevitable part of their work. These top performers sell effectively and need only be managed in a way related to their key motivations and not managed in a way that would demotivate them. These are the superstars, about whom managers will say, "I just point them in the right direction."

The truth of the matter, however, is that you should not leave them alone. You should spend most of your time with them. Let them know how important they are to your organization, how valuable they are to your future. Learn from them. Share what you learn with people who have the potential to be your next top performers. And most important, celebrate your top performers. They are what will keep you one step ahead of your competition.

At the other end of the spectrum is the bottom 20 percent, those individuals who fundamentally lack the dynamics to sell or the particular personality attributes required to sell their product or their service. In all likelihood, these people derive very little pleasure from closing a sale, or if they do, they lack the qualities needed in their specific sales situation. Since you cannot make someone want to sell or feel the gratification that a real salesperson would obtain from closing a sale successfully, it is very unlikely that much can be done to develop this group.

Our advice is to determine the real basic occupational motivations of each of these individuals and, if possible, place them in more appropriate positions within the company. The benefit of this approach is that they do, after all, know the company and its products or services. If they have a positive attitude and fit in with your culture, and if there is an appropriate position, it is preferable to salvage the company's investment in such individuals by placing them in more productive positions. In addition, there is a valuable morale factor if this kind of job crossover can occur. If, however, there is not an appropriate opening in the company for these misemployed salespeople, the need is clear: You have to replace members of this group as quickly as possible with appropriate and productive new hires. You owe it to them and to your organization.

Not holding onto your poor performers is something that Edilson Lopes feels very strongly about. The founder and general manager of KLA Business Education, one of Brazil's largest training companies, told us: "Be quick in dismissing those who do not wish to work to their potential. If someone is not working out, create a clear performance plan, with clearly defined objectives. Have the timing be short but realistic and the goals measurable but attainable. Let them know that you are willing to work with them, if they put in the hard work. Then, if they don't have the skills or desire, you are better off separating your ways. That way, when you have to let somebody go, you, and they, will know you've given it your all, and there was nothing else you could have done. You cannot give somebody that skill set. The best you can do is to make sure that the person you hire to replace that individual truly has the potential to succeed. That way, at the very least, you won't be repeating your mistakes. You will have learned from the past to make your next hiring decision better."

So you have the top performers, who we focused on earlier, in a separate chapter. They are the ones who should become your blueprint for hiring. Then there are the bottom performers. Those are the ones who should not be with you very long. Either help them move up or help them move on. Then there is the middle group. In most companies, the average performers account for 60 percent of the sales force. This can, in many ways, be the most difficult, perplexing, and at times frustrating group to deal with. They produce sales, but not with consistently high performance. Their performance can be spotty, but they do well enough to hang in. Or they can just plod along, not functioning on all cylinders, producing enough to keep their jobs but hardly tapping their potential. Management has already invested time, money, and effort in them, so it is important to try to make that investment pay off.

At some point or another, every manager looks at the math and says, "Imagine if I could get this group to produce just 5 percent more. Imagine 10 percent." We have found that many of these individuals are capable of producing much more. What is needed is to know which specific strategy should be designed for each individual. How can you motivate him or her to produce at a higher level? How can you tap into his or her true potential? There is obviously no single solution or formula. Analyzing each person's strengths and limitations within a group and separating the overall group into subgroups with similar dynamics is the first step in determining management's strategies to overcome these limitations.

What we typically have found is that one group will need assistance in closing techniques. More often than not, this group can benefit greatly from coaching and training that build on their competence and their confidence. We saw this occur with one salesman who was hesitant to ask for the order because he knew the price was high. As he became more familiar with the benefits of the solution his company was providing, he recognized that the value far exceeded the price, and his ability to close improved with his confidence level. Another group may possess adequate amounts of empathy but be extremely impatient. Such individuals could benefit from coaching and training that focuses on improving their listening skills. Another group may be lacking in the area of personal organization. Acquiring tools that will assist these individuals in time management might be all they need to function more productively.

The list could go on, but these examples should be sufficient to make the point. Often these average or marginal producers can be helped enormously by focusing on their strengths and limitations and through coaching, targeted training, and supervision that helps them to overcome their limitations so that they can perform at a substantially higher level.

A batter in a slump takes extra batting practice. A basketball player who does not shoot foul shots well practices shooting from the line. In the same way, the salesperson dragged down by one weakness can be helped by working to improve that specific area. Let us examine why some people, given proper management and training, can succeed, while others, under the same circumstances, will turn up empty-handed. *Marginal*, as we will see, turns out to be a very big word.

The key factor is to determine whether an individual's modest performance relates to his or her fundamental lack of appropriate dynamics or is limited by some particular personality factor that can be changed. We also must determine whether outside factors might be working to lower productivity in relation to the individual's real potential. Let us look at three cases from our files that exemplify this point.

We assessed the sales potential of a young man—we will call him Phillip—who was working for a large manufacturing company. He had great references, he had impressed the management of the company in the initial interview, and he had scored well on our in-depth personality profile. Yet, with all that going for him, and after a good start by making three important sales in the first month, he had sunk into a six-month slump.

The vice president of sales was perplexed. She asked to review all the facts to see whether there was a better solution than terminating Phillip, who had seemed so ideal at first. Phillip's in-depth personality profile indicated that he possessed very strong sales dynamics. He was empathic, enjoyed persuading, and could deal with rejection. However, he had a strong need for approval, particularly from authority figures.

Realizing this, we assessed Phillip's manager. When the personality profiles were placed side by side, the problem became apparent. The manager, who had come up from sales herself, was a hard-driving, extremely aggressive, and assertive individual with adequate empathy. She was an individualist. When dealing with salespeople, her tendency was to leave them alone—unless there was an obvious problem or concern that required her attention. She was from the school that believed that performance tells the story. "When I was selling," she told us, "the last thing I wanted was to have a manager looking over my shoulder."

The problem, as it turned out, was not with the manager because, after all, she had sold successfully and in fact managed a rather productive sales force. Nor was the problem with Phillip, the salesperson, who had the ability to sell. Rather, the problem related to the chemistry between the manager and the salesperson.

Had the company been small, we would have suggested that the manager try to provide more approval, guidance, and ongoing support to help relate better to Phillip and improve his performance. Of course, it is difficult to reprogram one's particular management approach and technique, but when possible, behavioral modification should be attempted to improve overall effectiveness.

Since the company had offices in other locations, however, what we suggested was that Phillip be shifted to another office where there was a manager whose more supportive style was a better fit for Phillip. The shift resulted in an almost immediate turnaround for Phillip, and today he is functioning at the level of production that was expected of him initially. By altering the outside factor, the management approach as related to Phillip's needs, Phillip's productivity was improved substantially.

The problem with Holly, a real estate salesperson, was much simpler to solve. She, like Phillip, had tremendous sales dynamics but was clearly not performing well after having been promoted to a position that called for selling commercial real estate. Interestingly, when management first reviewed her application and in-depth personality profile, she was not considered for that particular target market. However, after succeeding at selling moderately priced homes, she asked to be promoted, and fearing the company might lose her to a competitor, management complied. She was promoted to a position that called for selling commercial properties.

Holly, however, was impatient, hard-driven, somewhat disorganized, and desperately in need of instant gratification. She was a classic short-term, goal-oriented individual who wanted quick and frequent closes. As a result, she simply lacked the patience for long-term follow-up and service. Obviously, with commercial properties, long-term follow-up and service are as critical to success as the ability to sell. Thus the job that she was promoted to because of her strong sales ability was precisely the wrong job for her.

At our suggestion, the manager decided to move her into a listing responsibility. Selling listings involves a need for a strong close and the kind of immediate yes or no response that Holly's drive and impatience demanded. Listing, therefore, made for an ideal job match. The move was made with excellent results.

As a footnote, we should mention that management had been rightly concerned that Holly might consider the suggested shift a demotion, since the new position did not carry the prestige of commercial sales. However, the manager had emphasized that many of the listings Holly would be securing might be highly prestigious commercial properties or estate homes. The manager explained that the only difference would be securing the listing for the company, as opposed to going through the long, agonizing process of following up. By describing the move in this way, the manager was able to tap into Holly's basic personality attributes and so was able to save an otherwise losing situation.

The final example relates to Sally, a salesperson for a printing firm, who, unlike Phillip or Holly, was performing adequately. The problem was that she was performing just adequately. Her manager felt strongly that given her presentation, appearance, knowledge of printing, and overall manner, her performance should have been near the top of the sales force. Her strong qualities included empathy and the drive to sell effectively, as well as time management skills, excellent service motivation, and the attention to detail and sense of responsibility necessary to follow up and to provide the kind of expertise often required in printing sales. However, she needed approval and was unassertive. She sometimes would hesitate to push strongly enough for the close, lest she incur disapproval. Whenever there was some resistance to a possible sale, her tendency was to back off a bit too soon.

Of course, no salesperson, particularly in the printing industry, should be overly pushy or aggressive. Yet there are times when an effective salesperson senses that the prospect is on the verge of making a decision and needs only a slight push in the right direction. However, when such an opportunity would present itself, Sally's tendency was not to risk that slight push. The sales she made therefore were the automatic ones—jobs that sold themselves or called for only the least bit of soft persuasion.

Far too many sales were slipping through her fingers because of her unwillingness to be assertive at the right time. She attended an assertiveness training program and a few counseling sessions dealing with her reluctance to risk rejection. The combination proved effective. Although she is still not selling at the very top level of the sales force, she has moved from below average to well above average, and her manager feels that growth will continue.

After gaining insights and a clear understanding of the key strengths and areas of concern for these three marginal producers, management was able to upgrade their production substantially by taking specific actions related to their strengths and weaknesses. Phillip needed only to be placed under a manager whose style played more effectively to his needs. Holly's job responsibilities had to be shifted from one involving patience and follow-through, of which she was constitutionally incapable, to one playing to her strength—assertive, highly persuasive closing. Sally simply needed some assertiveness training and counseling to overcome a particular weakness, thus freeing her to be far more productive.

By understanding the unique qualities of each marginal producer, a sales manager frequently can upgrade individual performance by making simple yet targeted modifications. We have seen situations in which merely attending the right one-day planning workshop or having a manager slightly modify his or her coaching approach made all the difference in the world. Sometimes these small modifications literally can convert a salesperson skating on the edge of termination into a highly productive contributor. The key in all these situations is gaining a clear understanding of whether the individual's performance is marginal because he or she is basically not suited to the position, or whether there is a specific concern that can be addressed by making the right changes.

24

Coaching: How Much Can You Help Someone Improve?

When it comes to coaching, it begs the question, How much can someone really change? One answer is, Consider your last New Year's resolution—and the one before that.

Change is difficult.

We believe that people can change—if they are committed and really want to make the change. But part of the solution is also realizing that we are all creatures of habit—our best habits and those which are not so good. In order to change a habit, you have to practice the change daily (even if it is just something as simple as flossing). You have to make the change part of your routine for at least a month. And part of the solution is also recognizing that there often will be one step backward for every two steps forward. As long as you're going in the right direction, the change you desire can happen.

With this in mind, we want to share with you some ways you can coach people to reach their true potential. Before we get there, though, we need to let you know that none of the advice we're about to share will work if one of two people is not ready: you *and* the person you are trying to coach.

And this can account for a very complicated formula.

Both of you need to be open, flexible, intrigued by solving problems, self-aware, and willing to listen and reflect—and both of you need to be convinced that you want to change.

Without this fundamental desire, nothing will change.

It leads back to the question, Does anyone really change?

We have come to believe that we can all change in huge ways—if we really want to. Keep in mind one thing, however: Psychologists love to debate exactly when qualities such as empathy, persuasiveness, and resilience become part of who we are. Are we born with them? Do we learn them by age two? Five? Twelve?

Wherever that fine line is drawn, it is generally agreed that by the time someone is old enough to apply for a job, those qualities are either there or not. And we have come to believe that it is not our job to try to change someone—to make them other than they really are. Rather, it is our job to help them to realize their potential. Those are two very different things.

Trying to change someone—to make them other than they really are—is fruitless. We might get someone to follow our rules, but it will be, as they say in those late-night commercials, for a limited time only. Real change can come from only one place—within. Advice either rings true, or it doesn't.

How does this connect with coaching—and trying to develop top employees?

First of all, not everyone responds to coaching in the way the organization desires or intends. After being coached, most of us get sucked into our busy lives and get distracted by the day-to-day demands of our jobs and forget to implement what we've learned. We are all creatures of habit. So we fall back on old habits. And coaching falls by the wayside.

To change, we have to want to. And we have to understand that there is an enormous disconnect between understanding and doing. Most coaching is based on a huge, and false, assumption—that if people understand, they will act. But why do most people who have had a triple bypass operation, a year later resume their old eating habits? If we're not going to change when something is life-threatening, then why are we going to change one of our habits at work just because our boss wants us to?

In order for coaching to stick, it requires desire, understanding, commitment, support, being open to feedback, and constant follow-up.

This is a tall demand. And it assumes that someone really wants to change.

For coaching to succeed, you have to start out by truly understanding the strengths of the individual you are coaching. Coaching is a one-on-one activity. It starts with you and the individual with whom you are working. You need to know how you can connect most strongly with the individual you are coaching. Is the connection through your desire to succeed? Your optimism? Your empathy? Whatever the connection, it is your starting point.

Let the individual know that you know his or her strengths, even if he or she is too modest to say them out loud. Then, with their strengths as your foundation, you can both work on one behavior that you would both like to change.

Let us tell you a quick story about one of our clients—and how coaching for her connected at just the right time.

We were recently working with one of our client's most productive salespeople. She consistently got the highest ratings from her customers, but she had a remarkable ability to drive people inside her company absolutely crazy.

After spending some time with her, her manager, her clients, and some of her colleagues, we told her that we were very impressed with the way we'd seen her connect with her clients. She had a true gift. Then we told her that we'd like for her to be able to share her talents with other, younger salespeople—which we knew was one of her desires.

But . . . and we paused. Then we told her that after conducting a 360-degree evaluation, we had to share with her that she was perceived inside her own company as someone who was pushy, bossy, difficult, demanding, and sometimes even insulting—and someone who doesn't seem to care about anything but her own success.

She was taken aback by that assessment.

Part of her could not deny it. But she felt that she was pushing to get everything she could for her clients. And it never occurred to her how she was coming across.

When we asked her if that was how she wanted to come across, she said, "No, of course not." Then she talked about some people in the company who she was sure did not have that opinion of her.

Rather than challenge her on her beliefs, we said that what we'd like is for everyone in the company to think as highly of her as her clients do. Since we knew she was competitive, we added, "We'd like you to take this on as a challenge. Let's set a goal to change your perception within this building by the end of this year." Then we said, "You know how the Chinese have a year that is dedicated to a certain animal—which is said to embody certain qualities? Well, we want this to be your year of diplomacy. Whenever you are dealing with anyone in your company, whether it's in customer service, marketing, sales, or operations, we want you to think about coming across diplomatically."

And she took the challenge. What she even added, which we admired, is that she said to people, "This is my year of diplomacy. I know it might not come naturally to me, but I am intent on coming across more diplomatically."

And in her saying that, she was telling people what she is working on. And they gave her a chance. After all, if someone said to you, "I am working on being more diplomatic," wouldn't you be more open and accepting of the fact that they were honestly trying to change? And without that admission, she actually could be changing her behavior, but because of preconceived notions, people might not recognize that she was changing. Sometimes it can help to clarify things if we just say out loud what we are doing. This is something that we've seen help immensely. Sometimes the things we think are obvious are not as obvious to others. And just by saying them out loud, we can clear the air—or at least start to change things.

The thing to keep in mind is that as a coach, you are dealing in a very personal realm. It's the place where the professional and personal connect. Start with your connection with the person you are coaching. Then build on his or her many strengths. Say them out loud. Then talk about the one behavior that you would like to see change. At most, we can change one thing at a time—with focus, drive, desire, support, and follow-through.

One thing to keep in mind as we are trying to change is that we cannot change the past—we can only change the future. If you are coaching someone, don't concentrate on what was wrong. Jackson Browne, in his song, "These Days," wrote, "Don't confront me with my failures; I have not forgotten them." We are all keenly aware of our mistakes. We're not looking for someone to be another thorn in our sides—to point out our shortcomings. What we need is someone who can help us to envision a different future.

What would it be like if we were succeeding? This is what we want to know. If you are coaching someone, help them to create that future. Help them to be clear about what it could look and feel like. This is the place where coaching connects. This is where the best coaches connect with each of the individuals with whom they are working—and connect with themselves.

To become a better coach, you need to be comfortable about providing developmental feedback. And you want to create a safe, productive, open, and challenging coaching environment—where you and the individual you are coaching are both striving to be your best—one step at a time.

Bill Eckstrom, president of EcSELL Institute, told us: "We've seen leadership becoming way more interpersonal, focused on relationships, as opposed to what used to be a kind of hero model of leadership. *Coach* has become a verb and a noun. It is active and constant, a strategic component of what a leader does. As in sports, there is just a very small percentage of people who played the game who also have the ability to coach. And great organizations are built on finding that small percentage."

How much time should you spend coaching?

At Avis Budget Group, every one of the 600-plus salespeople in the organization has had an in-depth personality profile, which is matched to their performance, background, and aspirations, Tom Gartland, president of the company's North America Division, told us. Then developmental plans are created for each salesperson. And their manager works very closely with each individual to make sure that their current performance and their career aspirations are on track and aligned with the company's goals. The time the individual and the manager spend together on this accounts for a solid three weeks over the course of a year. This is a deep commitment and a rigorous process that clearly conveys to each individual how committed the organization is to them—today and in the future.

Curt Nelson, president and CEO of the Entrepreneurial Center, makes an interesting distinction between coaching and training. He told us, "I think coaching is in the moment, day to day. It is checking in, helping someone get unstuck, showing a way out of a situation they find themselves in, keeping them motivated. Training, from my perspective, is more of a formalized process. Training has more to do with developing specific skills or learning about products in a more formalized, scheduled session."

When Mark Dennis, vice president of sales and marketing for Veolia Environmental Services, was with his previous employer, the company tapped him to be a national sales and management trainer. In this position, because he had field and classroom experience, he would work with the sales managers to help them become better coaches.

What were some of the most common concerns he would coach to improve?

"Often it was helping the sales manager to create a systematic approach toward assessing a rep's performance. Did the manager understand the skills? Was the rep applying them?"

"Then it was helping the manager to develop effective ways to work with individual sales reps depending on what they needed. For some, it had to do with attitude; for others, it centered around their willingness to listen to feedback. Some were more familiar with the features but couldn't convey the benefits or solutions that were tied to the needs of the prospect. And we would incorporate what we knew about them from their in-depth personality profiles. So we had a clear sense of their potential, and we could map it to their performance. We would videotape the coaching sessions so that everyone could see how they were coming across. Then we developed a 30-day action plan for the rep to work on changes, with coaching and follow-up built in. This involved working with the manager and the rep to improve the level of communication and performance in a systematic way."

One of the fundamental coaching messages is to be in the present—to trust in your abilities and to tune into the client—so that you are both in the moment and can cocreate an ideal solution.

John Brubaker, chief performance officer at The Sport of Business, told us, "Peak performers have an almost innate ability to be present in the moment. That's what makes the best better than the rest. They're able to be present—in the moment. In sales, that means really listening to and connecting with the buyer."

What coaching advice would he have for an athlete or salesperson who just missed an enormous opportunity?

"They have to learn what I call 'intentional amnesia.' When you make a mistake, what you want to do is recognize it, admit it, and then forget it, literally flush it from your memory banks. Afterward, you can review what happened and learn from it. But at that time, in that moment, you've got to carry on. Athletes and salespeople have to get back in the game. So they need to have a mistake ritual, which is a focal point or a go-to process that they can use to move past an error, past a bad outcome."

The idea is not to focus on what just went wrong?

"Not immediately. There will be time for that later. But when you're in the game, whether it's an athletic event or selling to a prospect, you have to replace that fear with trust. Trust is the antidote to fear; it's the antidote to performance anxiety. It is important to trust in yourself. Perhaps you stumbled over your wording in the close. And the buyer turned you down. You've got to redirect your energy and focus on what is next—either with this prospect or with another customer. 'What's next?' That has to be your mantra. There is nothing you can do about that last failed attempt. And if you focus on it, it will cloud your judgment, and you'll carry it with you to your next appointment. Instead, you've got to shake it off—and focus, with confidence, on your next appointment. That will shine through on all different levels. You want to keep focused on the next play. This is what the best performers do naturally."

So you need rituals—one for letting go of a failed attempt and another for visualizing success.

"It's the voice inside your head. The messages you give yourself. You want to have your own reaffirming remark that you say to yourself to remind you of how good you really are. Even say it out loud to yourself. You'll hear it in a completely different way. It even has to do with how you carry yourself. Our emotions respond to motion, motion creates emotion, so if you're walking slumped over with your head down, that is going to create a negative emotion. Holding your head up and throwing your arms up in the air creates a completely different set of emotions."

You have to sell yourself on how good you are—and believe it. Of course, there's a big difference between understanding and doing.

"That's where coaching becomes very real and very personal. Truly effective coaching occurs when the coach and the person they are working with connect in a very real way. Then the coach is able to help an athlete or a salesperson see something in themselves and bring about real change."

This brings us back to the question, How much can someone really change?

"Here's an exercise. Stand up, and reach as high as you can. Now try to reach just a little higher. And now just a little higher. Are you as high as you can go? Whenever I do this, most people can reach just a little higher the first and second time. That's after they started out reaching as high as they thought they could."

We can all reach a little higher.

CHAPTER 25

Learning and Development

At a recent corporate management meeting, tension was palpable. The company's president was angry, and it was clear that someone was about to catch hell.

"I don't care whether you call this training, learning, or a development program," he said to his top sales executives, "this week-long program you insisted on fell on its face—and these charts prove it."

Sales charts were flashed onto the slide screen, and the president was in no way disposed toward understatement in pointing out the source of his displeasure. Despite an extensive and costly countrywide sales learning program for which salespeople had been taken out of the field for a full week, the charts showed only a modest initial sales increase, which almost immediately fell to the original base figure.

While the sales vice president and the regional sales managers squirmed, the president noted the high costs, both direct and indirect, of the training program and demanded an explanation: "It's obvious that the training failed. Now I want to know why."

As is typical in such situations, fingers were pointed, and blame was spread somewhere between the development team and the development approach. They were likely, and easy targets. The automatic assumption, however, that the fault lies with trainers and/or the training program is simplistic and, as often as not, simply wrong. In fact, in many instances, the fault lies elsewhere—it lies with the sales trainees.

Over the years, we have discussed this problem with many top professional learning experts, and most agree that, all too often, valid development programs fail because they are expected to teach people who are simply not capable of doing the work. Most of these pros will affirm that sales development often ignores the most basic reality not only of selling but also of human personality: People cannot be taught to do what they are fundamentally not suited to do. Attempting to make someone do what he or she is not capable of doing will only result in frustration and failure.

Indisputably, every salesperson can benefit from appropriate sales development. The person who is new to selling—someone just out of college or a converted schoolteacher, customer-service representative, or technician—must be oriented to the business of selling and given insights into some of its techniques and requirements regardless of the person's inherent abilities. Experienced salespeople can benefit from more advanced learning in areas such as the development of proposals and presentation skills and closing techniques. There is a continuing need in many businesses for ongoing product training, particularly now, when rapid change is the norm, not the exception. This development can range from a basic review of product features on simple product lines to detailed, scientific instruction in advanced technological equipment. In addition, training must precede the introduction of new products into the marketplace.

There is, then, an important place for several varieties of sales training. And with the large investments that companies make to build and maintain their sales forces, there are invariably large amounts of money riding on the outcome of sales development programs.

However, when these development programs do not produce the expected results, there is a predisposition to characterize trainers and sales training programs as failures. The truth of the matter, however, is that these trainers and their training programs are often given the impossible task of turning sows' ears into silk purses.

We are convinced that development can succeed only if selection succeeds. Good raw silk must be provided before the learning department or consultants can be expected to produce a purse of the requisite quality.

Appropriate development can make the inherently successful salesperson more productive. But people devoid of sales potential— for example, rigid, opinionated, and unempathic individuals—rarely respond to training, no matter how thorough and scientifically valid the training may be. People lacking ego-drive, those who gain no personal gratification from the sales process or from closing a sale, are not likely to respond to sales development because they simply do not enjoy the process of persuading others. They may go through the motions prescribed by the instructors, but the long-term results are likely to be nil.

Another place where development often misses the mark is in not recognizing the individual differences in each of the students. Effective learning succeeds by recognizing that no two people operate in precisely the same way. The salesperson who is extremely impulsive and ego-driven needs little urging, through training or otherwise, to push for a close. His or her development more appropriately should stress the best techniques for listening and for acquiring insights into the customer's needs and point of view.

In a development class, however, the individual seated near this impulsive, driven salesperson may very well be in need of help in closing sales. He or she may be extraordinarily empathic when relating to prospective customers but somewhat too hesitant to move toward a close. The development for these two individuals obviously should have different emphases. Development that is not tailored to recognize and focus on such individual differences will, of necessity, fail one person or the other or both.

A genuinely successful development program for 25 people must take into account the individual differences of all 25 individuals. Only this approach can show each person how to operate to his or her fullest potential and in accordance with his or her own personality makeup—assuming that they all possess the potential to succeed in the first place.

While, at first, this approach might appear to be an outline for chaos in the training room, the results can be dramatic. Such a program does, however, require somewhat more careful preparation than is usual and certainly precludes the purely canned training program. With knowledge of the specific makeup of the group in terms of both experiential and personality factors, instructors can design role plays and other targeted exercises that will truly connect with each individual.

These specific learning exercises can be configured to deal with the specific strengths, concerns, and motivations of the individuals within the group. If development is to be effective, it must be geared to the individual as opposed to providing an approach that supposedly covers everyone in one fell swoop.

In addition, skilled professional instructors, whether on company staff or retained to carry out a specific development project, must acquire knowledge of the company's products, marketing approaches, and support systems. Only then can the learning be geared to the individual in terms of personal qualities, as well as to the job function that person must carry out.

If an outside development firm is to be effective, it must overcome the concern that it characteristically works across a broad spectrum of business and industry. The team instructing mutual fund sales representatives this week may be instructing salespeople from a light machinery manufacturing firm next week and software salespeople the following week. There are certain similarities among selling jobs, but problems differ so vastly from one industry to another and, in fact, from one company within an industry to another that a realistic grasp of the sales situation within the specific company by the instructor is a vital prerequisite for maximally effective learning. This grasp can best be attained by the instructors spending several days in the field with salespeople and their sales managers, experiencing the selling firsthand, experiencing sales resistance, and developing successful responses to that resistance. The best consulting firms with which we have collaborated are perfectly capable of reaching this goal.

With a prior evaluation of each person to be trained, and with a thorough, firsthand study of the field sales requirements, the group facilitating the learning is ready to put the program together and proceed. However, there remains the concern of personalizing the development for each salesperson. This can be handled by structuring a development format that allocates minimum time to lectures and maximum time to a combination of intensive individual counseling and group sessions, both small and large.

The individual evaluations are used to structure groups. Individuals possessing intense ego-drive may be put together in a group, whereas other individuals needing help with personal organization might be doing other exercises. A group might be made up of ego-driven people and individuals with less ego-drive but outstanding listening skills. In short, prior knowledge of the dynamics of the individuals in the training group allows the instructors to use the strengths and weaknesses of those individuals as a key part of the learning process. It allows for the most ideal learning situation, where the instructors will be working to train each other through participating in joint activities.

Admittedly, the overall approach to development we are describing is more difficult and requires some innovation on the part of the trainers. But it meets the three requirements we consider absolute:

1. It offers a thorough picture of each person's real abilities and personality dynamics.

2. It optimizes each person's potential.

3. It is tailored to the needs of the unique challenges and needs that the sales force encounters on a day-to-day basis.

Effective learning and development recognize that there is no single best way to sell to which all can conform. There are no perfect formulas, no magic words that apply to all salespeople equally. Development should be seen as an approach to help salespeople maximize their unique abilities in their own way. Forcing them into another mold simply does not work, and if anything, it helps to guarantee failure for a person who may have enormous natural potential.

Alyson Brandt, executive vice president, general manager Americas, for Forum, a firm that has pioneered in linking learning to strategic business objectives, paused when we asked her: "How much do you think you can actually improve someone's performance?"

Then she said, "That's the ultimate question. Because we all have our own stripes or spots, and I don't think you can dramatically change those. So, if someone is not oriented toward developing relationships, I don't know that you can, nor that you would want to, change that. But I do think you can enhance someone's people skills. I do think you can adjust their attitudes and beliefs based on example, based on story, based on helping provide context and clarity around a value that makes sense to them. So, with the perspective of attitude and behavior, I think you can help someone develop their people skills and capabilities over time."

What does it take to work?

"It has to be both active and reflective. You've got to have supporting resources in place to help continue that growth. And it has to be applied, it has to be relevant, and it's got to be continuous. Reward and recognition are also important."

But how much can someone really change, assuming that they want to—10 percent? 25 percent? 50 percent? 100 percent?

"Let me share an example that is quite close to home. My sales team was excellent at developing relationships with their current clients, but we weren't focused on cultivating new clients. So we put a year-long prospecting change process in place. First, we created a tool kit, and we put everyone through training, and we helped clarify what was expected of everyone, why it was important, and what it would do for them. Then we introduced them to skills, processes, and tools that would help them to achieve their new goals. Then we started managing to those standards and goals. And we had everyone create their own goals with us. We were very specific about what we were driving to accomplish. Then we started measuring, coaching, and rewarding based on performance. And, as an organization, we moved the needle significantly with two years of concerted effort. Did everybody achieve their goals? No. But I would say that everybody moved the needle. And in many cases it was significant. The change was different for each person, based on their motivation and their desire. The net effect was an increase in our client mix portfolio that was beyond our expectations—over 20 percent increase in new logos/clients."

How much learning goes on with a coach, how much in the classroom, and how much on the job?

"We believe that roughly 30 percent of learning should be formal—which doesn't necessarily mean it happens in a physical classroom, but means that it's structured, it's led by a facilitator or coach, and it provides a space and time for reflection on new concepts and practice of new skills. And 70 percent should be on the job—where people apply the concepts and skills, see how they work and get in-the-moment feedback and coaching. So, when we are crafting our learning solutions, we start from the premise that it can't just be an event that you invest in because that alone won't drive behavior and give you a return on your investment. It's got to have more legs. It's about having a more systemic approach. How does your manager coach and reinforce what is being taught? How might you apply this in action learning? What would success look like six months down the road? So it is really taking key concepts, then giving them a version of formal learning experience, and then using technology and services and systems to continue to reinforce the learning and drive the change so that new skills can be acquired through actual application on the job, leading to the results your desire."

Kevin Higgins, president of Fusion Learning, told us: "I believe that people can improve enormously—if they are learners and capable of changing."

What does it take to be a learner and capable of changing?

"It starts with being open. People who know it all are not open. So they will learn how to stay exactly where they are rather than change and grow. So someone has to be genuinely open, interested in learning new things about themselves and about the world, and willing to change."

What percentage of salespeople are learners and capable of changing?

"In my experience, I'd say that open to learning is a pretty high number. I'd say 70 to 80 percent of salespeople are open to learning. But then, of those, I'd say that maybe one out of two is capable of changing."

So this would leave somewhere between one-third and one-half of an average sales force that is interested in learning and capable of changing. This is a real challenge for a sales manager trying to develop the talent, skills, and potential of his or her team. And, of course, it depends on the degrees and speeds as to how quickly someone will change. Some people will take to change very quickly. They'll take it in, really get it, and then put it into play and implement it immediately. For others, it's two steps forward, one back.

Would a successful development program be one where a salesperson was able to apply one new thing the next day that had an impact on his or her performance?

"If you can't use it tomorrow, don't put it in the program. You want to be practical, absolutely. But I'd like every salesperson to come out of a developmental course with three things they could apply the next day. One would be to know how to question better. The second would be to confirm more. And the third would be to respond less. It is to develop their questioning skills, get better at listening, and not to be so enamored with the sound of their own voice. The goal is to get them to be much more self-aware, both of their strengths and of their opportunities to change. The goal is to get them to ask better questions, listen at a higher level, talk less, and to be able to self-assess their strengths and opportunities on a daily basis."

CHAPTER 26

Compensating to Achieve Results

Compensation as a sales motivator has been explored, scrutinized, pondered, and analyzed by experts countless times. No reasonably good business library fails to yield innumerable books detailing the "best methods" of sales force compensation. This embarrassment of riches turns out to be of dubious value. A sales force is composed of individual human beings with broadly varying needs, points of view, self-perceptions, and psychological characteristics who cannot be infallibly categorized, measured, and punched out according to a set formula. It therefore follows that there is no one best plan for compensating all of them.

It is safe to make only one generalization about compensation: The program that motivates best or, perhaps even better put, that does not serve to demotivate is one that is geared to the specific needs of each person.

For example, a highly ego-driven salesperson with inordinate self-confidence is likely to be most acutely motivated by a compensation system based on incentives, that is, one that offers little base in the form of draw or salary but has a steeply graduated top end. This individual would be demotivated and frustrated by a program limiting top-end potential, even if it provided for more security.

On the other hand, such a commission-oriented program would be inappropriate (and, in fact, may have a reverse motivational effect) for a person with less confidence and ego-drive. In all probability, he or she would respond more positively to the higher draw or salary base that his or her associate might find unappealing.

Obviously, one compensation plan cannot have equal motivational effects on both these individuals. So why not introduce a flexible plan that provides both individuals with the kind of compensation to which each will respond best? Clearly, many firms, particularly smaller firms, cannot, as a practical matter, have a number of compensation plans—a different one for each salesperson. Yet, even in these situations, some creativity and imagination could result in subtle differences within basically similar plans to produce a positive impact on individuals. A number of our clients, including some relatively small companies, have prepared three or four plans. They sat down and worked with individual salespeople to select the plan with which the salespeople were most comfortable. In a small company, where people tend to know each other's business, there is the danger of jealousy when an individual under one compensation plan outearns someone working under a different plan. However, if an open discussion were held and the individual voluntarily chose his or her plan with all the facts (including the earnings potential and the security) laid out, such jealousy would be less likely to occur.

Edilson Lopes, founder of KLA Business Education, underscores this, saying: "One of the most important assets for an effective sales manager is to thoroughly understand the motivations, drives, strengths, limitations, and potential of each of the salespeople he or she is working with. It is vital to truly understand what makes each them tick—and to work with them individually."

Edilson goes on to tell us that he would even create individual incentive plans that are distinct for average performers and top performers. "Most organizations create a really great top prize," he told us, "that they, and everyone else in the organization, know is only likely to be attained by a select few individuals. So the top performers are motivated by that top prize, perhaps being in the President's Club or receiving a dream vacation, but most of the salespeople don't view it as attainable. So they don't perform any differently. Instead, we would recommend creating a plan where if they produced by 5 percent more than they did last year, there would be a significant bonus for them. That becomes achievable—and rewarding for them and the organization. The average performers might not reach the top 20 percent overnight, but they will come closer. And that is good for everyone. That way, their coaching, training, development, and incentives are based on them raising their standards. It is a way to improve their performance and the organization's."

What we are suggesting here, just as we did in our discussion on training, is a far more difficult approach to implement. It is certainly easier to set up one unified compensation plan that covers the entire sales force, whether a company develops a compensation program itself or brings in outside experts to help. Yet, as tempting as taking this easier road may be, thought should be given to how much is invested in the sales force and how critical maximum sales productivity is to the success of the company. Thus, if—with a little more effort and a little more creativity—compensation plans can be created to help maximize the productivity of each salesperson, isn't that extra work well worth it? A compensation plan that speaks to each individual's motivations not only will enhance productivity but also can play an important role in substantially increasing the retention of the most productive salespeople.

Another aspect of compensation that should be touched on is the fact that salespeople, regardless of their personality dynamics, are not totally immune to the lure of the "golden handcuffs." An attractive pension and retirement package, profit-sharing program, and frequent bonuses help to develop identification with the company, a feeling within the salespeople that they are in fact part of a team. We have found that the more an individual feels a sense of participation in the overall success of the firm, the more he or she will be motivated to contribute to that success. This applies to the full range of sales personalities. Security-oriented individuals like bonuses and profit-sharing potential because they can get side benefits without having to run the risks inherent in straight-commission sales. To commission-oriented salespeople, bonuses and profit sharing provide more opportunities to share in the big money and, in addition, enable them to feel that they are working for themselves, which is often the real desire of hard-driving salespeople.

Before completing our discussion of compensation, we want to stress this point: As important as money is, and as potentially valuable or inhibiting as a compensation plan can be, the key to sales success still remains whether the individual possesses the basic dynamics or motivations and whether he or she has the other requirements necessary to sell successfully in a specific sales job. It is that inner motivation that drives the salesperson to the next prospect and propels him or her out the door the next morning. Money helps the successful salesperson to keep score. Like a medal in the military, a trip to Hawaii, a pat on the back, or number one ranking on the sales chart—money is a symbol of success. But it is the inner motivation, the desire to get the "Yes," and the emotional gratification that closing brings that constitute the force behind the real salesperson's performance.

Obviously, no one can live on emotional gratification alone, but as we have suggested here, it is critical that the financial rewards be tied closely with the kind of emotional gratification the individual requires.

In concluding this discussion of training and compensation, it is important to reemphasize the fundamental point that the key to an individual's sales success is the attributes and motivations that exist within the individual. Training will fail if it is not geared toward helping a person to play to his or her unique strengths and overcome specific weaknesses. In the same way, compensation will fail if it does not enhance each person's unique attributes. Only with this kind of individualized approach can training and compensation achieve what they are designed to do—enhance, rather than inhibit, performance.

CHAPTER 27

What Team Building Really Means

One of the main things that you want to do with your top salespeople is to keep them engaged and motivated. As we've said, this has to do with understanding what drives each of your top salespeople—what really motivates them. But how do you keep an entire team of salespeople engaged and motivated? Building a top sales team will enable your company to exceed expectations. Whether your company is large or small, success often depends on forming a cohesive group out of people who, in other situations, might not even get along, let alone work together toward the same goal. This is the fundamental challenge of team building.

Basically, success in team building is measured in two ways: by keeping conflicts down and performance up. Building a winning sales team can be challenging because many salespeople relish the independence that their job brings them and may resist working in a team environment. When it comes time to hold quarterly sales meetings, some salespeople might look for reasons to avoid spending time together. "I'm sorry, I have a call with a client who I'm just about to close. Can I come by next time?" Or "I have a meeting set up in the next town over that I can't reschedule. Rain check?"

However, in reality, a sales team has to collaborate and work well together if it's going to achieve a common goal despite the independence associated with a job in sales. Ask anyone who works on a sales team if they trust the others on their team, and they will probably say yes. However, if you probe a little, you may get a yes, but only in certain situations. So what exactly is team building? Most people think of team building as a one-time event that usually involves the entire team going on a retreat, perhaps rock climbing or doing some other group activity. Many people also think of teams practicing trust falls and engaging in some bonding experiences.

The truth is, though, that team building is not a one-time solution. Rather, it's an ongoing, evolving process. While a meaningful team-building program can be challenging, the results are extremely rewarding, including strengthened relationships and improved performance. Meaningful team building is never easy. But knowing that more productive relationships will be the result makes it well worth the time and effort. As the people involved get to know themselves and the others on the team better, they often make some interesting discoveries. On an all-star team, for example, every individual may be a star player in his or her own right, but they still may not know how to work together toward a common goal.

And what are the downsides of not having a strong sales team? Well, first, chances are that team members will all fail to recognize and benefit from one another's skills and experiences. Newer salespeople might be reluctant to ask for assistance, or more seasoned employees might hesitate to provide constructive feedback. And even more damaging, they could jump to conclusions about the intentions or aptitudes of others, thereby wasting more time and energy than are needed on what their colleagues are doing or saying.

But where do you start? First, it is crucial to begin establishing open lines of communication and building trust. And this starts with understanding your team. We use surveys, interviews, and our in-depth personality assessment to gain a deeper understanding of all the individuals involved, including the sales manager. Those tools allow our consultants to work with the sales manager and each member of the team to fully understand the team environment and identify each individual's strengths and developmental opportunities. From there, our consultants are able to provide objective information about the interactive dynamics among individuals on the team.

The second step to developing a strong team is giving each team member the chance to get to know the people around him or her.

Another major advantage of using an in-depth personality assessment is that everyone gets to know everyone else from the same vantage point. Knowing the strengths and limitations of each individual allows everyone to connect with each other in a real and meaningful way and to work together at a much higher level.

Each person then will know what he or she needs to do to support the whole team, as well as what abilities he or she has that others may not. In addition, each person will be aware of the areas in which he or she struggles and see how other team members can help him or her. Team members soon may begin to think, "Now that I know my colleagues better, what can I do to help them when we work together and in what ways can they help me?"

Curt Nelson, founder of the Entrepreneurial Development Center, told of how "one of the best things he ever did from a team-building perspective" was to bring his executive team together and have a consultant share insights from each individual's in-depth personality profiles and help them each to understand how they were working together and could improve as a team.

He told us: "A consultant took one profile at a time and projected it on a screen. Then she described the individual, but no one knew who she was describing. We all had to guess who it was based on her description. And as she described each individual and we realized who they were, we came to know them, and each other, with a real depth of understanding. It was extremely meaningful. We understood what made each of us tick, the qualities and motivations that made us all unique. And it gave everybody in the room a completely different perspective about each other and about ourselves."

Can you give us an example?

"One of the individuals on my team is extremely bright. Your consultant talked about his unique ability to solve problems and to see things from a different perspective. But then she added, 'I'll bet sometimes he seems extremely cooperative and willing to help and other times he can seem a little distance and preoccupied. For instance, if you need him for a meeting right now, perhaps there is a customer problem, and he may not be very responsive. But I'll bet if you tell him you'd like to have him in a meeting tomorrow and describe to him the situation that needs to be solved, he is always accommodating and can add meaningful insights to the discussion.' And everybody was like, 'Yeah, so why not today?' And she said it was because he has a need to be right 100 percent of the time. So he does not want to put himself in a position that he cannot prepare for. Then she asked, 'Has he ever been wrong when you have him in a meeting he has prepared for?' And everyone said, no. 'Well, then, there you go. So if you want the best of him, you need to give him time to prep. He wants to be accommodating; he just doesn't want to let you down.' And that changed everybody's feelings about him. Then she went through all of us in the same way. And afterwards, everyone in the group got so much better than they had before. There was a sense of understanding and openness and appreciation for who we were, as individuals and as a team, and a renewed realization that we were all in it together."

TEAM BUILDING IS ONGOING

The last step is to keep the process going—realize that it's an ongoing process. The goal is to organize team assignments in such a way that everyone's strengths are capitalized on, and everyone's limitations are minimized. When the entire team operates from this balanced perspective, you won't be trying to reinvent or change anybody, to turn someone into something that they are not, or to force people to do things that run counter to who they really are. Instead, by operating from a base of mutual respect, team members can ask meaningful questions to learn more about each other rather than make unfounded assumptions and misjudge one another.

In short, everyone is reassured that it is okay to be who they are, but now they have this shared knowledge and the teamwork tools to work together much more effectively. Maximizing a team's success stems from being able to coach new salespeople on the selling environment.

Tim Barr, director of cloud sales at iDashboards, told us that top performers express a contagious combination of optimism and self-assurance. And those are qualities you want to make sure are evident throughout your organization. Part of establishing an effective team is to create an environment where the best are able to share what they've learned along the way. Success stories breed success stories. "Top performers, in my experience, have all those qualities, and they just come in every day and take care of business with an even nature," Tim shared. "When they close a big deal, they celebrate. But then it's back to finding some more business. And they do that consistently, over and over and over again. In fact, I've heard some of our seasoned top performers say to a new, young salesperson who has just landed a big deal, 'That's great. Way to go. Take it in. Then get back on the phone because now is the time to call. Are you ever going to be more excited than you are right now? And you know what? Your customers are going to understand that. They're going to hear that in your voice. So get on the phone and go find another one because now is your time.' So there absolutely is that feeling that when you close the big one, it's time to go get another one."

This is a great lesson. And one of the most important responsibilities of a sales manager is to create an environment where your team is able and willing to share. This is team building at its best—a supportive, engaging, collaborative environment that generates enthusiasm for both seasoned sales veterans and new employees alike. By tapping into each individual's motivators and personality, the sales team ultimately can work together in a more cohesive way. The common goal is clear: more business, more client engagements, and more revenue. And for the motivated, driven salesperson, this means more recognition, more rewards, and more money. Team building can help to facilitate this. Communicating the benefits of team building can help your hard-driving salespeople to feel more willing to join those quarterly meetings and exchange information with their colleagues.

Once a sales team knows each other's strengths and how they play out, it helps to create an environment of openness, collaboration, and trust.

PART 6

THE SALES MANAGER

Making sure that goals are met, salespeople stay motivated, talents are developed, the best applicants are hired, and clients remain engaged, as well as preparing for the future, constitute quite a juggling act. It takes a special mix of talents and personal qualities. This is what sales managers do.

You might think that the best salespeople would automatically make the best sales managers. Sometimes they do, but more often, this is not the case. All too often the very qualities that enable someone to excel as a salesperson can cause him or her to be an ineffective sales manager.

In this part, we'll explore the underlying differences between what drives someone to be effective in sales and what motivates someone else to manage effectively. We'll also explore the difference between managing and leading, which can mean the difference between winning and losing in cutthroat markets. Pure managers make the system work. Leaders make things happen. And in the process, leaders make the people around them better.

CHAPTER 28

Why the Best Salespeople Often Don't Become Great Managers

U p to this point, we have been focusing on how to hire and develop your next top sales performer. Before we close, we want to spend just a little bit of time talking about the psychology of sales managers: what makes them tick, what separates the best from the rest, and why you don't necessarily want to promote your top salesperson into your next sales management position.

To promote the star salesperson to a managerial position often induces a classic application of The Peter Principle. This practice seems, on reflection, to be almost purposefully self-defeating because it removes that rare breed, the top sales producer, from the opportunity of continuing to produce sales and places this person in a job for which his or her competence may be, at best, questionable. Yet this practice would appear to be the rule rather than the exception. In fact, it is almost institutionalized by some company recruiters, who promise young people that a beginning in sales is the sure and usually the straightest road to a managerial career.

The philosophy underlying this strange practice is that if a person can sell successfully, he or she can manage salespeople with equal success. On its face, the assumption can be recognized as patently wrong. Certainly, some salespeople can manage, and some managers can sell. But the psychological realities strongly favor less than desirable results when the roles are indiscriminately interchanged.

Most frequently, executives live to regret the promotion of their top salesperson into a management position. The first and most obvious result is the loss of an outstanding salesperson and the gain of a mediocre, or worse, manager. The misfortune is compounded by a secondary consequence: The former salesperson who fails as a manager often will not, indeed cannot, go back to the sales force of the same company because this is a tacit admission of failure to his or her associates. This person will be more inclined to leave the company, sometimes taking a sales job with one of the competitors, and then he or she will have an even renewed reason to tap into his or her inner sales abilities, which will cause you even more harm as he or she woos away your clients.

This problem will come as no surprise to many experienced managers. In fact, when discussing it, they almost invariably tell us that they know the automatic promotion of top salespeople to managerial responsibilities is an unwise policy. More often than not, though, they follow this acknowledgment with a shrug and an admission of bafflement: "Where else can we find sales managers?" or "Our people want to be promoted or rewarded, in some way, for good and faithful performance. What else can we give them?"

No matter how genuine their frustrations, such solutions are short-lived.

But there is a rational approach that can lead to a permanent solution: By all means reward your best salespeople in the most imaginative and suitable ways. But promote to management only individuals who have the ability to manage.

While successful people strive to grow in their careers, it must be kept in mind that not all salespeople are cut out to be sales managers. In fact, the characteristics of the best salespeople are often in conflict with the tasks required of sales and operational managers.

Salespeople like to persuade, and they enjoy the win and derive great satisfaction from being the "one who makes it happen." And they can use those abilities to try to convince you that they truly want to be a sales manager. However, once a successful salesperson beats out the competition and persuades the organization that he or she is the best candidate to become sales manager, this individual often finds out that the nature of the sales management role is not what he or she thought it would be. In fact, in order to succeed in management, most salespeople would have to turn themselves inside out. It's like our parents told us so many times: Be careful what you wish for—you may get it!

A BALANCING ACT

Leader, mentor, trainer, taskmaster, coach, monitor, liaison, administrator, babysitter, disciplinarian, organizer, herder of cats. When performed well, the sales manager's role is the force that keeps salespeople on course. It is the sales manager who cultivates, monitors, and protects the precious revenue streams on which every business depends. Often the key communication pipeline between field operations and internal operations, the sales manager plays a critical role in the selection, development, coordination, and productivity of the people who, in turn, generate the revenue lifeblood of the business.

Clearly, the sales manager's role is critical. However, as noted earlier, while the sales manager's role is the obvious next step up the proverbial corporate ladder, not every successful salesperson is cut out to climb the rung.

It would be a significant understatement to say that salespeople can be difficult to manage. Just ask any person who has held the role. By their very nature, salespeople tend to be demanding and impatient and have little tolerance for routine details. "Expense report? Sure, I'll get it to you next Tuesday!" "Lead documentation? No problem. I'll do it over the weekend." "New-product training? I've got this great appointment . . . maybe next week." "You want my calendar and call plan for the next month? Are you kidding?"

The sales manager's role requires organization and discipline, a high level of patience, the ability and willingness to delegate, and the capability of deriving satisfaction from seeing someone else win. When you say it out loud, it becomes obvious that these qualities are actually the opposite of an ideal salesperson's qualities.

Consider this: Very few star athletes are able to become coaches or general managers. While some are able to develop the technical skills, few have the temperament to subordinate their own desire to "make the shot" or "score the point." Some do succeed in making the transition. However, the star performer who can't give up the satisfaction that comes from scoring the winning point runs the risk of being in competition with the very people he or she must coach, mentor, monitor, discipline, and develop. It is this conflict of motivational interests that can inhibit a very successful salesperson from becoming a star at the management level.

THE DIFFERENCES

There is considerable evidence that argues that sales and managerial abilities are actually quite different. In essence, the personality dynamics that make a top salesperson successful and those that make a manager excellent are frequently in unremitting conflict.

Over the years, we have had the opportunity to study and evaluate the underlying personality characteristics of thousands of salespeople and managers. In looking at traditional hunter salesperson dynamics compared with those of top-rated managers, a number of key differences come to the surface in study after study.

Most recently, we completed a cross-industry study that contrasted the personality profiles of 629 top-producing sales hunters with the profiles of 1,470 top-performing sales managers who were working for 267 companies located throughout the United States, Great Britain, Canada, Brazil, Mexico, and Japan. In general, our findings clearly confirm that successful salespeople exhibit fundamentally different personality profiles and characteristics than successful managers.

More specifically, as can be seen from the graph in Figure 28-1, the successful sales hunters we profiled scored significantly higher on measures of

- *Ego-drive*—the motivation to persuade
- *Assertiveness*—the inclination to be proactive and forceful in expressing ideas
- *Urgency*—the need to get things done
- *Risk-taking*—the willingness to consider and take chances

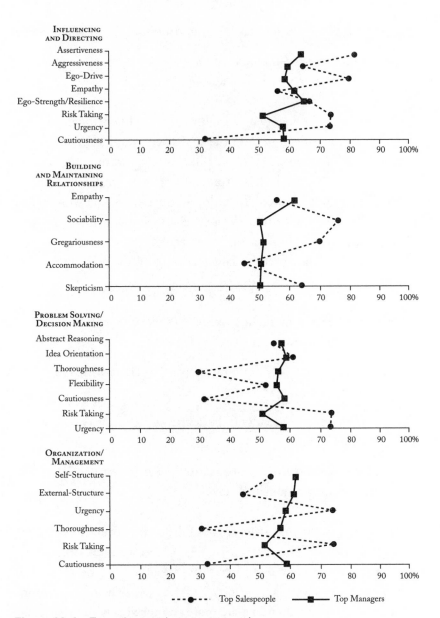

Figure 28-1 Top salespeople versus top sales managers.

- *Sociability*—the desire to be around and work with other people

  Gregariousness—the inclination and confidence to network and proactively establish new relationships

By and large, the salespeople in our study are likely to derive considerably more gratification from the act of persuading others than are the managers. They are also more inclined to be proactive and forceful in expressing their ideas, have a strong need to get things done, and are more willing to take chances. In addition, the salespeople will tend to be naturals at meeting and developing relationships with new people. The top-performing sales managers, on the other hand, while having more moderate profiles on the characteristics just noted, exhibited significantly higher scores on

- *Cautiousness*—an inclination toward due diligence and "looking before you leap"

- *Thoroughness*—an orientation toward working with and managing details

- *Self-structure*—a tendency to define priorities and exercise self-discipline

- *External structure*—an orientation toward working within and maintaining established rules

Quite simply, the managers are built differently from the top-performing salespeople. They are more likely to have a natural orientation toward structure and details and do not have as strong a need to score every point themselves. As a result, the best sales managers are more able to work through others and are more comfortable with delegating, coordinating, organizing, coaching, and monitoring aspects of the role.

TO PROMOTE OR NOT TO PROMOTE?

Still, the question arises: To promote or not to promote? On many occasions, exasperated managers have told us that a sales management spot has just become open in the company and that several top salespeople are not very bashfully yearning for it. Our advice is unvarying: Give your best salesperson anything that is feasible—a big private office with a thick rug and a huge desk, medals with oak-leaf clusters, increased commissions, the opportunity to mentor, dinners in their honor—anything to show the degree to which their performance is valued and appreciated. But under no circumstances make him or her sales manager without being certain that he or she has the proper dynamics to manage.

What are some other options? Jim Dickie, managing partner at CSO Insights, told us about one salesperson who was pushing to be a manager. It was clear to the leadership of the company that this individual really didn't want to be a manager. He had just reached a crossroads in his life, where he was asking, "Is that all there is?" He was a top producer who was looking for recognition, for a nod, for a message that his career was on the right track and moving forward. Therefore, the leadership of the company provided this top-producing salesperson with his own administrative assistant. It made him feel special, which is what he was looking for. And the assistant has helped him become even more productive, more than making up for the additional salary. "It keeps my top producer going" is what the manager told us.

We've worked with other sales leaders who have created mentorships for their top performers, enabling them to share their expertise and knowledge with new salespeople but not taking the veterans away from what makes them so successful.

At Virgin Media, Andrew Marshall, the former sales director, told us that the company created what he calls "The Journey of a Salesperson." Someone could start out there with an entry-level position, just out of university, and, depending on his or her potential and performance, move through telemarketing teams into the corporate sales force, which has four different levels, culminating in a strategic account manager position. Our managers are very focused on working with individuals on their learning and development plan and helping them achieve their objectives so that they can continue to move forward on their career path. At the end of the journey, a senior-level salesperson will be perceived as just as successful as a salesperson who went along a management route," he told us.

It may be difficult to make salespeople understand that, in the long run, neither they nor you will benefit by the wrong promotional move. Although difficult, the attempt must be made.

The underlying problems seem to be rooted in salespeople's perception of the managerial role. First, they frequently feel that greater status is attached to managing than to selling. The salesperson in the field often perceives the manager as the person who "has it made"; the manager has his or her name and title on the door to the big office, is under less pressure to produce, and is judged only on the basis of others' performance.

What salespeople need to recognize is the importance of their profession. Through their individual contributions, they are absolutely pivotal to the growth of their organizations. Yet many top-performing salespeople don't feel this way. If we could just wave a magic wand and make it happen, we would elevate the status of sales as a profession to the level it rightly deserves. The best salespeople, after all, are well compensated. In fact, of all the people in business earning over $100,000 a year, more than half are salespeople. Sales also offers unusual opportunities for fulfillment and nonmaterial personal gain, including maximum opportunity for freedom to do a job in one's own way.

Therefore, our strong advice would be for salespeople to carefully avoid managerial jobs *unless* they are convinced that their best talents and greatest opportunities for gratification lie in managing.

Admittedly, these are not easy points to sell a salesperson who hungers after the prestige and ease that he or she thinks comes with a managerial position.

Paul Knee, managing director at Verathon, a United Kingdom–based, global company producing ultrasound diagnostic equipment, told us how he slowly groomed a top-performing salesperson for a management position.

"After one of our very successful salespeople had been here a year, he approached me about being a manager. He had just taken a brand-new product from zero into a really strong market position. So, with that success in his back pocket, he told me that he wanted to show other people how to do what he was doing and to grow with the company as a manager. I liked the idea that he had the initiative to come to me and that he had ambitions. So I told him that I believed in him and thought that he had the potential to manage but that he would have to spend more time with me, exploring the possibility, and that he would have to trust me. We talked a lot about trust. I assured him that his career was important to me and that I wanted to help develop his career. But I wasn't going to just drop him into a management spot because it is different. Very different. And I had to be sure—for him and for the organization—that he was ready."

So how did he proceed?

"Over the course of the next year, I spent a lot of extra time with him. At first, we talked about the difference between becoming a salesperson, where you're totally responsible for your own revenue and everything is down to you, and becoming a manager, where you've got to coach salespeople to manage their customers. It is a massive shift. Your will have to relinquish the day-to-day customer contact. My expectation is that you will teach our salespeople how to become better. And you're going to earn your revenue through the ability of those salespeople to improve."

How was the salesperson responding to this?

"He was saying that nobody could sell better than him, so it was only natural that he could show others how to do it. And I explained to him that because he loved selling so much, giving up the constant customer contact was going to be hard for him. And, equally important, he was going to have to learn that everyone else was not going to learn to sell his way. They all had different strengths, motivations, and potential—and he was going to have to learn how to tap into each of those for each person on his team."

How long did these conversations go on?

"Over the course of a year, we talked about what stepping into management would mean. Then a position opened. But I told him I was not just going to give him the position. I said that we were going to look externally as well and that he would have to compete for the position on that basis. And he said that I could bring in whoever I liked, that he was still going to get the job. So we did a full interview process with him and the other final candidates, reviewed their personality profiles, and weighed all their strengths and limitations. And he was competing with three people who already had management experience.

We had a team of executives making the decision. And he won, hands-down. It was a unanimous decision. I couldn't offer the job to anyone else. I had to give it to him. And he is succeeding very well. His enthusiasm is contagious—with his team and with the other sales managers."

In this case, moving a top-performing salesperson into management worked because the process was gradual, the mentoring was targeted, and the individual had the qualities needed to succeed.

Paulo Nascentes, vice president of Tigre Brazil, told us that because it is so difficult to identify whether a salesperson has what it takes to succeed as a manager, his company has developed a formalized methodology that includes identifying whether someone has the right personality profile, placing that individual in a management development program, and then, afterwards, having five executives on a committee all agree on whether the individual is ready for a promotion. "Because the chances of failure are so large and the impact can be enormous, we have become very careful about deciding who moves into a management position," he told us. Before starting this formalized process, the company had one too many experiences where a salesperson was promoted to management, didn't do well, and then left to continue his or her sales career with one of their competitors. "That can be a double-edged problem," Paulo underscores. "You lose a top-performing salesperson. *And* he or she goes to work for a competitor, against you. We developed our very formalized approach to deciding who would move into a management position, and then we prepare them for success to make sure that we never lost a top-performing salesperson to a competitor again."

Amy Addison, internal sales director at John Hancock, shared with us the stories of two salespeople she promoted to management positions who completely surprised her. "The one guy had a very laid-back style as a salesperson. He was very accommodating, and if there was a problem, he would be the one to reassure everyone that we would work through it. So I was completely taken by surprise when he became a manager and started coming across to his team as very heavy-handed."

It was like a Jekyl and Hyde?

"Exactly. He took on a very aggressive tone with his team, telling them to step it up or you may have to find new jobs. What he was trying to do was motivate them to do better, but, in fact, he quickly 'demotivated' them."

So how did you handle the situation?

"I spoke with him about it. Then, when his 360-degree results came back and he received the feedback, he became much more receptive to improving the situation, which he did."

And how did the other salesperson promoted into a management position surprise you?

"She was almost the opposite story. As a salesperson, she was perceived by others in the department as very abrasive. When I announced that she would be a manager, some of the others were very hesitant about being on her team. They actually came to me and said that they'd prefer to be on the other team. But she quickly surprised them. She became very effective in her management role. I believe that because she started with the right qualities and she really wanted to be successful, she was very open to feedback from me and her direct reports. So she could make the appropriate adjustments to her management style."

Here are a few things we recommend you tell a top-performing salesperson who, you suspect, wants the title of sales manager but doesn't really want the responsibilities. Make sure that he or she is prepared to

- Sublimate his or her own ego. Let the people under him or her get the glory.

- Learn how to handle detail, for there will be lots of it, including, in addition to his or her own reports and administrative record keeping, all the sales reports and expense vouchers of every salesperson in the territory.

- Organize his or her own activities and those of the sales staff.

- Induce the staff to act without forcing compliance, an exercise that requires infinite quantities of patience (a characteristic not notably abundant in top salespeople).

- Make decisions of a more far-reaching nature than those which affect a single sale; this requires that he or she gather and evaluate all pertinent information and consider the consequences of his or her decisions.

- Plan and analyze—for countless hours—prospect lists, advertising programs, and marketing plans instead of dealing with people.

- Figure on attending frequent meetings, listening to the problems and complaints of the salespeople, and justifying their performance—and his or her own—to supervisors.

- Handle such personnel chores as firing people he or she likes or recommending that they be fired.

- Function as a liaison between the needs of each salesperson and the company.

These are only a few in a long catalogue of sales manager responsibilities and tasks that can be anathema to a top-performing salesperson.

Another cautionary note that salespeople seeking a management position certainly would want to consider comes from Gerhard Gschwandtner, CEO of Selling Power. He told us, "The average tenure of a sales leader is 22 to 24 months. So, just consider: When you are put into a new sales management position, it can take you about nine months before you realize what is truly going on in your sales organization. You need to assess the people, the processes, the politics of the organization, the market conditions, the competitive situations, and where your firm is with technology. Before you can modify and optimize, you have to assess. And often by the time a sales manager has just started to implement his or her optimization process, two years have gone by—and if you haven't shown the right results, you are out the door."

Peter Byloos, chief executive officer of Handicare, a leading provider of aids for the elderly and physically disabled, has an interesting test that he always keeps in the back of his mind when it comes to promoting someone to a management position. He told us, "To switch from selling yourself to developing others is not an easy one. To move to management, a salesperson has to be motivated to identify talent in others, be keenly interested in developing that talent, identify where the team is going, and track how fast progress is being made. These management skills have very little to do with selling. So the one component I always try to assess is whether a potential manager has enough emotional talent. This is where success will come. One of the questions I always ask myself is, would I want to work for that person? If I'm hesitant, that tells me a lot."

THOSE WHO CAN

Okay, so most top-selling salespeople may not be cut out to be sales managers. Fair enough. But what about those who are? There are many potentially excellent managers who are now engaged in selling. So executives looking for a sales manager would be foolish to overlook the possibility that the right person for the job is already on the sales force.

We believe that every salesperson should be studied as a potential manager, virtually from the day the person is hired. The reasons are obvious: If the manager is promoted from the sales ranks, that person will begin his or her first managerial day with comprehensive knowledge of the company's products, clientele, sales force, sales problems, politics, and policies. The benefits of promoting qualified people to managerial responsibilities are so clear, in fact, that we have for many years evaluated and reported the managerial potential of all salespeople we have assessed.

Tom Gartland, president, North America of Avis Budget Group, has assessed the personality dynamics of every one of his 600-plus salespeople. "When we understand the potential and aspirations of a salesperson we have just hired, then we can work with him or her to make sure that they have a career map that fulfills their goals and ours. It might be to higher-level selling positions. Or, if someone demonstrates leadership capability, we can create a different career path that zigs and zags in and out of management and higher-level selling skills. So we will eventually have a population of people who could fit in my previous role as the executive vice president of sales."

The fact that there are so many salespeople who cannot manage does not invalidate the fact that there are many who can. Danger lies only in the belief that competence displayed in one area can be assumed to indicate competence in all other areas.

We have actually found far more people in the middle of a sales force who have turned out to be well-qualified managers than we have found at the very top. Again, as we noted in our research, those in the middle have tended to have somewhat less ego-drive and so are able to tolerate delegation better than their more strongly driven, perhaps more productive, sales colleagues. Also, a person with less ego-drive tends to have better tolerance of planning and follow-through and a more balanced ability to make decisions and to handle work in a more organized way. Again, this should not be thought of as an absolute because certainly there are top-performing salespeople who have gone on to become outstanding managers. The point, again, is that when you are looking for a salesperson, you are looking for sales dynamics (empathy, ego-drive, ego-strength, assertiveness, urgency, etc.), whereas when you are looking for a sales manager, you are searching for leadership ability, including the abilities to delegate, to make good management decisions, to handle detail, and to coordinate and follow up on the work of others.

If all these qualities happen to be combined in the same individual, that makes for the best of all worlds. If such a combination does not exist, however, be certain that the management dynamics are present regardless of outstanding sales performance.

As in so much that we have written about in this book, the critical element here is matching the dynamics of a particular individual to the dynamics required by a particular job. It is only through matching relevant dynamics that you are likely to fill the job successfully.

So, before concluding this chapter, let's explore in more depth the qualities an individual needs to succeed in the sales management role. A number of these qualities overlap attributes that are required to succeed in certain sales situations. To succeed as a sales manager, the possession of most of these qualities is essential.

Among extremely effective executives we have worked with, there are flamboyant extroverts as well as those who are painfully shy. While some stick to the straight and narrow, others give eccentricity a new meaning. Some are self-centered, while others are generous to a fault.

For every manager who suffers over decisions, there is one who seems to make decisions with great ease and aplomb. Some have broad interests, while others know nothing except their own area of expertise.

DEFINING THE MANAGEMENT ROLE

To be effective, managers have to sense opportunities, formulate new possibilities, build coalitions with peers, and convince those in positions of higher authority that their proposed solutions will help to achieve corporate goals.

Using interviews and reviews of various task and competency surveys, 360-degree tools, our in-depth personality assessments, and reviews of the general literature, we have concluded that leadership and management tasks can be divided into four dominant themes:

- Influencing and directing

- Building and maintaining relationships

- Problem solving and decision making

- Personal organization and time management

INFLUENCING AND DIRECTING

In order for any manager to be successful, he or she must be adept at influencing and directing the actions of others. Walt Disney's former CEO, Michael Eisner, believes that having a strong point of view is one of the most critical elements needed to be successful in management. He says, "Around here, a strong point of view is worth at least 80 IQ points."

Effective managers or leaders must be capable of assertively presenting their goals and ideas in a confident and straightforward manner without damaging the confidence or self-esteem of their audience. They must have the drive and empathy to be persuasive when necessary and able to provide clear direction, expectations, and feedback. The management role requires the ability to delegate and follow through without taking over or abdicating, which can be a tough trick for a highly ego-driven salesperson who is addicted to closing and has limited patience for people who might inhibit movement toward a sought-after goal or objective. Top managers need to be effective in negotiating "win-win" outcomes. And most important, they need to be capable of subordinating their own ego gratification to become masters at playing the role of coach and mentor. More simply put, they must change their frame of reference from "I" to "we" and derive satisfaction from a broader victory attained through others.

BUILDING AND MAINTAINING RELATIONSHIPS

The second theme shared by all top managers is the ability to build and maintain relationships. At the end of the day, this is the one area where salespeople and managers have the most in common. Sales and management roles are all people jobs. They require well-honed interpersonal skills, as well as the ability to maintain credibility and engender trust. The very best salespeople, managers, and leaders have the empathy necessary to relate to others. They are naturals at listening and understanding subtle cues and responses that other people provide. Effective communicators, these managers, salespeople, and leaders are able to adjust or modify their messages and styles of presentation to meet the needs and expectations of their audience while at the same time accomplishing their own mission. In addition, top-level managers, like top-level salespeople, have the confidence and assertiveness to express themselves, and sufficient outgoingness and sociability to network and initiate relationships. They genuinely like being around people. They don't wait for people to come to them. Rather, they are proactive in establishing rapport and in providing the warmth necessary to initiate and maintain ongoing working relationships. The best managers and leaders also have the capability of establishing and coordinating team efforts and building consensus. Thus they are able to create cooperative working environments in which everyone has the opportunity to be successful.

In general, the best managers, like the best salespeople, enjoy working with people and are very good at it.

PROBLEM SOLVING AND DECISION MAKING

The third dominant theme is problem solving and decision making. All management and leadership roles begin with the recognition of a need, opportunity, or problem. The most effective managers are able to spot trends, evaluate alternatives, and make decisions. They are able to synthesize and analyze vast amounts of information about performance, the competition, the marketplace, and company resources in a manner that balances the business's immediate needs with those of the future. They recognize problems and issues; analyze root causes; evaluate and consider alternatives; develop goals, strategies, and tactics; and most important, make decisions.

Top-performing managers and leaders have a high level of abstract problem-solving capability. They are open-minded and flexible in their thinking, and they balance the need to be careful and thorough with the ability to "pull the trigger." They are not afraid of risking the occasional wrong decision because they are confident in their ability to recover and move forward. The best managers and leaders have the courage to take action and the ability to learn from their mistakes.

The effective sales manager, in particular, is likely to be a careful diagnostician who has the ability to monitor and evaluate performance trends and define tactics for engineering improved results for both the individual and the business. Such analysis requires the patience and thoroughness to sift through data and the conscientiousness to plan a strategy while at the same time maintaining a sense of urgency about moving forward. Most salespeople are great on the urgency but fall short on the due diligence. Keep in mind that both are necessary.

PERSONAL ORGANIZATION AND TIME MANAGEMENT

And the fourth and final dominant theme is personal organization and time management, which are essential to managing effectively. The best managers are adept at setting and juggling goals, objectives, and priorities. Working within established rules, systems, and procedures, top managers must define key tasks, establish and/or implement measurement criteria for tracking results, assign priorities and resources, and follow through to ensure timely and accurate completion of assignments. It is the consistency of sticking to a defined set of tasks and a well-managed agenda that results in expectations attained.

Staying focused, managing interruptions and distractions, persisting, making adjustments to an established plan in a timely manner, and using time efficiently—these are the hallmarks of managerial performance. The most effective managers have a high level of discipline, a thorough style of working with details, and in addition, a strong sense of urgency. They do not focus on details for details' sake. Rather, they are achievement-minded and have the flexibility and confidence to make decisions or shift the agenda to respond to developing needs. Moreover, they have the focus necessary to balance near-term objectives with long-term goals.

UNIQUE COMBINATION

In essence, while managers approach their work with varying styles and methodologies, we have found that certain basic characteristics are needed to manage effectively regardless of the situation. To be effective, a manager must be able to analyze situations, be willing to make decisions and take risks, be able to communicate effectively, be capable of commanding respect from others, be able to delegate and motivate, be consistent and fair, and be willing to encourage growth in others as well as oneself.

Rather than trying to fit into a prescribed mold, the best managers with whom we have worked are those who thoroughly understand their inherent strengths and limitations. Then they build a team by doing what they do best and surrounding themselves with others whose strengths complement their limitations.

MAKING THE TRANSITION

One person who seemed to seamlessly make the transition from an individual sales contributor to sales leadership was Sean Sweeney, who was the first salesperson hired at Philadelphia Insurance in 1978. "Then

I was asked to start hiring other salespeople and to manage them. And I thought that I didn't want them to go through the same fumbling in the darkness that I did at the beginning. So I started to put together a sales process."

You were the first salesperson at Philadelphia Insurance and now you're the president and chief operating officer and a director on the board?

"It's been a great ride. When we just started, we were a small insurance agency, and I had a boss who sold, but we were just seat of the pants, smiling and dialing. I was right there in the front row of it all. He was making the strategies, and I was taking the beach."

What was it like for you moving from sales to management?

"Well, it was difficult because I had to initially take a step back financially, because I was going to be on a salary plus a bonus rather than on commission. But, when I did that, I felt that our company was moving, and if I moved with it, eventually I would be in a favorable position. But the main thing was that I wanted the salespeople's results to be a reflection of my coaching. And so I wanted to figure out how to guarantee their success. That's why I started trying to figure out how to put together a process that would ensure their success. From the heavy-lifting prospecting, to the way you presented yourself, to the style of your presentation, I wanted everything to be very orderly and highly professional. So I actually had tremendous joy experimenting with all types of presentation skills and trying to figure out what was best for our industry, and what was best for our customers, and what was most natural for the people who were working for me."

To succeed in sales, management, whatever your pursuit, you have to love what you're doing.

Another person who characterized the transition from sales to management as painless was Mike Nagel, president and chief executive officer of Vomaris Innovations, a leading regenerative medicine company focusing on wound care with bioelectric technology. He told us, "Although I did well in sales and was a high performer, at a certain point, I found myself getting a little bored with it. There was too much the same for me. So when I got my chance to be in management, I went for it." With a smile, he quickly adds, "Now, it was a long time ago, and maybe the executives who worked with me would argue that it wasn't as painless for them as I remember it being for me. But because of my personality profile, I like a lot of challenges and a lot of variety. And I am also motivated by teaching and coaching and motivating and trying to lead by positive attributes and really pulling people together as a team for a common purpose and focusing on making all of us better. So I found an enormous amount of personal gratification out of managing. I think because I am personally driven to lead a team that succeeds that it was a much easier transition for me."

So the transition was completely without any bumps in the road?

"Well, I think a big thing, when I look back on my career, is that I was willing to step sideways in order to step forward later. When I was at Abbott Labs, my sales manager at the time told me I should take a marketing position in house to broaden my understanding of the business. And I said, 'You're crazy. I have a young family. Why would I take a pay cut now?' But he said to me, 'You're young, you have the drive to go further, so suck it up now, because you're going to learn how the medical device business really runs. If a year from now you don't think you're on the right path, give me a call, and I'll put you back in the field. But if you want to be an executive, you need to broaden your experience.' So I know a lot of people who get hooked in sales. They get cranking along, and they don't want to take the pay cut to go into management. So they stay on the sales track but keep dreaming about replacing me. But if they don't get that global view of how a company works, if they don't reach out for a possible international experience, then they are unlikely to make the transition. What I say to salespeople like that is, do you want to be a sales leader? Or do you just want to be called a sales leader? Do you just want the title and all that comes along with that? Or are you really interested in leading others and preparing yourself for that journey?"

This is the real question any salesperson needs to ask himself or herself. The answer, either way, is fine. It just has to be right for you.

Allow us to close with an analogy. In sports, we have known that the moment a new record is set, every athlete throughout the world acquires a new dimension of accomplishment. For years, no one could run the mile in less than four minutes. Then Roger Bannister broke through the old record, and soon runners from every neighborhood athletic club were approaching the mark, and another generation of leaders began to break new barriers.

In human affairs, the distance between the leaders and the average remains constant. If leadership performance is high, the average will increase. Thus the easiest way to raise the performance of an entire company is to raise the effectiveness of its management.

CHAPTER 29

Managers or Leaders?

As was suggested in Chapter 28, salespeople, like many other employees, naturally look to the next step on the corporate ladder as a way to satisfy their motivation for growth, status, and development. Most of us want and need to keep moving forward with our careers. So what are the very best salespeople supposed to do if they want to climb the corporate ladder? For many of them, it would be like defying gravity. As our studies have shown, the characteristics of the best salespeople are often in conflict with some of the key tasks required of managers.

Yet many topflight salespeople have, in fact, gone on to become superb leaders. They bring vision, momentum, and energy to an enterprise that can be contagious. Being in a "power position" often can play to their strengths—if they know how to recognize talent in others, energize them, and make things happen.

But this begs the question: If so many top-performing salespeople go on to become ineffective managers, why do some succeed in key leadership roles? How do they overcome the odds? Part of the answer has to do with the difference between managing and leading.

We have just completed a study in which we evaluated the qualities that distinguish the best leaders, managers, and salespeople. We evaluated and compared the characteristics of 293 presidents and CEOs with the profiles of 1,470 superior managers and 629 top salespeople. Interestingly, from a personality perspective, what we found was a much closer relationship between top leaders and salespeople than between top leaders and managers.

Many of the best leaders and top-performing salespeople seem to be cut from the same cloth. Interestingly, during interviews, we found that many presidents and CEOs actually came up through the sales ranks. This is good news for some top salespeople who aspire to new challenges, but it does not leave the doors of leadership wide open to all top salespeople.

THE ESSENCE OF LEADERSHIP

Leadership is the ability that enables an individual to get other people to do willingly what they have the ability to do but might not ordinarily do on their own. In many ways, the entrepreneurial leader embodies many sales characteristics. This comes through when they are pitching an idea to an important client, negotiating a strategic relationship, persuading a key employee to take on a new challenge, or conducting a pre–initial public offering dot-com road show. And they too seem somewhat "challenged" when it comes to tasks requiring discipline, structure, and a conscientious focus on details and due diligence.

For most organizations, it is the leader's voice that sets the tone, defines the vision, and manages the agenda. Moreover, our research indicates that just as many salespeople are not likely to be well matched to a management role, most managers are not likely to be well suited to top-level leadership positions. They're just not built the same way.

Given these findings, organizations would do well to look within their sales ranks for future leadership candidates. For it is among these highly driven but sometimes detail-challenged individuals that the soul of the leader is incubated.

Like sales roles, the ability to assume leadership is, first and foremost, a function of who we are. Renato Munhoz da Rocha, president of Inepar, the Brazilian conglomerate, told us, "If you put leaders in a group, within a very short period of time they will stand out—either because of their conversation and the ideas they express or simply because of the way they present themselves."

How do you identify someone who has leadership potential? And how can you nurture, mentor, and coach someone with that potential so that, over the course of time, they will be prepared to lead when the time comes?

Many organizations have a tendency to suffocate future leaders by allowing only those at the top to have a chance to play the role. This is often the reason why salespeople who have a focus on moving forward are attracted to entrepreneurial opportunities where they can be in charge.

Warren Bennis, a distinguished professor and well-known author, describes leaders as "pragmatic dreamers, individuals with an original but attainable vision." He further suggests that "managers do things right, while leaders do the right things."

From our perspective:

- Managers focus on results. Leaders know that results are achieved through people.

- Managers are implementers. Leaders are initiators.

- Managers command through their position. Leaders inspire following because they can make great ideas come alive.

- Managers have their opinions. Leaders help to form opinions.

- Managers are followed because they are bosses. Leaders are followed because we believe in them.

What we are certain about is that leaders are different from managers—and in many ways more like some salespeople—in the underlying personality characteristics that define who they are. At their best, leaders are inspiring. They do not merely provide direction and ideas but rather create the music, orchestrate the resources, and engender environments where new achievements are realized.

THE MOST IMPORTANT ASPECT OF LEADERSHIP

We surveyed over 300 presidents and CEOs and asked them what they considered to be the most important and the worst aspects of being a leader. Among the choices we asked them to rank were

- Creating the right vision

- Getting people to embrace that vision

- Maintaining momentum (motivating, influencing, and persuading others)

- Managing change (strategic planning, problem solving, etc.)

- Surrounding yourself with the right people

- Developing staff (coaching individuals, managing performance, and facilitating teams)

- Delegating authority

- Orchestrating priorities

- Making tough decisions about capital, financial, and human resources

- Staying the course

- Keeping self-confidence

These leaders told us that surrounding themselves with the right people was among the best and worst aspects of leading a company. "Surrounding yourself with the right people" was selected 42 percent of the time, second only to "creating the right vision," as one of the best parts of being a leader. Interestingly, it also was selected as one of the three most difficult aspects of being an effective leader, just behind "maintaining momentum" and "developing staff."

When you are leading an organization, surrounding yourself with the right people becomes an either-or situation. Either you hire and develop people with whom you thoroughly enjoy working, people who are bright, engaging, conscientious, and adept at solving problems, or the chemistry is not there, and leading becomes a constant battle.

In general, the leadership group we surveyed recognized the critical importance of first having the "right idea" and then getting other people (who embrace that idea) on board and engaged in the tasks of implementing that idea and effecting change.

SALESPEOPLE HAVE A LOT IN COMMON WITH LEADERS

In Chapter 28 we compared the qualities of top-performing salespeople with the underlying personality characteristics of top-performing managers. We concluded that there were considerable differences between the two groups. However, as can be seen from Figures 29-1 through 29-4, the characteristics of top salespeople are, in many ways, similar to those of top executive leaders.

Influencing and Directing

Compared with the profile of top managers, both the salespeople we evaluated and the top executives who participated in our study scored significantly higher on measures of assertiveness and ego-drive (see

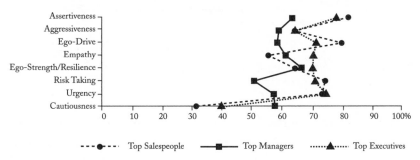

Figure 29-1 Influencing and directing.

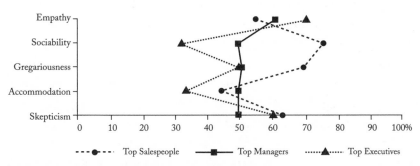

Figure 29-2 Building and maintaining relationships.

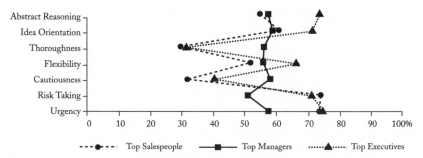

Figure 29-3   Problem solving/decision making.

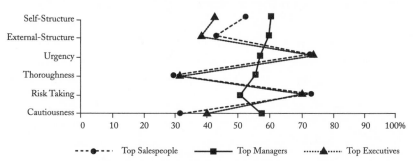

Figure 29-4   Personal organization/time management.

Figure 29-1). In general, the executives and salespeople are far more likely to be dominant, proactive, and persuasive in expressing their ideas. More to the point, the executives and salespeople we assessed generally will be more competitively motivated and will derive gratification when their point of view is adopted. In addition, the executives and salespeople who participated in our study are far more likely to exhibit impatience and take risks and are much less cautious in moving forward than are the top-performing managers. In general, both salespeople and executives are likely to present themselves in a direct, driven, although somewhat intense and impatient manner.

The top managers, on the other hand, present a more "balanced" profile of characteristics. Compared with the salespeople and executives, they are likely to be more willing to subordinate their own ego gratification in favor of an individual contributor or a team win. In addition, they are far less likely to take risks and generally will be more cautious and less impulsive in their interactions with others. While they are capable of directing and influencing others, the top-performing managers are more likely to take a facilitative role rather than a dominant role. As a result, they may be more effective in supporting, coaching, and mentoring others, including the leaders they report to, than in taking the dominant leadership position.

For salespeople who are "leaders in waiting," here's one important point to consider: From an influencing and directing perspective, the executives we profiled differed from salespeople in at least one important quality. Top executives are likely to exhibit a higher level of empathy than salespeople in general. This suggests that in order for top salespeople to ascend the leadership ladder, they must be capable of guiding their vision and presenting their persuasive message with great sensitivity to the needs of their audience.

Another cautionary note is that top-performing salespeople are more ego driven than most leaders, although leaders clearly have a strong need to persuade. This is certainly something that top-performing salespeople would have to be aware of and attempt to temper if they are interested in leading. Too intense of a need to sell one's point of view can keep others around you from expressing their true thoughts and feelings. And that ability to connect with others and to consider all perspectives is one of the hallmarks of great leaders. Again, it is a balancing act.

With these caveats—of listening better and not just pushing their own agenda—many top-performing salespeople possess definite leadership qualities.

Building and Maintaining Relationships

When it comes to working with and interacting with others, there are some key differences between the salespeople, leaders, and managers we profiled (see Figure 29-2). The salespeople, as noted, generally scored somewhat lower on empathy than did the leaders. In this regard, they were more similar to the top-management group: able to identify with another point of view but a bit inflexible on occasion. The most significant differences between the leaders and salespeople centered on sociability and gregariousness.

In general, salespeople are strongly outgoing. Likely to be proactive in networking and establishing new contacts, they will be comfortable in putting themselves into situations where there is an opportunity to interact with other people. Top executives, on the other hand, while having great empathy and the ability to relate to others, are, for the most part, likely to be somewhat private. They have sufficient gregariousness to "play the game" but will be highly selective in terms of whom they choose to spend their time with. Top-rated managers are empathic in their ability to relate but generally moderate in their outgoingness, accommodation, and skepticism—not nearly as extreme as the other two groups.

Given these differences, it is clear that not all salespeople will be entirely comfortable in the solitary role of leader. We are reminded of the old saw, "It's lonely at the top." Leaders seek the advice and counsel of others but will not seek out social situations just for their own sake. Most salespeople need and want to be around people.

PROBLEM SOLVING AND DECISION MAKING

As problem solvers, salespeople are, in many ways, more like the top executive group than the management group (see Figure 29-3). While the top leaders generally score significantly higher than both salespeople and other managers on abstract reasoning ability and idea orientation, their style of problem solving and decision making is similar to that of salespeople.

Leaders tend to be somewhat more creative and bring tremendous problem-solving ability and flexibility to the core leadership tasks of recognizing issues and opportunities, developing strategies, and working through barriers that impede progress toward important goals. However, like salespeople, they tend to be impatient to reach conclusions and take action, and have limited tolerance for minutia and aspects of detail that could impede progress. Again, the managers tend to be more balanced and moderate in their approach to problem solving—more comfortable with details and likely to be less impatient with the process of getting to the right conclusion.

Leaders and salespeople are less concerned with issues of due diligence and thus are much more likely to take actions based on instincts.

Here is one more important caveat for salespeople who see themselves as leaders and want to move forward: Given their superior problem-solving capabilities, top executives are far more likely to survive on their instincts, and thus their decisions usually will be more accurate. For salespeople who have a more moderate abstract reasoning capability, there is no substitute for exercising a small degree of restraint.

PERSONAL ORGANIZATION AND TIME MANAGEMENT

Neither leaders nor salespeople are likely to be highly organized or disciplined in their approach (see Figure 29-4). While top-level managers are generally oriented toward defining and setting goals, establishing and budgeting priorities, implementing tactics, tracking performance and other details, and managing follow-through, salespeople and top executives share a tendency to be spontaneous, easily distractible, opportunistic, and impatient. These groups thrive on chaos and are often responsible for creating it.

Exemplary managers, the people whom leaders surround themselves with and who are responsible for directing the efforts of salespeople, "do things right." Salespeople and top executive leaders, on the other hand, because of their approach to personal organization and time management frequently leave a mess in their wake for others to clean up.

KNOWING WHO YOU ARE

Given our overall findings, there are many similarities between the characteristics of top executives and those of salespeople—more, in fact, than between salespeople and sales managers. This poses a dilemma both for the salesperson who wants upward mobility and a chance at the "golden ring" and for the organization that has a need not only to retain its sales force but also to safeguard its future talent pool of potential managers and leaders.

You have to start out by being true to yourself. Self-awareness is one of the most fundamental concepts of getting on in the world.

People who are highly self-aware know where they are headed. And perhaps more important, they know how to play to their strengths.

From our perspective, it is vital in managing a top-performing salesperson's future career growth and development opportunities to know "who you are." Taking the wrong job even for the right reasons can have a catastrophic effect if not managed with a high degree of self-awareness. Are you someone who likes working through others? Do you enjoy the challenge of creating and managing systems? Do you get a kick out of seeing a plan come together? Are you patient? Do you like implementing and tracking plans and seeing them through to the end? Or do you like "taking the shot" and being the "star"? Do you thrive on being around people, or are you as comfortable being alone as with others? Or, in the final analysis, do you get the biggest kick out of selling?

These are important questions for salespeople looking to take their career into management or leadership to ask themselves and quite relevant when they are thinking through how and if they should push forward. For some salespeople, the best answer may be to keep doing what they do (and like doing) best—selling. For others, sales management may be a perfect fit. And for those of you who are "leaders in waiting," there are two alternatives: First, you can define a well-thought-through strategy to go for that management role and "grit through it" with a clear knowledge of your ultimate goal of becoming a leader. Or second, you can create a unique path either within your organization or elsewhere.

In the end, we are all responsible for managing our own destinies. Knowing who you are is the basis for engineering a future that "fits."

Tom Gartland, president, North America of Avis Budget Group, knew that he wanted to be in sales for as long as he can remember.

"When I was 14 years old, I went to work for a place called Robert's Rent-a-Tux. I lied about my age and told them I was 16. So there I was renting tuxedos but, more important, driving incremental commission by selling cufflinks, shoes, and bow ties. I understood how to make money. And that's what has driven me my entire life."

We're trying to picture this 14-year-old fitting us for tuxedos.

"Then flash forward to my first job as a district manager. I was a little clumsy in the beginning because I went from being an individual contributor to managing 15 people. The shift for me then was a major one—but one that I am able to articulate much better now than I could then and one that I am absolutely crystal clear on today. The shift was realizing that the difference between being a top performer and a manager is ensuring that you have the right people in the right jobs and that you provide them with the necessary training and coaching in order for them to be successful. With the right people in the right jobs, your success as a manager becomes almost automatic. At that point, it is my belief that the most important job of a leader is to develop individualized plans for each of your top performers and a succession plan for the organization. This is the single most important role I play, I believe, here at Avis Budget Group. And it starts with entry-level sales all the way to the executive vice president of revenue generation because the succession plan is a long history of individualized development over the course of a decade. And what we do today has implications 10 years from now."

As a leader, you are hiring somebody for a certain position now, but you are also hiring them for the future, a future that is yet unknown.

You knew that you always wanted to be in sales. Did you also always know that you wanted to be a leader?

"I probably knew that I wanted to lead when I was selling in the tuxedo store. I was thinking how I could run the store better. Leading has always been part of my DNA. I believe that you can develop leadership skills, but I'm not sure you can develop a leader. It's either part of who you are or it is not. I was the captain of my hockey team when I was in school. For me, it's been about being driven myself but also wanting to surround myself with a team of equally driven people. I don't have to be the smartest guy in the room, but I know how to recognize the smartest people and the best talent, and I know how to position them to succeed. That gives me tremendous satisfaction."

Mark Dennis, vice president of sales and marketing at Veolia Environmental Services, learned a lot about himself as he moved from being an individual contributor to a manager. "I went through quite a few a-ha moments. I was put into a sales management position without any training. So I was trying to coach my peers whom I'd been working with before, and I stumbled and fumbled for about a year-and-a-half. I had no training, no direction. So I tried to coach everyone to sell the way I sold. And I quickly realized that the way I was succeeding as a salesperson was not the way others were succeeding. And my way wasn't going to work for everyone else. Early on, I was not coaching. I was just trying to force my way of selling onto others. And they would look at me and say, 'I don't do it that way. And here's why.' And I'd say, 'But if you do it that way, you'll be more successful.' And they'd push back. And I was young and didn't know better. And it took me awhile to realize that people have their own styles, and I'm not there just to push my style on somebody else. That's not how you get results. That was one of my a-ha moments."

What did you do when you were stuck? How did you get unstuck?

"I stared reading every management and self-help book I could get my hands on. I would listen to management tapes over and over again in the car, and I took several sales management training courses. And eventually, I learned that I needed to understand each of my people's individual styles, their strengths, and their natural approaches and guide and lead them from where they were. I had to understand and connect with them individually and then coach them and foster and encourage them on improving their personal style."

Can you give us a for instance?

"We had certain guidelines about information that we needed in our CRM [customer resource management] system so that we could track what was going on with our prospects and clients. And it was a continual struggle with most of our salespeople, who are, generally speaking, not focused on details and not well organized. So rather than continually struggling, I brought in a sales coordinator who helped them with some of these duties and freed them up to go out and sell, which is what they wanted to do."

How did you know you were succeeding as a manager?

"It was a transition. As an individual contributor, when you make a sale, you feel great. There is nothing like it. As a manager, you get that same sense of personal pride and gratification when someone on your team breaks through and hits their numbers or makes the President's Club. That becomes very exciting. Knowing that you had something to do with it, but it was really helping somebody else discover what they had. And that becomes fun. You're competing, and you're winning, and you're all in it together. And it is enormously fulfilling."

That is an amazing transformation.

"An enormous part of my transformation was when my manager at the time, Cookie Zeuch took me under her wing. She was a wonderful mentor. She saw something in me and believed in me and brought me up to corporate headquarters and put me in as a national sales and management trainer. And for three years I did that and learned an enormous amount from her about being a much more effective coach to others."

There is one other thought we'd like to share with you from Laurie Dalton, vice president of human resources for Gate Gourmet. She told us, "I always remind leaders, particularly new ones, that everyone is watching them, and everyone takes them home at night." They often pause and look at me quizzically. Then I remind them, "You have more influence than you can ever imagine. Just think about your boss," and then they start to nod. "Your boss goes home with you, so to speak. And as the boss, things you don't even realize you said or did become the focus of dinner conversations. And you remain on your employees' minds over the weekend. So your energy or lack of focus, your positive attitude or negative comments, carry on and have an impact far beyond what you probably realize. As a leader, my message is to remember this. And focus on your attitude. Because it will become contagious."

THE CORPORATE CHALLENGE

While individuals have a need to manage their future career growth and opportunities, organizations have an equally strong need to retain their top talent. As we have pointed out, not every employee has the underlying characteristics that will result in a successful move into a sales management or a leadership role. Yet this path is viewed by salespeople as a coveted goal. Organizations therefore must be strategic in identifying and targeting future talent. The earlier that talent and potential are recognized, the sooner the development process can begin, and the more likely it is that talent will be retained—and have an opportunity to grow with your company.

By their very nature, both salespeople and an organization's future managers and leaders need to be recognized and have career paths that help them to realize their potential. The managers and leaders of the future are extremely valuable, and the sales organization is a good breeding ground for their development, provided that management is aware of the potential that resides within its ranks.

In order for sales managers and future leaders to be developed, they must be

- Identified

- Mentored and coached

- Brought to the attention of the organization

- Given responsibilities

- Nurtured and developed

At the same time, organizations must be creative in professionalizing and improving the status of the sales role so that top performers who continue as individual contributors do not, in any way, feel that they are not achieving their full potential in terms of material rewards, status, social rewards, and future growth opportunities.

PART **7**

THE SUCCESSFUL SALESPERSON IN TODAY'S WORLD

From a business perspective, the boundaries of countries have disappeared. What does this mean for those who are trying to succeed in selling? Our studies show that the profile of the successful salesperson is essentially the same in America as it is in Japan, Sweden, England, Brazil, Canada, Hong Kong, or virtually anywhere else in the world. It all comes down to motivation.

CHAPTER 30

The Global Salesperson: What Does It Take to Compete In the New Reality?

How has sales changed? Another way of asking this question is, How has the world changed?

Let us tell about Jian Xie to give you a sense of the scope and speed of how things are changing.

Jian told us, "I came back to China about 15 years ago. I never thought I would come back. I was born here in Shanghai. After graduating from college, I bought a one-way ticket to the United States. I had two suitcases, one small briefcase, and $60 in my pocket. That was it. And I was determined to succeed in the United States. So I went to graduate school at Marquette, and then I started working for a company in Milwaukee, A.O. Smith. And I worked in virtually every position you could think of—from technical to sales to management—over the course of 10 years. The way I saw it, for me, this was a freebie training program, preparing me for the future. And along the way, I got my American citizenship."

Then, in the mid-1990s, Jian saw the paradigm start to shift.

Fast forward to now: Jian is the president of Actuant, China, part of a $1.5 billion diversified industrial company with operations in more than 30 countries.

"I never thought I'd be back. But China now is like the United States was in the 1950s, with everything buzzing, jobs everywhere, the country growing, and life getting better. Our colleges are graduating an enormous number of students who are bright, open-minded, have language skills, and are willing to work hard and leverage their talents to get ahead. It is a very exciting time to be here. And the energy here, where things are happening very quickly, suits my personality."

How does a salesperson adjust to the seismic shifts in culture, technology, and buying habits that are occurring?

Stephen Inman, director of human resources at Kohler Company, who has worked in China, India, France, and England, told us that working in different countries has given him an enormous appreciation and insight into people—and into himself.

"When people ask for my advice about working in different countries, I always tell them to look for the similarities. Don't get hung up on the differences. They have a job; you have a job. They have a family; you have a family. They have aging parents; you have aging parents. They have a mortgage; you have a mortgage. If you look for the cultural differences too soon, you'll stumble on them and highlight them and be confused by them. Instead, look to what you share in common, which is often enormous. If you focus on the similarities, they will trust you. Then they will share with you what the cultural differences are so that you can appreciate them—rather than have them separate you."

Focus on the similarities. That's an important message.

"The Chinese consumer shares may similarities with the North American consumer. They are middle class, aspirational, want to differentiate themselves, and are willing to spend money to make themselves feel good in their environment. So it is important for us to present our products as a shared global experience."

As you consider whether someone has the potential to succeed in different countries, what do you look for?

"First and foremost, I look for somebody who is has a track record of success in doing what they are doing in their current country. Then I want to know if they are adaptable, flexible, open, and curious. Can they listen well and reflect on what they are hearing? I also want to know if they are skeptical while being empathic. I know that might sound funny, but they've got to have enough skepticism to ask what somebody means when they say, 'It's different here.' They need to probe, to make sure that they understand. But they also need to have enough empathy to listen to someone and not just dismiss what they are saying but to truly seek out what is meant by the difference."

Mark Nechita, senior director of international human resources for Calloway Golf, is truly a global citizen. He has lived and worked in over 40 countries throughout Asia, North and South America and the Middle East. In addition to being naturally curious and genuinely interested in others, Mark told us that "people who succeed in various and diverse situations are willing to take risks. Moving out of a comfortable space can have risks. And if, for whatever reason, you don't take those risks, you can stay within the space you know and not venture forth. Some people are more comfortable leveraging their knowledge and capabilities in their current network. Others are driven by new experiences, new challenges, and new opportunities. It really comes down to how people are wired."

Selling in this new world with fewer borders will belong to the explorers—to those who are interested in being where change is occurring.

Ron Rubin, Minister of Tea (owner) of The Republic of Tea, has just hired an individual to head up the organization's international sales efforts. "While the majority of our teas come from India, Japan, South Africa, Taiwan and China, our sales have all been in the United States since the company's founding over 20 years ago. And because we don't have international experience in selling, we knew that bringing on the right person was paramount. This is a very strategic decision for us."

Beyond looking for someone with combined qualities of a top-flight salesperson and a dynamic leader, what else were you looking for?

We also wanted someone who has an entrepreneurial spirit, has a passion for tea, has a global perspective, is strategic, and wants to help shape the future. We've heard suggestions about starting in Canada because of the similarity and proximity to the market in the United States. We also heard the case for going to England or Japan because those regions have strong traditions for appreciating tea. Also, China or Brazil have been recommended because they are emerging markets that are open to new ideas."

To succeed in this global marketplace, this new sales leader will have to be bright, strategic, and enjoy developing plans. He or she also will need to be able to convey ideas and initiatives in a forthright manner, be persuasive, and be equally inclined to listen to ideas from others. The ideal candidate also will need to be flexible, highly organized and driven to succeed. Setbacks will have to be perceived as nothing but learning experiences. Competing in the global marketplace calls for an ideal blend of the qualities that distinguish top-performing salespeople and leaders—at hyper speed.

WHEN THE BUSINESS MODEL CHANGES

Responding to the technological, global, and competitive changes taking place, many companies are finding that they have to transform their business models. What worked in the past will no longer sustain them. Some of these changes have been minor; others significant. And they are occurring at record speeds. As a result, salespeople are being faced with unprecedented challenges. And what once made them successful may have very little to do with helping them to succeed in this new world.

Consider Gate Gourmet, the world's largest independent provider of catering to the travel industry. Until a few years ago, a salesperson's job for Gate Gourmet was to convince an airline or railroad company to carry their food rather than a competitor's. A successful salesperson would focus on quality and menu distinctions, but, of course, those were easily copied. So, as is often the case in sales, much depended on the relationships that each salesperson developed.

Then most of the airlines decided to no longer serve food as part of the cost of flying. And all of a sudden, the business of catering to the travel industry was turned on its ear.

Before it was hard enough to compete against the other firm's trying to service the airline companies. But, at least, you knew who they were. And you knew how to position your strengths against theirs. And if you won a contract, you were safe, at least for a while.

Now, the game has changed. Completely. Now, you have to serve a complete menu of low-priced options. And you are vying for each individual flyer to open his or her wallet and buy one of your offerings, based on quality, price, and convenience. And now you are not just competing with the other catering providers, but you are also competing with every other food chain that is right next to the gate where the people flying are getting ready to board.

So your business has changed, the model is completely different, the menu is more complicated (you need to have enough of just the right items rather than just one of everything for each passenger), and the profit margins have dwindled.

You are still selling—in the same business, theoretically. But everything has changed. Completely. And without a moment to spare, you still need to be one step ahead of the competition.

This is where selling takes on a whole new meaning. When the business model changes, some people who were succeeding before will be able to adapt and make it. And some might find that they have to take their talents elsewhere.

SELLING TO THE C-SUITE

Many executives today are looking for the rare breed of salesperson who can sell to the C-suite. They are looking for an experienced salesperson, with all the essential personality dynamics required of the best, along with a level of gravitas and the ability to think globally and come across as a trusted and valued consultant. A little bit of gray around the ears also would be welcome.

How can you tell if a top-performing salesperson has what it takes to be promoted to a position as a global account manager? How does the conversation change at the C-suite? And how do you prepare someone for those conversations?

Alyson Brandt, executive vice president, general manager Americas for Forum, told us: "We are really looking for a unique balance of a number of different priorities and requirements for selling. It is more of a value-add, complex solution–based approach to selling, particularly in our business. What we're looking for are people who understand how to bring insight to their clients, and how to build relationships, not only with their buyer, but across the organization."

This requires an elevated level of skill sets.

"Right. It is about influencing in a way that is welcome, bringing insight that couldn't be gained elsewhere, facilitating conversations at a deeper level, thoroughly understanding our client's business, bringing resources to bear to build firm-to-firm relationships, being unfailingly responsive, and bringing unquestionable value."

How can you tell if someone is ready to step up to that challenging job description?

"You need to evaluate someone and help to develop their potential on four levels. First is about relationship capabilities. Second is about consulting capabilities. Third is understanding how to navigate the sales process. And fourth is about the team-building and collaborative skills they bring to each engagement."

And someone has to be ready on all four of those levels.

How can you prepare someone to sell to the C-suite if they have never sold into it before? How can you help someone to change their conversation? To realize that what worked like a charm for them before will not fly at this altitude?

"It is all about evolving as a sales leader. There are specific conversations and skills you need to enter the C-suite. It is knowing what your audience is interested in. In our business, for instance, you would talk about learning, motivation, and systems at the human resources level, but you also would need to be able to talk about business impact, speed to market, and enhancing performance for a line leader."

Can you give us an example of someone who has most of those skills but not all of them—and how it could be holding his or her career from moving to the highest level?

"That's an interesting question. There is one person I'm thinking of who is a phenomenal relationship builder. She is the first person to show empathy. She'll acknowledge everyone's contributions, stay in touch, and exudes strong relationship capabilities in everything she does. And everyone feels her genuine warmth and caring about them and the project they're working on together. But she hesitates to make that courageous jump to call higher or call more broadly, to expand her connections within the client organization. And what is holding her back is that she is concerned about what she might not know.

"So, if you had a two-by-two framework with one side being the relationship and the other side being the information, using the information to build credibility is her weak spot. So she depends on other people to bring that to bear, which isn't necessarily a bad thing as long as the client is getting what he or she wants. But it holds her back from being able to advance where she sells in an organization and where she has relationships—because selling at a higher level requires this balance. It is not that she is not curious, but her curiosity is going to defer to the relationship side as opposed to the information side. She is still excellent selling at her current level. But she won't be ready for the C-Suite until she increases her knowledge and confidence on the information side."

Gerhard Gschwandtner, CEO of Selling Power, told us: "Anyone can talk with people in the C-suite. I have people at my reception desk who talk with senior-level executives all the time. The question is not whether you can have access to the C-suite. The real question is how productive is that person talking to the C-level executives. And I would say that 80 percent of the time when salespeople finally get to the C-level executive, they are wasting their time because they don't know the right questions and they don't know how to hold a conversation for longer than five minutes. It comes down to content. What kind of meaningful content can you share with a C-level executive in the right language so that you don't take three paragraphs to explain something that a truly professional salesperson could explain in one sentence? How much value are you bringing?"

The key lies in realizing that whenever a senior executive has a difficult situation to resolve, it is unlikely that he or she will call his or her executive assistant and say, "I've got a problem. Get me a salesperson." Global account managers earn the respect of the senior executives with whom they work by coming through consistently, time and time again, and by lending insights that prove valuable. They may have previously shared a perspective on the marketplace or on what a competitor was doing. As a result, when one of their C-level clients finds himself or herself wrestling with a difficult situation, they feel comfortable calling on their global account manager, as a trusted advisor, as someone who can lend a valuable perspective and unexpected insight. This is where truly professional salespeople bring real value.

IN CLOSING

Sales is a profession that is completely and entirely transportable. It travels very lightly. With the right potential, knowledge, skills, capabilities, and passion, a talented salesperson can make it anywhere—and can continually enhance his or her position, moving into more complex and engaging sales roles or into management and leadership.

Aside from transportability across product lines, industries, and companies, the sales profession is also transportable across borders. It exists everywhere in the world. And our research in the Americas, Europe, Asia, and the Far and Middle East supports the notion that despite a few cultural differences, there is a unique and recognizable sales personality that cuts across all cultures.

A quick, interesting finding from our studies is that the best salespeople in various countries sometimes defy stereotypes. For instance, the top British salespeople are a bit more freewheeling and aggressive than the best salespeople in the United States. These differences, while intriguing, are minor, and they take into account that the best salespeople around the world are all driven to persuade, empathic, able to bounce back from rejection, conscientious, and motivated to come through for their clients. When these basic, underlying sales dynamics are in place, success will follow.

Successful salespeople in New York City share similar personality strengths with the best salespeople in Tokyo, once we adjust for a few stylistic and cultural considerations. In our studies, we have found that the best Japanese salespeople are just as motivated to persuade as their counterparts in the United States. The only real difference is that they tap into their empathy and adjust to the subtler, more refined approach needed to be effective in Japan. While the cultural differences may appear striking between Japan and the United States, they are equally strong between midtown Manhattan and rural Texas. In both cases, our studies have proved that top salespeople are able to succeed by playing to their strengths and adjusting their approach to the needs of each situation.

This is all very good news for top salespeople and for the organizations that need them.

CHAPTER 31

It's All About Motivation

So here's the deal: Whether in sales, management, or leadership, people who are most productive over a long period of time have found a set of activities and tasks to engage in that is consistent with their skills and their basic personality dynamics. As a result, they are the lucky ones. They really like what they're doing, or at least most of what they're doing most of the time. If you find a job that's consistent with who you are, you'll never have to work another day in your life.

This is at the heart of our message.

Over the course of consulting with over 25,000 companies around the world throughout the past half century, we frequently come across executives who are disappointed in the results of their hiring and development processes. As we shared with you in the Introduction to this book, the percentage of sales representatives making quota dropped to less than 50 percent last year. Obviously, something isn't working.

The irony is that many of the executives who are complaining about the productivity of the salespeople they hire don't realize that they are, unwittingly, reinforcing a broken process—a broken process for hiring and a broken process for developing top talent.

In this book we have shared with you—through our own experience and the voices of many of our enlightened, thoughtful, and insightful clients—how to replace these broken processes.

Hopefully, we have conveyed our firm conviction that you cannot fix these broken processes. Instead, you have to replace them. Replace them with a renewed sense of looking for potential rather than experience. Replace them with a clear understanding of the qualities that distinguish your top performers. Then use your top performers as your blueprint for the future. Replace those broken processes with a thorough understanding of who and what you are seeking.

If what you are doing is not working, don't keep doing it.

Instead, to find your next top salesperson, first you have to ensure that your expectations are clear and that you know what you need. Do you need a hunter or a farmer? What is involved in succeeding in this role? It all starts by understanding the job and being clear on what results you hope to achieve.

Then screen out people you know won't cut it in your organization. Integrate your company's values and culture into the interviewing process. You not only want a top salesperson, but you also want someone who shares your company's values and motivation to succeed.

Using a personality assessment in your hiring process can help you on many levels. It will help you understand what distinguishes your top performers. What sets them apart from those in the middle of the pack, and those at the bottom? Who in the middle has the potential to become a top performer—if they were, perhaps, working with a different manager; or given coaching in a specific area?

Equally important, the insights from a study of the qualities that distinguish your top performers will help you to recognize those strengths in promising job applicants. Such insights also will help you to uncover even the most cunning of interview stars. And what you learn about your current top performers will help you to discover people already in your organization who possess the qualities to be your next top producers—but they may be doing something completely different.

By looking for potential rather than experience, you will hire and develop top performers.

Don't look to the past to change things.

Look to the future, to someone's potential, to what they, and your organization, can become.

For top salespeople, selling is rewarding because they are outgoing, persuasive, empathic, confident, and willing to take risks. Put most simply: Successful salespeople are built to sell. They thrive on getting the "Yes" and feel motivated to bring others around to their point of view.

What you want to find are the 25 percent of the population that are naturally built that way—those who have the potential to succeed.

Then groom them by connecting with their strengths and potential. Ultimately, selling is what drives business.

Yet, because too many of the wrong people are attempting to eke out a living through selling, the profession has gotten a reputational black eye. Phrases such as *selling out, selling a bill of goods*, and *selling you down the river* clearly convey that selling has taken on a negative connotation.

We are suggesting that by replacing the broken hiring and development processes to which many organizations still cling, the profession of sales can be elevated to the level it deserves. More salespeople will be hired who are ideally suited and built to succeed. The number of salespeople exceeding quota will increase dramatically. And the profession of sales, as a result, will be truly recognized for all its strengths.

After all, selling provides an opportunity for salespeople to receive recognition, status, and rewards. Salespeople contribute to their organizations in the most measurable way—the creation of revenue.

And, as we have emphasized throughout this book, for those who you have what it takes to succeed in sales, the career path is wide open. They may have additional strengths and motivations and be able to adapt to roles in sales management or entrepreneurial leadership. Some of our best leaders started out as salespeople. For others, the freedom to continue succeeding in sales can be endless as they set new personal achievements and chart new territory.

For top sales managers and leaders, success is all about who you surround yourself with. Succeeding first begins by understanding your personal strengths, where you shine, and the areas on which you need to work. Then you want to focus on the strengths, potential, and motivations of the salespeople with whom you surround yourself.

Focus on the qualities needed to succeed in sales. Then magnify them. Help to turn up the volume on those qualities: the ability to read others, the drive to persuade, the ability to bounce back from rejection. When these basic underlying sales dynamics are in place, success can follow. This is where potential reigns.

Potential is what you are looking for. This is why there is always a picture of flowers on a packet of seeds. We really don't care what the seeds look like. We want to know what they will become.

If we could leave you with one last thought, it would be this: Open yourself to uncovering and developing the potential of individuals. We have found that the real winners in this world are the individuals who know who they are, know what they're after, and know how to play to their strengths. And they are willing to take a risk on someone else's potential. Find that in yourself. Look for it in others. And you will be well on your way to hiring and developing top performers.

How to Discover
Your Own Defining Qualities

As our gift to you, we'd like to provide you with a way to get some objective insights into the qualities that drive and distinguish you. Consider this to be our contribution to your journey.

We are offering you the opportunity to take our online, in-depth personality profile, which can provide you with an introductory assessment of your defining qualities. This personality profile is the same assessment used by Johnson & Johnson, SAP, Avis Budget Group, and thousands of midsized and small companies to assess the potential of applicants and employees.

You are welcome to take this free profile and receive a report pinpointing the qualities that distinguish you.

This developmental guide will provide you with some interesting and valuable insights into the qualities that drive you, highlighting some of your key strengths and motivations, along with suggestions for developing your potential.

If you are a leader or a manager, the results can help you to reflect about how you connect with others and help you to consider how you might think about the individuals on your team differently.

If you are a salesperson or someone aspiring to go into sales, the results can help you to clarify whether your strengths and motivations are aligned with your goals.

To take advantage of your free online assessment, go to YourNextTopPerformer.com. Click on the button that says, "Take

Caliper's Free Assessment." Enter CALIPEROFFEREB23. Then follow the directions.

Of course, if you are interested in further assessments, coaching, or counseling, we are always available to you. And if you are a leader, manager, or employer, you can always reach us to receive guidance in hiring, developing, coaching, team building, succession planning, and organizational development.

Index

About the Authors

Herb Greenberg, PhD is the founder and CEO and **Patrick Sweeney** is the president of Caliper, an international management consulting firm.

Headquartered in Princeton, NJ, with a dozen offices around the world, Caliper consults with executives on hiring, employee development, team building, executive coaching, succession planning and organizational performance. For over a half-century, Caliper has assessed the potential of over three million applicants and employees for Fortune 500 companies and some of the fastest growing, mid-size and smaller organizations around the world.

Herb and Patrick are coauthors of the *New York Times* best seller *Succeed on Your Own Terms* published by McGraw-Hill.

Inspiring speakers, they have presented at international conferences on: How Leaders Surround Themselves with Top Performers; Coaching for Success; Developing Your Dream Team; How Women are Refining Leadership; The Psychology of the Sports Champion; and Succeeding on Your Own Terms.